Michael and Me

Michael and Me

The Untold Story of
MICHAEL JACKSON'S
Secret Romance

Shana Mangatal

An A Cappella Book

To maintain the privacy of individuals, some names have been changed.

First edition
Published by Chicago Review Press Incorporated
814 North Franklin Street
Chicago, Illinois 60610
ISBN 978-1-61373-617-3

Library of Congress Cataloging-in-Publication Data
Is available from the Library of Congress.

Interior layout: Nord Compo

Printed in the United States of America
5 4 3 2 1

This book is dedicated to my wonderful parents,
Emmanuel and Janice Mangatal, and my aunt Vera Bell Schnur.

My father "Mano" and Aunt Vera will always live on in my memories.

Janice—Thank you for your endless love and support . . . and
for encouraging me to Go Be My Dream.

There are no secrets that time does not reveal.

—Jean Racine

PROLOGUE

Dreams do come true. It could happen to you.

—Walt Disney

It was March 5, 1988.

The city lights soared past me as the Yellow Cab wove in and out of busy traffic. The energy of New York City was an intoxicant, invigorating every moment. The city had a pulse so strong, it felt like it must be the epicenter of the universe.

As we pulled up to Madison Square Garden, the butterflies in my stomach flew faster. I felt that I was about to step into a piece of history. I was right: this night would set me on a course that would change my life.

We had arrived in New York just a few hours earlier after a four-and-a-half-hour drive from our hometown in Largo, Maryland, a suburb of Washington, DC. My aunt Vera had driven my friend Tracy and me in her brand-new silver Nissan Maxima. That car was all the rage that year because it talked, telling you important things like "Your lights are on." I always got a kick out of riding in it. Sometimes we would purposely leave the lights on just so we could hear it talk.

We were here to see Michael Jackson in concert—he was on his Bad tour. I had been looking forward to this day for months. I was seventeen, and Michael was my idol.

We found our seats, which were behind the stage. At first I was upset that they were so bad. When I purchased the tickets, they hadn't informed me that the seats would be in an obstructed view area. As the show went on, however, I grew to like them. It gave me a different vantage point. From behind, you could catch a glimpse of how the magic was made, and I could see him walking off and on stage before the curtain was raised. I had always been obsessed with magicians like David Copperfield. I was the type who would watch a trick over and over so that I could figure out how the illusion was created. The creation of an illusion is what fascinated me about Michael. I always suspected his Peter Pan image was just a facade. And now I could glimpse the real Michael, behind the curtain.

After a couple songs, the charm of sitting behind the stage wore off, and we decided to walk around to see if we could snag some better seats. Since we were already behind the stage, we easily made our way onto the floor without anyone checking for tickets. We spotted an empty area in the front row, and blended in there as if we belonged. We managed to stay in our newfound front-row seats for the remainder of the concert. I couldn't believe how lucky we were.

This experience was completely different from sitting behind the stage. Michael was *right there*, as if he were performing in my living room. And he was overwhelmingly sexy. He wore black pants with silver buckles, which showcased his perfect body—especially his round backside. They were so tight; I could see *everything*. It was like he was dancing naked in front of me for two hours. It was so intense and exhilarating, inspiring feelings that I had never felt before.

During the song "I Just Can't Stop Loving You," he and Sheryl Crow, who was his background singer back then, came together and started dancing closely. He started rubbing his crotch while he was singing to her, so much that he became noticeably excited. I could not believe my eyes. I felt like I was going to faint from shock. It was like I was seeing something I wasn't supposed to see. I was overwhelmed. I had read so many tabloid stories painting Michael as this asexual man-child that I was not expecting this at all.

He then launched into a beautiful rendition of his hit song "Human Nature." "See that girl—she knows I'm watching. She likes the way I stare." As his smooth voice effortlessly glided over the lyrics, he pointed right to me. I squealed so loud, he started smiling. I had been screaming the whole time, so there was no doubt he had noticed me before then. He kept glancing at me for the remainder of the concert and I was sure we had made a love connection.

I talked endlessly about that magical moment with my aunt Vera and Tracy during the entire cab ride back to the hotel. "Did you see him point to me when he said 'See that girl'? We made eye contact! He was looking at me the whole concert. I know he saw me!"

"Yes, he did point at you. I saw it." Tracy said, probably just hoping I would shut up.

We had left at the beginning of the last song, "Man in the Mirror," to beat the traffic. We also wanted to arrive back at the hotel before Michael so that we could try to catch a glimpse of him returning from the show.

The Helmsley Palace on the corner of Fiftieth Street and Madison Avenue was a luxurious, majestic skyscraper fifty-five floors high, directly across the street from St. Patrick's Cathedral. Stepping into the lobby made you feel like royalty—the decor was classic, literally like a palace. I had read in magazines that this was Michael's favorite place to stay while in New York and I was hoping this time would be no different. When we had checked in earlier, we noticed a group of fans waiting across the street, and I knew that my research had paid off. Michael *was* staying there. I was so relieved.

As our cab pulled up to the entrance at around eleven, the group of about a hundred fans were still gathered across the street behind a barricade. A glimpse of Michael was all they wanted. Some held signs with Michael's picture; others were decked out in Michael's signature costume: high-water pants, a fedora, and one sparkly white glove. They were chanting, "Michael! Michael! Michael!" hoping to get his attention. New York City police manned the area, making sure the crowd didn't get out of control. This scene would repeat itself in every city Michael traveled to. At this moment, he was truly the king of the world.

Whenever Michael came to any town, the place stood still. It was as if pixie dust had been sprinkled over it. Everything seemed more alive, more beautiful—more *magical.* I distinctly remember being excited simply because Michael was breathing the same air, feeling the same weather, and seeing the same sights as I was.

Back then, Michael mania was in full effect. When he came to town, vendors would set up on every block, selling buttons and T-shirts and anything else they could stick his image on. It seemed like the entire world was under Michael's spell. New York City was no different on this balmy night.

We exited our cab and a surly hotel security guard stopped us at the revolving doors. "I'm sorry, but only guests of the hotel are allowed in the lobby." Aunt Vera proudly produced the card key to our room. That was the magic ticket. The guard's demeanor instantly changed to warmth and we were promptly escorted into the elegant lobby.

I felt so special as I looked back at the growing crowd of screaming fans being held at bay across the street. Some shouted, "La Toya!," mistaking me for Michael's beautiful older sister. I chuckled under my breath but felt honored to be mistaken for anyone in the Jackson family. I reveled in the moment and waved to the crowd. They screamed even louder.

We headed for the elevators to our room. Just then, I saw Michael getting out of a glass elevator from the parking garage. We had managed somehow to arrive at the hotel at the same time. He walked in with a black towel around his neck and a big brown coat. He spotted me and started staring. I waved. He waved back.

"Oh my God, Tracy! Did you see that? He recognized me! I know he did." I was so giddy, I was talking a mile a minute. "I know he saw me in the audience! I cannot believe this. Did you see him wave? We have got to meet him tonight, no matter what."

In my teenage mind, Michael's wave was all the proof I needed that we had made a love connection. There was no way I was going back to Maryland without at least *trying* to meet him. I had caught his attention. I couldn't turn back now.

With a cool swagger, Michael strolled onto one of the special elevators that were guarded by security. These private elevators only stopped on the top floors, where the penthouses were located. Through our investigations, Tracy and I had found out that Michael's suite was on the fifty-third floor. We started devising a plan. The elevators we had access to didn't go to those floors, of course. They could only be reached by those private elevators. We decided that the only way to reach his floor would be to bypass the elevator altogether and walk . . . up the stairs . . . fifty-three flights.

When you're young your brain thinks differently. You feel invincible and don't think about consequences. Yeah, we were young and crazy, and clearly in good physical shape. We trudged up those stairs without a second thought. Our minds were focused on one thing and one thing only: getting to Michael.

When we finally reached the floor, I opened the door that led to the hallway. To our surprise, our plan had worked. As we turned the corner, I spotted Chuck, Michael's main bodyguard, with his trademark black top hat that I had seen him wearing in pictures with Michael. I thought that we would immediately be kicked off the floor, because he looked imposing. Michael's entire security staff was there.

I boldly approached Chuck and told him that I had seen him in Japan.

He said, "Oh, you were there?"

"No, on TV," I said.

Everyone laughed. I guess they were used to fans following Michael all over the world.

Tracy asked Chuck if he could get Michael's autograph for her. He said that would be no problem at all.

Just then, Emmanuel Lewis, famous for playing Webster on the sitcom of the same name, emerged from what appeared to be Michael's suite. He was shockingly tiny, only a little taller than my knee. I think we were close to the same age. Chuck asked Emmanuel if he could get Michael's autograph for Tracy. He said, "Sure." Then I decided I wanted one too.

"Get me one too, please," I said as I ran after him.

"Whose do you want? Mine or his?"

Not wanting to hurt Emmanuel's feelings, I said, "Both."

He said, "No, you probably want Michael's. I'll get it." Before walking back into the suite, he asked us to write our names on a sheet of paper so that Michael could personalize our autographs.

Back then, an autograph was equivalent to a selfie. We didn't have cell phones, so a camera wasn't always readily available; an autograph was the only proof you could show your friends that you actually met a celebrity. I hadn't even brought a camera on this trip. None of us had. Times were different then. Our memories and, in my case, my diaries, are all we now have.

Hilary, another member of Michael's security team, whispered to Chuck, "Janet just called. She'll be up in a few minutes."

Janet Jackson was at the height of her fame at this time, having recently released her chart-topping album *Control.* I had just performed the title track at my high school talent show with my best friend, Tirina, learning every move of the groundbreaking choreography from the music video and singing over Janet's breathy vocals. We received a standing ovation for our performance, and I won Most Talented of my senior class shortly thereafter. Needless to say, I was a fan.

Emmanuel came back with our autographs and handed them to us. My heart nearly stopped when I saw the ornate silver handwriting that was uniquely Michael's. He had *touched* this picture of him in his motorcycle jacket, which also meant Michael was actually in the room just a few feet away. A rush of excitement surged in my veins. He was *so close.*

The elevator door opened. It was Janet with her boyfriend at the time, Rene. I smiled with anxious anticipation as she approached. Dressed in a silk black blazer and black slacks, she looked as gorgeous in person as she did in pictures. I greeted her with a warm "Hi!"

She stared coldly, not saying a word, as she sauntered by.

I was so disappointed.

Jimmy Jam, Quincy Jones, Sugar Ray Leonard, and a parade of other celebrities I had only dreamed of meeting started exiting the elevator after Janet's arrival. At this point, I could no longer contain myself. I said to Chuck, "Can we please go in to the party?"

He said, "You really want to go in?"

"Yes, please."

"What would you do if you went in?"

"We'd mingle. We'd be nice." I was practically begging at this point.

Then one of Michael's other bodyguards said, "Why is it that pretty girls always get their way?"

With no other choice at this point, Chuck reluctantly said, "OK. Go ahead in."

Chuck, wherever you are today, *thank you.*

As we opened the door and walked into the room, the bright lights hit me. Everyone was staring. We were probably the only non-A-list people in the room. They must have wondered who we were and thought we were important too. I was wearing a black leather jacket, black leather pants, black high heel boots with silver buckles, and toy handcuffs hung from my belt. Of course, I hadn't even kissed a boy yet, so my "bad girl" look was all for show.

I stopped and stood in the foyer of this immaculate suite and took everything in. Here I was, in Michael Jackson's penthouse at the top of New York City. Even in my wildest dreams, I hadn't imagined this. I scoped the place out, wanting to soak up every detail of this room that only royalty and very special people had inhabited. It was an elegant suite, with a massive window that encompassed the entire side of one wall and displayed a breathtaking view of Manhattan's sparkling skyline. To the right of the foyer was a winding staircase that led to an upstairs bedroom—obviously Michael's room. In front of me was a beautiful black baby grand piano.

I looked behind me and Janet and Rene were sitting on a sofa, keeping to themselves, people-watching. I was now slightly afraid to even cross Janet's path again. Her cold stare was enough to ward me away for life.

Next to the piano, Michael's personal photographer, Sam Emerson, was standing taking pictures. I knew that Sam only took pictures of Michael, so I figured he couldn't be too far away. I walked closer and *there he was*, leaning against the piano; guests surrounded him, getting their pictures taken. I walked and stood next to Sam. I didn't dare ask for a picture, fearing he would discover that I was a mere mortal. I wanted to just blend in with the scenery, in fact. Surely everyone must have known we didn't belong.

But then Michael spotted me. A big smile spread across his famous face and his eyes widened through his Ray-Ban sunglasses. He vigorously waved like a schoolboy spotting a familiar face in the crowd. I slightly smiled and looked over my shoulder to see whom he was waving at. Surely, it couldn't be me.

But it *was* . . .

I waved back.

Suddenly, not only did I belong at the party, but the host himself had welcomed me. I started to relax as I felt a million eyes staring even harder. Michael's welcome had inducted me into this crowd of A-listers and transformed me into one of them. Everybody was suddenly extremely nice. Even Janet's attitude softened a bit.

Too afraid to actually speak words, I walked closer and stood behind Michael. He was acting as the perfect host, chatting with his guests and making sure everyone was happy, taking pictures with anyone who asked. *Boy, I wish I had brought my camera.* He was gracious, humble, and friendly. He was the Michael I had always dreamed he would be. He had been famous for almost twenty years at this point, but fame still hadn't quite taken complete hold of him. He was just a normal, extremely nice guy entertaining guests in a hotel room. No one would have ever guessed that this dude had just finished performing in front of twenty thousand screaming fans at Madison Square Garden.

His skin was perfectly smooth and a lovely chocolate color. He wasn't wearing any makeup and was simply beautiful. Onstage, his skin had seemed much lighter, even white, but I was happy to see that he still had his original beautiful brown complexion just like when he was a little boy. His lighter-looking skin was all a result of stage makeup, I surmised.

Even back then there were rumors that he was bleaching his skin and nasty tabloid stories about it. I was so happy to see that that couldn't be further from the truth. His hair was nice and freshly washed, with a wavy ponytail—a short one. *He must wear a fake one sometimes*, I thought, because it was longer in concert just an hour earlier. He had on black Ray-Ban sunglasses and a red corduroy button-down shirt that was tucked into his black slacks; his belt was silver and glittery. His amazingly cool black lace-up shoes had silver plates on the tips. His right arm was adorned with two bracelets, one silver, the other black. He had a noticeable dent on the side of his nose, but nothing looked fake. In fact, he was more handsome in person, with no makeup on, than I had ever seen him in pictures and videos. He was small, though. His waist must have been smaller than mine, and I only weighed ninety-eight pounds. I had on high heels, which made me about five foot six. He wasn't much taller than I was—maybe five foot nine.

I also noticed he was chewing gum. I had never seen Michael chew gum before and it made him seem so *normal.* Up until now, I had only seen him on TV and in pictures, so in my mind he was this perfect dream guy who didn't do normal stuff like chew gum or go to the bathroom. He was a *star* and stars didn't do normal stuff like us regular folks.

I overheard Sean Lennon, who was twelve years old, begging his mother, Yoko Ono, to let him spend the night. He begged and begged until finally she agreed . . . just a regular mother and son having a typical conversation.

It appeared that Michael was going to have a slumber party with Sean Lennon, Emmanuel Lewis, and a couple of other kids I saw running around. Although Michael was in his late twenties and in the prime of his superstardom, no sexy female groupie types were roaming around like one would expect at a concert after-party like this. Michael was different: he preferred the company of kids. This made him even more endearing to me. His Peter Pan persona appealed to those of us not ready for actual relationships. He was safe.

Jimmy Jam sat at the baby grand and started playing a few songs, his fingers gliding seamlessly over the ivory keys. I walked over to the window, gazed upon the sparkling lights, and thought, *Is this really happening?* It all felt like a dream. There was Michael, *staring at me.* Nights like this just didn't occur in my world.

I strolled over to the bar, where an array of minibottles lined the marble counter. Too young to drink alcohol, I poured myself a 7Up. I wanted to seem cool, with a drink in my hand. Even the 7Up tasted better than it ever had before. To this day, when I drink a 7Up, I am transported back to Michael's hotel suite on that spring night when I was seventeen.

All of New York's elite seemed to be in the room. I spotted New York artist Keith Haring, who had spread a bunch of buttons with his political sketches on them on Michael's coffee table. Keith would pass away two years later from complications of the AIDS virus. I still have some of those buttons and cherish them.

Tracy and I found an empty sofa and relaxed, hoping to blend in. I glanced up and spotted Quincy Jones walking over. He asked if anyone was sitting in the spot next to me. I managed to nervously mutter that the seat was empty. He plopped onto the sofa and placed his icy brown cocktail, which he had mixed himself at the bar, on the coffee table. I tried to remain calm as I watched him coolly sip his beverage and chat with other nearby guests. After all,

I didn't want to blow my cover. No one needed to know that I was still in high school and dying inside, sitting next to the man who had produced *Thriller*. I felt like Cinderella, worried that the clock would strike midnight at any minute and I would have to return to normal life. Surrounded by legends, I could only think about how out of place I was. These people had accomplished so much. I had watched them win Grammys, perform concerts, and create masterpieces. And here I was, just a girl from Largo, Maryland. My life had only just begun.

I then saw Michael spot Janet and Rene. Determined to at least shake Michael's hand, I walked back over to him. I overheard Rene say, "Great show, man!" Michael shook his hand and said, "Thank you." Then Michael leaned over to Janet and whispered something in her ear. As if Michael had just shared the most amazing secret ever heard, she widened her already big eyes and said, "Really? Get out of here!" Michael smiled and said, "I'll call you." They seemed like typical siblings, Janet looking up to her big brother.

Then Michael turned around. He was just a few inches away. He was so close I could smell his perfume. He looked at me, smiled the biggest smile, with the whitest teeth I had ever seen, reached out his hand, and said, "Hi. I'm Michael."

It felt like the entire world stopped. The man I had dreamed about since I was a child was standing in front of me, reaching for my hand. It was the moment I had been waiting for.

I silently composed myself and took his hand in mine. "Hi. I'm Shana."

His hand was so soft. It felt like a warm, billowy cloud. It was the softest hand I had ever felt. I was so nervous. I was afraid to hold it too tight. So I delicately held it as if it were a porcelain doll, not wanting to disrespect the hand that wore that famous white glove.

But Michael took me by surprise and grabbed my hand tighter. I opened my hand to let go of his tight grip, but he *kept holding on*. I was stunned. He then slid his large thin hand down my entire hand, lingering on every finger and sliding down to the tips of my fingernails. The whole while he was smiling that big beautiful smile and nervously biting his bottom lip.

Michael Jackson was flirting with me.

It was one of those rare moments that will be flashed before my eyes when my life is at its end. This moment was *everything*.

Then other guests started closing in on him, vying for his attention. He was the man of the hour and everyone wanted their moment with him too. We looked at each other and smiled as I slinked back to the sofa where I had been sitting. Michael stayed a little longer, mingling with his guests, before heading up the spiral staircase, saying good night to everyone as he disappeared into his room. Sean Lennon and Emmanuel Lewis ran up the stairs behind him.

I thought that this would be one of those stories I would tell my future grandkids over and over until they were sick of hearing it, when I was old and gray: my one memory of meeting the most famous man in the world.

But it was only the beginning.

1

It's the possibility of having a dream come true
that makes life interesting.

—Paulo Coelho, *The Alchemist*

The Jackson Five exploded on the scene with four number-one hit singles, launching the seventies and securing their place in history. My parents and brother Todd watched their debut on *The Ed Sullivan Show*, which occurred just six months before I was born. I suppose I was there too, witnessing it from the womb.

Growing up, Todd and I loved to pretend we were the Jackson Five. He always insisted on being Michael. I protested, "No, I want to be Michael!" But Todd was five years older than I and he invariably won, making me Marlon. We acted out our parts in our living room, dancing and belting out all of the hits in front of an imaginary audience of screaming fans.

Our warm home in Largo, Maryland, was the backdrop for what I remember as the perfect childhood—akin to a family life one might find in the 1950s. My father, Emmanuel, who preferred to be addressed by his nickname, Mano, worked as an electrical engineer. My mother, Janice, carved out a career as an IT/computer manager at prestigious government agencies in the DC area, including NASA. Although both of my parents had busy work schedules, my brother and I never had a babysitter. My parents took us with them everywhere, or one figured out a way to be home with us while the other worked. We had yearly summer vacations to Disney World in Orlando, Florida, and ate dinner together every night as a family.

My father had moved to Brooklyn from the French Caribbean island of Martinique in the early 1960s. He spoke with a romantic French accent and looked just like Johnny Mathis, who was my mother's idol. Suave and handsome, with thick, wavy black hair and a beautiful reddish-brown skin tone, he was what we call a pretty boy.

For my mother, it was love at first sight. She had relocated to New York City around the same time with her mother, whose family all lived in the New York area. She was working at a dry cleaning store when one day my father walked in to drop off some clothes. She was nineteen years old, and he was eight years older. They were married for forty-two years, until my father passed away in 2005.

On Christmas morning of 1973, I remember waking up before the sun to find an abundance of presents under our white Christmas tree. I spotted the Jackson Five board game and the other presents became invisible. Todd and I tore open the box and played as soon as we could take the pieces out. I was just a toddler so I wasn't very good at the game, but I tried my best to join in on the fun. Every Saturday morning our routine included playing that game in our pajamas while watching *The Jackson 5* cartoon and *Soul Train*, followed by *American Bandstand.*

We combed through *Right On!* magazine every month to see what Michael and his brothers were wearing and what they were doing. *Right On!* was like our bible. If we saw Michael wearing a fringe suede jacket, then of course we had to get one too. When I think of the 1970s, my memories are painted with a kaleidoscope of colors and rose-colored dreams. It was a great decade filled with disco, soul, Afros, bell bottoms, peace, and love.

Computers, cell phones, video games, DVDs, and CDs didn't exist. We used our imaginations to have fun. Nothing was immediate or readily accessible and the world felt more enchanting and mysterious because of it. Hollywood resided in a land far, far away—a place inhabited by glamorous, pretty people and only reached in our fantasies. My brother and I incessantly asked our mother what movie stars were really like. They seemed so perfect; we couldn't imagine them doing normal things like going to the bathroom. My mother, always wanting to maintain an air of wonder and magic in our lives, responded that, in fact, movie stars did *not* go to the bathroom. We believed her wholeheartedly and viewed Hollywood as a mystical place where all of your dreams came true. From that early age, I knew that California was the place I was meant to be. My mother had instilled in us the motto "Go be your dream."

The first concert I attended was the Jacksons' Triumph tour in 1981. Todd took me—he was sixteen years old and I was eleven. We hopped in my father's station wagon, the kind with the wood paneling along the sides, and drove the short distance to the venue. I wore my coolest outfit—a colorful, braided headband and a purple jelly-bean jacket. This jacket was a must-have among us preteen girls. Although it was made of cheap, plastic, see-through material, wearing it made me feel like a part of the in-crowd. My hair was in its usual style, two long braids and curled bangs in the front. In elementary school, I was known as "that Indian-looking girl" because of my long hair. It was the envy of all of the girls in my class.

We arrived at the venue of the concert, the Capitol Centre, which was a few miles from our house in Largo. The tickets for our nosebleed seats were an expensive twelve dollars each, which took many months of weekly allowances to save.

Stacy Lattisaw opened the show. She had the voice of an angel, was just a few years older than me, and also hailed from the Washington, DC, area. Seeing someone so close to my age, from my neighborhood, on TV and the radio, inspired me. I idolized her. Every day I locked myself in my room imagining I was Stacy, singing her songs and recording my voice in a cassette recorder. I also performed her songs at family get-togethers. Everyone knew to expect a one-woman show from me at all of our parties. I'm sure they were all sick of hearing me sing Stacy's hits "Let Me Be Your Angel" and "Love on a Two-Way Street" at every event, but enduring my little performances was the price you had to pay to eat the delicious food my mother was cooking at our frequent Maryland blue crab feasts.

Whenever Stacy had a new album coming out, I begged my parents to drive me to the record store on the first day of its release. The joy of seeing that big album cover sitting on display for the first time is one of those indescribable feelings that future generations will never know.

At the Jacksons' concert, Stacy performed all of her hit songs. Mesmerized, I sang along. Her initials, SL, were spray-painted on top of her hair. . . and the top of her hair was all I could make out from my seat in the upper deck. But that didn't dampen anything. I was fulfilling one of my girlhood dreams—being able to sing along with her live.

Stacy took her final bow and the lights in the arena dimmed. The crowd stirred with anticipation. After about twenty minutes, the arena went completely dark and a huge video screen dropped down in front of the stage. A short film starring the Jackson brothers played. The audience went crazy. There they were, up on the screen, singing their powerful anthem "Can You Feel It," which was one of the hit songs on their *Triumph* album. As the song boomed out over the large speakers, the excitement in the air intensified. Everyone screamed and sang along until it ended. The video screen disappeared into the air and huge colored spotlights rose from the darkness. All five of the brothers stood onstage, posed like statues of gods. With Michael in the center, they remained frozen for five minutes. The audience screamed louder and louder. The song "Can You Feel It" exploded back onto the sound system, and the brothers burst into their dance routine, singing the song live.

Stacy Lattisaw became a distant memory as I sat enthralled by the power of Michael's performance. He was no longer that little boy in the Jackson Five. He was a grown and sexy man now—a confident superstar. Michael made me a believer that night.

After the concert, my brother and I walked to our car, which was in an outside parking lot. We noticed circles of teens gathered. Curious, we approached one of them. Two teens were in the middle of the circle performing a weird dance we had never seen before. It baffled us. They were gliding as if on air and spinning on the ground with acrobatic moves. As it turns out, it was *breakdancing*. It was the first time my brother and I had ever witnessed it.

From the moment MTV launched its rocket ship in 1981, it was on all day in my house. And no artist was more brilliant when it came to music videos than Michael Jackson. I always had the VCR ready to record anything that had to do with Michael, and

I amassed a stack of tapes that I watched over and over again. I remember running home from school to catch the world premieres of Michael's short films from the *Thriller* album. Michael didn't call them music videos, he called them short films—and they really were. These were not the cheap videos with cheesy special effects and bad choreography that filled MTV all day. Michael's videos each had a story line, expensive sets, great cinematography, a respected director, and breathtaking choreography. And thus, MTV treated the premiere of a new Michael video as an *event*.

In my teenage years, I wasn't like most other girls. I wasn't crazy for boys and I had no interest in partying. I preferred to keep to myself. I was a loner. I always felt I was on the outside looking in on life—never feeling like I fully fit in with anybody or anything. The song "At Seventeen" by Janis Ian became my theme song. At school, I became known for my unique wardrobe—wearing mismatched socks, sparkly gold boots, and three watches on each arm. I was a cross between Madonna, Jody Watley, and Cyndi Lauper. I dared to be different and the other kids respected me because of it. But I knew that living in a small town was just not for me. California was the only place I wanted to be and dreams of living there consumed my mind.

While other kids partied, I took the subway to Washington, DC, to visit the Smithsonian and other places filled with culture. Alone, I attended plays and concerts of classic singers—soaking up as much as I could. I watched old movies and read every book that ever existed on Hollywood. The entertainment world was all I cared about, and I was determined to learn every piece of its history.

At the age of fifteen, I became fascinated by ballet legend Mikhail Baryshnikov. I saw him in a movie called *White Nights* with Gregory Hines and I fell in love. I just had to meet him.

Baryshnikov was the star dancer of the American Ballet Theater and the revered company was scheduled to perform a few nights at the Kennedy Center in downtown Washington, DC. My friend Cheryl and I came up with the bright idea to dress as ballerinas and sneak backstage so we could meet him. There was one small catch—there were no black ballerinas in the American Ballet Theater. We knew we would stand out like a sore thumb, but we were willing to try anything. Believe it or not, our crazy plan worked.

We dressed in ballet workout clothes—leg warmers, shorts, and a T-shirt—and strolled through the backstage door. No one stopped us at all. *We were in.*

The first night was called the gala. This was huge in the ballet world. Politicians and the upper crust of Washington, DC, were all in attendance, having paid lots of money to witness the brilliance of Baryshnikov.

We found our way to the stage and stood in the wings, watching the entire gala from that location. We were actually on the stage, just behind the curtain, waiting with the other ballerinas who were taking turns dancing on and off stage. At one point, Baryshnikov, his entire body drenched in sweat, twirled off stage and reclined in a chair right next to me. He flexed his leg muscles, warming up for the next sequence. I thought I had died and gone to heaven. No one said a word to us all night and we were glad. I suppose they figured we belonged.

We tried our luck and went back the next night, hoping for the same results. We managed to watch half of the show from the same location until a crew member told us we were in the way and couldn't stand there due to insurance issues. We left, sad but with a feeling of accomplishment. Our goal of watching Baryshnikov dance, up close and in person, was achieved. I think some of his sweat might have even dripped on me on his way off of the stage.

This sense of adventure was the driving force behind my decision to leave Largo, Maryland, at the age of eighteen and drive across the country to California. I had attended precollege courses in high school from the University of Maryland, graduating with honors and straight As, and my mailbox was flooded with scholarship offers from prestigious universities. But California was calling. Every second that passed was a second that I could be in Los Angeles. I felt I was wasting time by not being where I knew I belonged. College would always be there, I figured. And if I moved to California, I could go to my dream school, UCLA, while working a part-time job. All of these thoughts swirled in my mind as I packed my bags and loaded them into my 1984 gray Chevrolet Cavalier, which I received as a graduation present from my parents.

My friend Evelyn joined me on my adventure and we hit the road, taking turns driving. We had formed a singing duo a few months before and we were determined to get a record deal—writing a new song every day and recording them on our cheap, portable cassette recorder. Evelyn played the keyboard and I wrote the lyrics and melodies. We figured we could record a real demo when we arrived in L.A. and find a record company interested in us. Yes, we thought it would be that easy.

On our journey across the United States, we recorded and wrote five new songs. I sang as I drove through the cow pastures of Texas and the majestic mountains of Arizona, while Evelyn operated the tape recorder. We were focused on having a few songs to give record companies upon our arrival. We didn't have any other jobs lined up—we just figured it would all work out somehow.

An invisible force was pulling me to Los Angeles and I wasn't going to let a minor detail like a job or lack of money stop me.

My dreams were big, and it was time to chase them.

2

Life is either a daring adventure or nothing.

—Helen Keller

WELCOME TO CALIFORNIA. Evelyn and I screamed with joy as the words on the dusty green sign came into view. After driving nonstop across the United States for two and a half days, we had arrived.

It was 1989 and Los Angeles felt like paradise. There was a sense of hope here, a feeling that anything was possible. The sun was bright and hot and the sky was deep blue, with no clouds in sight. Just waking up every morning and seeing palm trees swaying outside of my window made me happy.

Evelyn moved in with her sister in the rich neighborhood of Brentwood, just down the street from O. J. Simpson, and I settled into a Holiday Inn in Glendale, a sleepy town just on the edge of the San Fernando Valley, which was not considered a desirable area back then. But it was cheap, safe, and offered monthly rates for extended stays. At $650 a month, it couldn't be beat.

Incidentally, Michael's final resting place would be in Glendale at Forest Lawn Memorial cemetery. And, by some twist of fate, I was there on June 25, 2009, when I learned of his death as I was driving by the cemetery. But I still had twenty years to go before any of that happened. We'll get to that later.

Between trips to Fat Burger, Evelyn and I wrote and recorded songs in a makeshift recording studio inside the pool house in the backyard of Evelyn's sister's Brentwood mansion, located just off of Sunset Boulevard. We purchased a four-track recorder, microphone, reverb machine, and keyboards—just enough to get by. After polishing our demo of three pop/R&B songs, we pounded the pavement, hoping for a lucky break.

The lucky break came, but not in the music industry.

Evelyn's brother-in-law introduced us to an attorney named Stephen Barnes, who set up a meeting for us with a young African American movie director named Reginald Hudlin. Inside his small office in Hollywood, Reggie told us about a movie he had just finished writing called *House Party*. The film would also mark his directorial debut. The casting process had just started and, despite our lack of acting experience, he gave us both nonspeaking roles that were showcased throughout the film in memorable scenes. Starring in the film were Martin Lawrence, rappers Kid 'N Play, and a host of other young unknown talent also just arriving in town. We were ecstatic to be a part of a real Hollywood production.

We filmed the majority of the movie on a soundstage at Culver Studios in Culver City. *Gone with the Wind* was also filmed there back in the 1930s, and I felt honored to stand where Clark Gable and Vivien Leigh once recited their famous lines.

Next door to our stage was the set for the Saturday morning children's show *Pee-wee's Playhouse*. I was a huge fan of Pee-wee Herman and his movie *Pee-wee's Big Adventure*, having watched it many times. I couldn't have been more excited. Every morning, as I sat outside in the chilly air, sipping a steaming hot cup of coffee from the craft services table, I watched Pee-wee walk from his trailer to the stage. I hoped to catch a glimpse of him without the pancake makeup he always wore. Not only did I see him bare faced and in street clothes, I spotted him smoking a cigarette. I was shocked. Pee-wee Herman a smoker? Wow. The illusions created by the Hollywood image machine were starting to unveil themselves.

House Party was a hit. It became one of the most popular films in the history of African American cinema and is now considered a classic. Not a bad way to start my career in Hollywood.

After *House Party*, I won small roles in sitcoms such as *Family Matters*, *A Different World*, *2 Guys a Girl and a Pizza Place*, and *The Fresh Prince of Bel Air*. My dreams of a singing career never panned out, however, and my friend Evelyn moved back to Washington, DC, to live a normal life.

I was now alone with no steady income in this big city. On a whim, I interviewed for a job as a tour guide at Universal Studios. Actually, it wasn't an interview—it was an audition. I competed against hundreds of other young hopefuls, all with dreams of having this seemingly fun and glamorous job. The grueling weeklong interview process ended with a test that included reciting a one-hundred-page script verbatim, over a microphone, as we cruised on an empty tram through the historic back lot. Remembering every detail of Universal Studios history was not easy and most failed. But I was a show biz history junkie, which helped me pass the test with flying colors. I got the job.

Every day, I conducted three tours on a tram filled with two hundred wide-eyed guests, narrating the extensive route as we passed by such iconic locations as the *Psycho* house and New York Street. It was fun but hard work. Being a tour guide was definitely more difficult than it looked, and I only lasted three months.

If I wanted to stay in L.A., I needed to find a *real* job—fast.

3

> We shall never know all the good that a simple smile can do.
>
> —Mother Theresa

It was a breezy spring day in Hollywood as I circled Cahuenga Boulevard looking for a metered parking space. The streets were bustling with tourists and parking was always elusive in this part of town. I endured this daily ritual to visit my favorite newsstand, World Book and News. Filled with every periodical you could imagine, this place was heaven for people like me who devoured magazines. The owners probably hated me because I never bought anything—I stood leafing through entire magazines, sometimes for hours. My first item of business was always the trades—specifically the *Hollywood Reporter* and *Variety*. Back then, the trades were the sole places to find office jobs in the entertainment industry. I had no office experience, but I figured if I mailed out enough resumes, at least one would stick.

I spotted an ad in the *Hollywood Reporter* that read, "Top Music Management Company Seeks Receptionist." That sounded interesting. I wrote down the address and mailed my résumé the next day. I didn't expect anyone to respond, since no one else had, but it was worth a try.

Two weeks later, I received a phone call requesting an interview. The person on the phone never mentioned the name of the company, just the address. I figured I had nothing to lose, so I scheduled an interview for the next day.

Wearing the only business attire I owned—a conservative blue dress, black pumps with heels worn down, and a pair of panty hose that had a rip in them—I hopped in my Chevy Cavalier and embarked on the route I would eventually take every morning for the next seven years.

I lived in North Hollywood, located in the San Fernando Valley section of Los Angeles. An ethnically diverse town with mostly young, struggling actors, singers, and dancers, it was where a lot of us landed upon moving to L.A. It was affordable, offered an endless array of acting classes and dance studios, and was not far from the action on the other side of the hill in Hollywood.

The valley was as close to suburbia as you could find in L.A., with an abundance of sidewalks, cheap apartments, houses filled with barking dogs, backyard pool parties, and barbeques. It got so hot in the summer you could often see the heat rising from the blacktop.

My weekend nights usually consisted of combing the aisles of Tower Records on Ventura Boulevard in Sherman Oaks, searching for rare vinyl records, or reading foreign magazines at the local newsstand on Van Nuys. Yeah, I was a nerd. No wild parties or crazy friends for me. The valley was a fun place to live if you were young but most of us dreamed of living on the other side of the hill, where it was cool—and expensive. Even though it was only seven miles away, it felt like the other side of the world, with its beautiful beaches, movie stars, and fast cars. We valley kids were all striving for one thing—success in Hollywood and a way over there.

I pulled out of my garage and drove down Lankershim Boulevard, passing dilapidated old apartment buildings, gaudy car dealerships, and Universal Studios. I made a right onto Ventura, where tall palm trees lined the sidewalk in front of trendy clothing boutiques and cafés. Every street in the valley offered a different experience, which was one of the great things about it. I turned left onto Laurel Canyon and proceeded over the hill.

Let me tell you about Laurel Canyon. When I first moved to L.A. and drove down this curvy, narrow, scary road for the first time, I was terrified. I couldn't imagine ever driving it at night. It's one lane in each direction and any wrong move could equal disaster. Somehow, though, Laurel Canyon would soon become my best friend, offering me an escape route out of the boring valley to the glamorous world of Hollywood. Each morning I would look forward to traveling down its shady lanes lined with imposing trees and hippie-looking houses straight out of the 1960s, anticipating the exciting adventures that awaited me on the other side. It would become the yellow brick road of my life—offering hope and endless opportunities to make dreams come true.

Laurel Canyon ends at Sunset Boulevard, right where the legendary Schwabs drugstore used to sit. Every time I approached that intersection, I imagined it still being there, filled with young starlets hoping to be discovered.

I made a right. My attention was focused on finding the address they gave for the job interview: 8730 Sunset Blvd., Penthouse West. I didn't have much experience with job interviews, so I tried to imagine all of the questions they might ask. As I silently rehearsed every possibility, I reached the tallest building on the block—a brown, modern glass structure sitting in the middle of Sunset Plaza. This section of Sunset was considered trendy because celebrity hot spot restaurants such as Le Dome and Nicky Blair, along with upscale designer clothing boutiques, lined the block. Across the street was Spago, where chef Wolfgang Puck became an icon, and the annual star-studded Academy Awards after-party was held. In my mind, there was no way I would ever be lucky enough to work in a location like this. I wasn't hip or cool and would never fit in with these fancy people.

I parked and wandered around the packed underground garage searching for the elevators. Every space seemed to be filled with brand new Mercedes, Jaguars, and shiny sports cars.

There was an East Tower and a West Tower, which, as I read on the directory, housed entertainment companies, including the *National Enquirer,* BMI Music, and Levine/Schneider Public Relations. The West Penthouse, where I was headed, belonged to Gallin Morey Associates. I entered the mirrored elevator and pressed PENTHOUSE. I tried to contain my nerves as the door swished closed and I ascended to the top floor. The door opened and, to my surprise, it deposited me directly into the suite. Gallin Morey encompassed the entire floor. The first person to greet me was the front desk receptionist. This was the job I was interviewing for, and I started imagining myself sitting there smiling. I bubbled with excitement at the prospect of working at this glamorous place.

As I waited in the lobby on one of the plush leather couches, I recalled a strange dream I had the night before. The dream was about the interview about to take place. All I could remember of the dream was that the person interviewing me kept saying, "All you have to do is smile."

I kept that in mind as Lisa, the human resources coordinator, came out to get me. She was tall, with long, flowing brown hair, and she was beautiful, just like everybody else. Lisa led me down halls lined with framed movie posters and past offices filled with platinum records with intense, young assistants pecking on typewriters. Music blasted out of slick conference rooms as brash executives ranted on phones. They wore colorful Armani suits that looked straight out of the wardrobe department for *Miami Vice*. This wasn't your typical office. This was a rock-and-roll office, filled with energy and passion. And I now wanted to work here *bad*.

Lisa was nice and easy to talk to, and the interview went well. After it was over, as I was heading out of the door, she stopped me. With a knowing look, she said, "You have an amazing smile. That's just what we need for this position."

About a week later, I received a call from Lisa informing me that I had *gotten the job*. I could not believe it. The advice from my dream had worked. I have no doubt that my smile was what sealed the deal.

Even though I was excited, I was apprehensive about accepting. I had never had a full-time job before, so the thought of being stuck at a desk from 9 AM to 7 PM every day was daunting. Plus, I wanted to be an actress. How on earth would I be able to go on auditions if I were stuck at a desk all day? I called my mother, who always found the positives in every situation, and asked what I should do. She said, "Well, everything happens for a reason. You never know what the reason may be. Go ahead and try it out for three months. You just might like it." I took her always sage advice and accepted the offer.

4

We are the music-makers,
And we are the dreamers of dreams

—Arthur O'Shaughnessy, *Ode*

Gallin Morey Associates was one of the hottest music and talent management companies of the '90s. Its doors were often referred to as "the gateway to the stars." Everybody who was anybody came through them, and for seven years, I was front and center in this exclusive enclave of dream makers. Some of our clients included Dolly Parton, Neil Diamond, Mac Davis, the Pointer Sisters, Martin Lawrence, Milli Vanilli, Whoopie Goldberg, Korn, Nicole Kidman, Renée Zellwegger, Paul Walker, Mariah Carey, and, to my surprise, *Michael Jackson.*

Sandy Gallin was a flamboyant and charming Hollywood power player. His best friend was billionaire David Geffen. Together they knew everybody. They were a part of the so-called Velvet Mafia, which consisted of some of the most powerful gay executives in town.

Another of Sandy's best friends was screen legend Elizabeth Taylor. Several times a day, Elizabeth called Sandy to discuss the latest Hollywood gossip. Her favorite topic of conversation—Michael Jackson. Sometimes she called so often Sandy had to dodge her calls by asking me to tell her he wasn't there. The funny thing is that she always knew when I was lying. She would say, "Suuure he's not there." Laughing, I would respond, "No, I'm serious. He just left." I could never fool her though, and we laughed about it together, both knowing the truth.

I had many conversations with Elizabeth (who didn't like to be called Liz) and she was always funny and kind. I remember her calling the day after she announced her engagement to construction worker Larry Fortensky. She left a message for Sandy, and then called right back five minutes later. When she heard my voice she said, "Hi, this is Elizabeth." Then, she caught herself, remembering that she had already called. "Oh, didn't I just talk to you?" she said.

"Yes, you did," I said.

She started chuckling. "Oh my goodness. I must be losing my mind. Well, I guess that's what happens when you're a blushing bride."

We both laughed and I congratulated her on her engagement. Even though it was her eighth, she still seemed excited at the prospect of marriage. She still believed in love.

Elizabeth's speaking voice was elegant, with a singsongy happy tone as if she were on the verge of laughter at all times. I always looked forward to speaking to her because I knew she would make me smile. She was down to earth, much like Michael. I started noticing that the bigger the star, the more kind and grounded they were. Sandy's other prized client, Dolly Parton, was the same way. She always asked me how I was doing when she called and shared jokes with me. She even listed me in the thank-you section of her autobiography. I can't say enough wonderful things about Dolly.

Interesting people ambled off of the elevators in front of my desk all day. I never knew whom to expect when those silver elevator doors opened. I remember sitting at my desk one afternoon when an office assistant named Josie approached me. A young hunk with deep blue eyes and bulging muscles accompanied her. His handsome face took my breath away.

"Shana, this is Brad. Would you mind giving him some parking validations?"

Brad reached out his hand and introduced himself.

Unfortunately, I had decided to eat lunch at my desk that day—Taco Bell. Brad caught me right in the middle of taking a bite out of a Soft Taco Supreme. I was so embarrassed I wanted to crawl under my desk. Sour cream and hot sauce dripped from my hands as I ransacked the Taco Bell bag, looking for a napkin.

"Hi, Brad. I'm Shana. Nice to meet you . . . I'm sorry I'm eating, but I haven't had a chance to go to lunch."

Brad peered over my desk to see what I was munching on. The sight of the familiar bag and my half-eaten taco excited him. "Taco Bell! That is my favorite place to eat. I'm not kidding. I go to the one on Beverly Boulevard almost every day. That's some good stuff."

Brad became even more handsome after he told me this. "Yes, it is good!" I responded, my mouth filled with ground beef and cheese. "Brad, what's your last name? I have to write it down for the parking validations."

"No worries. It's Pitt. P-i-t-t. Brad Pitt."

Brad's first successful film, *Thelma and Louise,* was released a few weeks after our meeting and his fame ascended into the stratosphere. I'm quite sure he was never asked for his last name again.

I wonder if Taco Bell is still his favorite place to eat.

Sandy Gallin was one of those bosses you could only find in Hollywood. He meditated daily with a turbaned guru named Gurmukh and fired his assistants on an almost weekly basis. I often heard him screaming at them for making the smallest mistake. I watched as they ran out of the office crying, never to return.

Sandy liked to eat a baked potato with grilled onions and steamed vegetables from Le Dome (which was located on the ground floor of our building) every day for lunch. If his assistants didn't have it delivered at the exact time he wanted it, he yelled at them. Sometimes he would even throw things at them. The more they showed fear, the more he would attack. Most didn't last long. But Sandy had a charm about him that made him difficult to dislike. He was funny, with an edgy wit, and was always nice to me. I grew to love him and, thankfully, I was never subjected to any of his tirades.

Jim Morey was the opposite of Sandy: loved by all. He was friendly and a genuinely nice guy, a family man, married with kids, and a dream boss. He was the more conservative one, wearing designer suits, smelling of rich cologne, and always carrying a briefcase. He and Sandy evened each other out—yin and yang—the perfect partnership. He gave me advice and helped me navigate the crazy world I was now a part of.

My desk was the calm in the middle of the storm and often I acted as a therapist, encouraging the assistants to hang in there. Some of those assistants were the young, gay, handsome boys Sandy met at his famous weekly pool parties, which were held at his sprawling mansion in Beverly Hills or his beach home in Malibu. Most of these boys were fresh off the bus from small towns across the country. They harbored dreams of becoming rich or famous—or both. I chuckled every time a new one stepped off the elevator for his first day on the job. They were so fresh-faced and eager. That excitement never lasted long.

I somehow managed to stay at the company for nearly a decade—a record, I'm sure. Over those years, I witnessed the birth of many legends and had a front-row seat to the wild and wacky music industry, which was thriving in those heady days of the '90s.

My first month on the job, I was invited to one of Sandy's famous parties. They were a thing of legend, something you only read about in magazines. Think *The Great Gatsby*. This would be my first real Hollywood party. I hadn't even turned twenty-one yet, so to say I was naive and unsophisticated would be an understatement.

My old Chevy Cavalier trudged up the winding palm tree–lined road that led to Sandy's expansive mansion. His house sat high atop a hill, just above Doheny Drive. As I reached the gate, a valet/aspiring actor greeted me to park my car. I had never seen a valet at someone's private home before. Something told me this was not going to be an ordinary party.

The bash was being thrown in honor of Sandy's boyfriend, Tom. It was his birthday. Tom was drop-dead gorgeous, with impossibly deep dimples and a sweet midwestern personality. He worked at Gallin Morey as a junior music manager. I had no idea he was gay or Sandy's boyfriend until this night. He was so cute I'd actually developed a crush on him during my short time at the company. Sandy was obviously besotted as well, because this party was extravagant.

A hot, young waiter holding a tray filled with crystal flutes of champagne greeted me as I entered the opulent foyer. It was like stepping into a page of *Architectural Digest*. Everything seemed to be bathed in white, yet was cozy and comfortable. These kind of houses had to be seen to be believed. It was stunning.

While I stood in awe, not knowing which way to turn first, I spotted Madonna. Yes, *that* Madonna. I had gone through my Madonna phase as a teenager, emulating her unique style of dress and watching her videos nonstop, so this was exciting. As I walked closer, I became disappointed. She didn't look anything like she did in her music videos. She barely had on any makeup. Her hair was jet black and looked like it could use a wash—it was pulled back off her face. She wore a baggy T-shirt and shorts that were too big for her, with flat shoes and knee-high socks. She was also short, which I didn't expect. Her date for the evening was Alex Keshishian, who directed her hit documentary, *Truth or Dare*. She was thirty-two years old at this time but looked like a schoolgirl gone bad. Her demeanor was that of someone who was under the influence of something. I'm not sure if she actually was, but she was acting spacey. I overheard her saying, "I don't do the blue ones." I imagined she was discussing pills, as most of Hollywood seemed to be on them and other drugs.

Madonna had met Michael for the first time a few months earlier, at Sandy's previous party. They had spent the entire night sitting on the steps in Sandy's foyer talking. Shortly after that meeting, they attended the Academy Awards together.

Michael loved to tell the story of his first date with Madonna. According to him, she came to his condo in nothing but a robe and tried to seduce him. But Madonna's plan didn't work. Her aggression turned him off.

Although he rebuffed her advances that night, he seriously reconsidered his decision, wondering if perhaps he should've tried it out. He asked a few of his male friends, including music producer Teddy Riley, for advice. "Should I do her?" he asked. His friends all told him to go for it. Most guys weren't turning down Madonna at that time. She was just as famous as Michael and considered a sex symbol, having just released her controversial book, *Sex*. But he decided against it and the great hookup of Michael and Madonna never happened.

The drinks were free and endless at this Sandy Gallin party and everybody was indulging except me. I kept the same glass of champagne in my hand the entire night. I knew that I wouldn't be able to drive home if I drank more than that. Terence Trent D'Arby, whose hit song "Sign Your Name" had recently made him a star, was also there and appeared to have had one too many. I stood behind him in line for the bathroom. He became impatient because whoever was in the bathroom was taking a long time. After about ten minutes of waiting, he banged on the door shouting, "You're taking too long!"

I couldn't help but laugh, but I was happy he had the guts to do it, because we all had to go. To our surprise, when the door opened all three members of the Pointer Sisters came stumbling out, looking embarrassed. Terence hurried in without speaking another word and was out quickly. I went in after him and could smell the distinct scent of marijuana. That night I learned why people in Hollywood always went to the bathroom together and took forever to finish.

Sandy's best friend, David Geffen, was also there. At that moment, he was the richest, most powerful man in town. He sported a perpetual tan and a certain *je ne sais quoi* that made him irresistible. David and Sandy were both in their late forties but in incredible shape, able to attract any young, hot guy they desired. Everyone wanted to know David and, at this time, Michael Jackson was no different. David and Michael had become fast friends, and David introduced Michael to Sandy. That's how Michael became Sandy's client. There were even rumors that David and Michael were secretly dating. I wondered if this was true. No one really knew what Michael's sexual orientation was at this time but everyone speculated about it. He had managed to keep that side of himself ambiguous even to those who knew him well.

Years later, I asked Michael about David and why they were no longer close friends (Michael managed to fall out with most of his friends every few years). I don't know how true it is, because Michael was known to exaggerate on occasion, but he said that David had tried to seduce him, attempting to kiss him, and, according to Michael, he refused. Their friendship was strained after that. This story sounded surprisingly similar to the one about Madonna.

One thing was for sure: men and women were both intrigued by Michael's natural charm. To know him was to be in love with him. Many had tried and failed to seduce him. I started to wonder if it was possible for anyone to ever succeed.

5

When you want something, all the universe conspires in helping you to achieve it.

—Paulo Coehlo, *The Alchemist*

Back at the office, I spent most of my hours answering our busy phones and greeting visitors. It was a fun and easy job but the hours were long. Chatting with the various characters that worked at the company is what kept things interesting.

Sandy had a loyal and longtime executive assistant named Sheila. She was older and caring, much like a mother figure. The moment she first saw me, she declared that I would make the perfect wife for Michael. I agreed with her, of course, and we had fun discussing how we were going to achieve this. One day, after having enough of our daily meaningless chatter, she blurted, "That's it. I'm going to call Michael's assistant Norma right now and tell her I have found his wife."

Always high-strung, Sheila bolted up to her office to call Norma Staikos, Michael's longtime trusted assistant. About ten minutes later, she came back to my desk.

"I called Norma. So, now we're both plotting to get you and Michael together. Don't tell anybody. This is just between me, you, and Norma." Her voice then lowered to an almost conspiratorial tone, as if she were about to impart the most secret information in the world. "Norma told me what Michael likes in a woman. He likes them sexy, yet feminine. Quiet, with a twinkle in her eye, and not pushy or aggressive." She pointed her finger at me and whispered, "These are all you! You might be too young for him though. I don't know."

Michael was twelve years older than I was, but I knew he was young at heart. I told Sheila that I didn't think my age would bother him. She also said that she and Norma joked that we were both so shy, when we met we probably would stand in silence the entire time.

All of this talk was making me increasingly excited to see Michael again. At this point, he had only called on the phone to talk to Sandy and I had been too shy to say anything to him.

When I first started the job, Michael was putting the finishing touches on his *Dangerous* album, which was being recorded mostly at Record One in Sherman Oaks and Larrabee Studios in North Hollywood. I lived not far from those studios at the time, and I often saw Michael driving his white Chevy Blazer down Ventura. He led a seminormal, quiet life at this time—living in a high-rise condo he called the Hideout on Wilshire Boulevard and later a townhouse in Century City. Located right in the middle of the city, these condos were surrounded by people and neighbors. The ubiquitous cameras of TMZ didn't exist back then, so he was able to get around town without anyone noticing. It was not uncommon to stop at a red light, look over, and see Michael sitting next to you in his car, in the driver's seat. Those days would sadly end soon, however. The release of the *Dangerous* album launched Michael back into the spotlight and out of his temporary anonymity forever.

Michael delivered *Dangerous* to Sony on October 31, 1991. He toiled in the studio until the last possible minute, having already missed numerous deadlines. He was never satisfied with any of his work, always thinking he could make it better. His perfectionism often hindered him from finishing things that would have been great for anyone else.

The first problem that had to be ironed out before the album was released was the credits. Bill Botrell originally produced a majority of the songs and Teddy Riley was brought in later to make them better. Bill felt Teddy's name shouldn't be listed in the credits as a producer for certain songs. And Michael, rightfully having a bit of an ego, felt that his own name should be the only one credited. He felt that he was being generous by putting anyone else's name on them and boasted that he had written and produced everything himself, that he only had help from others. In the end, Michael acquiesced and everyone was properly credited, avoiding a lawsuit from the other producers—but not before a few angry phone calls and letters were exchanged.

Propaganda Films made a deal to produce all of the short films for the album, with a total budget of $12 million. Michael felt that they were spending too extravagantly, though, and told Jim Morey that it was his job to make sure they stop. He said he was "sick of it." He was always pretty tough with Jim and Sandy. He may have appeared to be kind and gentle, but he was known to make unreasonable demands of those who worked for him. It wasn't easy managing Michael Jackson.

The first appearance Michael was scheduled to make for the *Dangerous* album launch was for MTV10, the network's tenth anniversary celebration. His insecurities started creeping in, however, and he asked to make the tape date as late as possible. He said to Jim, "I need some time to recoup and to just figure out where I'm going. And plus, I look awful. I need some rest."

I was put in charge of compiling Michael's VIP guest list for the show and was thrilled at the prospect of seeing him live again. The taping, which was to be televised, took place inside of a hangar at Santa Monica Airport on a warm November day.

After checking Michael's guests in, I grabbed a spot in the front row to enjoy the show. He made his entrance wearing a flowing white shirt, which was opened to reveal a white undershirt, and tight black pants with knee pads. He looked great and the crowd went crazy. He performed two songs from the *Dangerous* album, "Black or White" and "Will You Be There." After the show, I escorted some of the guests who were on the VIP list onstage to meet and greet Michael. He spotted me and shook my hand, saying hi, but I was too shy to tell him that I was the girl who answered the phones at his manager's office.

He called the office the next day and I mustered up the courage to tell him how amazing his performance had been. Before this, I had only transferred him to Sandy without engaging him in conversation. I was afraid to say anything because I wasn't sure how he would react. Some clients didn't like to be spoken to, and I certainly didn't want to be fired for overstepping my bounds. But I figured I would take a chance. I had to break the ice somehow.

"Michael for Sandy," he said. For years to come, this was how he asked for Sandy every time.

I took a deep breath and spoke fast. "Hi, Michael! Um . . . I just wanted to tell you . . . you were so good last night! I was there in the front row and I was screaming the whole time!"

Caught off guard, he paused for a second. *Oh no,* I thought, *is he upset that I spoke to him?* But to my delight, he was happy to hear my compliment. "That's so sweet," he enthused. "Thank you!"

From that moment on, I congratulated him after every TV performance or appearance he made. We became casual phone friends, and I think he looked forward to hearing how great I thought he was. I didn't hide the fact that I was a huge fan, and he liked that.

It was around this time that Michael started insisting on being called the King of Pop. The execs at MTV were particularly frustrated because they wanted him to perform on their upcoming MTV Video Music Awards, but Michael would only agree to it if they introduced him as the King of Pop. They countered and said, "Well, the only way we'll call you that is if you do a Rock the Vote public service announcement to encourage young people to vote." Michael wanted to be called the King of Pop so bad that he agreed to film the PSA, even though he didn't want to.

Many people working with Michael at this time started to think that his ego was getting a bit out of control because of these crazy demands—but that wasn't the reason he wanted to be called the King of Pop. Elvis was known as the King of Rock 'n' Roll and Michael felt that, because he was black, people didn't give him the same respect. He felt that racism played a part in how history was shaped and artists were remembered. He was also extremely competitive and wanted to be known as the greatest of all time—over Elvis. His plan was to keep pushing this self-made moniker on the public until it was engrained in everyone's minds. He was *demanding* to be respected. From that point forward, all the way up until his final appearance at the *This Is It* press conference in 2009, he refused to appear or perform anywhere unless it was written in the contract that he would be introduced as the King of Pop. And today, because of it, Michael is remembered all over the world by that title. He was a smart guy.

For this album, he insisted that it be the biggest and best promotion that any of his albums had ever had—a request he would repeat like a mantra for all of his future projects. He knew that without the proper promotion, an album was sure to flop—his biggest fear.

I still remember the day that Tower Records in West Hollywood unveiled its elaborate *Dangerous* album display. Facing Sunset Boulevard, the side wall of Tower Records was considered one of the most prestigious billboards in the world. Every artist dreamed of being featured there. Sony paid a large sum of money to ensure prime placement for *Dangerous*, and it was stunning—covering not only the wall but the roof as well.

Michael's longtime communications manager Bob Jones and publicist Lee Solters came to our office that day to walk over and see it. Our office was less than a block away from Tower Records, so we had a prime location to view it. I joined them on the walk down Sunset and took pictures of the amazing re-creation. Michael insisted that he did not want his face on the cover of the album, so instead Mark Ryden was hired to interpret the songs with a painting. The result was a hodgepodge of various symbols and images and was perfect for the new mysterious image Michael wanted to convey.

Michael's insecurities over his appearance increased as the pressure to promote the album grew. And there's one incident that stands out in my mind in particular . . .

It was late one evening and I was tidying up my desk, getting ready to go home for the day, when the phone rang. I picked it up and all I could hear on the other end were sobs. It was Michael. He had just received a rough cut of his recently shot video for the song "Who Is It"—and he hated it. He was panic-stricken.

I immediately conferenced him in to Sandy while I grabbed Gregg Mitchell, who was a junior manager at the office helping on the project. We both listened in to take notes.

"I look like a monkey," Michael cried. "Is there any way we can change it in postproduction?"

Gregg and I looked at each other and shook our heads in disbelief.

Sandy assured Michael that he looked great, but he was not having it. "If we can't change it, we have to reshoot it. Or else we'll just have to scrap the whole thing!"

Sony had already invested millions in this video, including hiring top director David Fincher, and they were not about to spend another cent to lighten it or reshoot it, especially since they also felt Michael looked good. In fact, he had never looked better.

We screened the video for the Gallin Morey staff the next day in our conference room to get their opinions and everyone agreed—it was one of his best ever. He wore a simple suit in the video, not his usual flashy attire, and it made him look sexy and mature. It was his most adventurous and adult-themed video yet, and it was sure to propel the single to number one.

Sony refused to cave in to Michael's demands. And because of that, he refused to shoot the rest of the scenes needed to complete the video. With no other choice, David Fincher hired a Michael Jackson double to film the remainder of his scenes.

It didn't end there, though. Michael was so upset that Sony wouldn't agree to reshoot his scenes that he demanded that they not release the video at all. After a lot of haggling, the video was released in Europe only. It was never released in the United States and the single stalled in the top 15 on the charts.

Michael sabotaging his own career because of his insecurities became a pattern that would only grow over the years. I couldn't understand it. Those of us around him thought that he was perfect just as he was. Every few months, it seemed his nose would take on a new shape or other subtle changes would appear. He always covered his face with a towel or surgeon's mask, as if he couldn't bear the thought of people looking at it. If only he could see what I saw—the most handsome man on earth.

Some have assumed that he did not like his skin color, but he was always very proud of his race. No matter how white his skin would eventually become, he always remained a proud black man. I think people get that mixed up sometimes, which is an unfair assumption. Race and color were two different things for him. In fact, his wish was to be colorless, which I suppose he achieved. I suspect it was his years of enduring the pervasive racism that he constantly spoke about existing within the music industry that caused him to want to be without color, almost to prove a point. With Michael, everything he did had a deeper meaning than what met the eye, and his actions usually stemmed from something that had happened to him earlier in life. He never explained any of his actions to the public and was deeply misunderstood because of it.

In an interview with Oprah, he mentioned enduring years of physical and emotional abuse at the hands of his father. This abuse clearly ruined his self-esteem. The stage was the only place Michael felt completely confident. It allowed him to live out his fantasies and become the cool, self-assured man he dreamed of being. His insecurities made most people who knew him feel like they needed to protect and save him. And it made girls like me fall in love.

Michael filmed and released a series of hit songs and groundbreaking short films for the *Dangerous* album, each one having its own world premiere on MTV and Fox, and they all caused a stir in one way or another. He knew how to keep the public talking and was willing to do anything to create controversy.

The album's release started off with a bang with the *Black or White* film. The record company was alarmed when they received the first cut and Michael appeared to be simulating masturbation on film. He had taken his crotch grabbing to a whole new level for this video. Instead of just grabbing his crotch, he was now *rubbing* it. In one scene that was eventually taken out, Michael unzipped his pants, put his hand inside, and rubbed. This was too much for Sony and they demanded that it be cut out.

Although Michael appeared shy in public, it was clear he reveled in the attention he received. In addition to the overtly sexual aspect of the solo dance piece, it was also violent. Michael jumped on cars and smashed windows with a crowbar. He knew that the public would be outraged, so he had his publicist, Lee Solters, draft a response to the predicted outrage a week before the video even aired. The night before it premiered on Fox, we were already prepared with a statement from Michael apologizing for any harm the video may have caused. Sure enough, when the video aired, the whole world exploded with discussion about it. Some were disgusted by Michael's behavior. Others were excited by this sudden bold change in his character. But either way, *they were talking*. Michael couldn't have been happier.

Another video that caused a commotion was the one for "In the Closet." The song was originally written to be a duet for Michael and Madonna, but once their relationship soured, Princess Stephanie of Monaco took over Madonna's parts. Directed by Herb Ritts, the video was Michael's sexiest to date. His leading lady was supermodel Naomi Campbell. Their scenes were filled with lots of bumping and grinding and feeling on each other's bodies, and Naomi developed a crush on Michael. She told a friend of mine who was on set, "I want Michael's body. I feel like I've already had Michael's body, so we might as well just take it further." But Naomi's wild personality scared Michael off and their relationship remained only for the cameras.

By the time awards season rolled around, everybody wanted Michael to be a part of their show. Dick Clark started calling every day, begging for him to open the American Music Awards with a performance. Michael insisted that the only way he would perform was if he received awards for best album and best single—pop and R&B—in addition to a special award named after him. Dick agreed to his demands, creating an award called the Michael Jackson International Star Award, and Michael opened the show with a memorable performance of his song "Dangerous." I never knew those awards could be determined beforehand—until that night, when I saw Michael accepting all of the ones he had asked for.

After being successful with that barter, he refused to appear on any future award shows unless he was given a special award or tribute. He figured if he was going to bring a show ratings just by appearing, he'd better get something in return. I don't recall any of the award shows denying his demands. The Grammys was one of the only shows that couldn't guarantee awards like best album or best song, but they did agree to honor him with his own special segment. When it came to Michael, people were willing to do almost anything to make him a part of their show . . . and he knew it.

6

> You are never given a wish without also being given the power to make it come true.
>
> —Richard Bach, *Illusions*

"Michael will be there in five minutes." Gary Hearne, Michael's loyal driver, was on the phone alerting me of Michael's imminent arrival. I called Sandy's current assistant, Linda, to inform her of this breaking news and she raced to my desk to escort Michael off the elevator. This would be his first time visiting our offices and I couldn't wait for us to officially meet again. Linda and I both stared at the elevator doors with nervous anticipation, awaiting the grand entrance of the King of Pop.

A few minutes later, the silver doors swished open and there stood Michael. He was wearing his trademark black fedora, a red button-down shirt, black slacks, and a black silk surgeon's mask that covered his entire face except his eyes. This mask had become part of his daily wardrobe. No one ever questioned why he wore it. I just figured it acted as a tool to deflect attention away from his ever-changing appearance. Michael dashed off the elevator, holding his head down, as if he were expecting a group of screaming fans to greet him. He glanced at me while he rushed past my desk without speaking. Linda looked at me and shrugged her shoulders as he followed closely behind her. She had been looking forward to introducing the two of us, but he was clearly in a rush. I supposed our meeting would have to wait until later.

He stayed at our office for three hours that day, videotaping an acceptance speech in our conference room for an upcoming awards show overseas. When he was finished for the day, I spotted him and Jim Morey heading my way. I heard Jim say, "Come on, let's go meet Shana." Jim had wanted this meeting to happen between us for a long time and he was almost as excited as I was. As they walked toward me, I overheard Michael say, "She's so cute!" Before they reached my desk, however, Michael ducked into the men's bathroom. Jim was left standing bewildered, wondering where he had gone. A few minutes later, Michael emerged from the bathroom and Jim led him to my desk. He had taken off his surgeon's mask.

"Have you met Shana?" Jim said.

Prior to him coming, I had wondered if perhaps he would remember meeting me three years before in New York. I figured it would be best not to mention it, unless he did.

Michael reached out to shake my hand and said, "Hi Shana. Nice to see you." He didn't say nice to meet you. He specifically said *see* you. I suppose he had been wondering who the face was behind the voice he had been talking to on the phone for the past year . . . or perhaps he did remember our New York meeting.

Jim continued, "Shana is one of your biggest fans. Every day she asks, 'When is Michael coming in?'"

I couldn't have been more embarrassed. I didn't want Michael to think of me as simply a fan, but I guess the cat was out of the bag and I couldn't hide it. I *was* a fan. I was also the only person of color at the entire company. These two factors created a bond between Michael and me that was different from my relations with everyone else who worked there. I would soon become his trusted ally as he became increasingly paranoid of everyone around him.

After that first time, Michael started coming to the office at least once a week for meetings. I would get so excited every time Gary called to tell me they were on their way. I always made sure I was dressed in my best outfit on those days—usually a blouse, short skirt, stockings, and heels. I didn't wear much makeup back then, just red lipstick and eyeliner.

One time, in the middle of one of Michael's meetings, Jim came racing to my desk. He was so excited he could barely get his words out. "Shana, you're not going to believe this. Are you ready?"

"What is it?" I asked, anxious to hear what could possibly be so astonishing.

"Michael wanted me to ask if he can borrow your makeup!"

"No he didn't. Are you kidding?"

"I'm not kidding. He really did." Jim had been trying for months to find an excuse to connect Michael and me and now here was my chance. His face fell in disappointment when I reluctantly told him that I didn't wear foundation, which was the kind of makeup Michael was looking for.

"Aww Shana, you've missed your chance," Jim said with sadness.

My mind raced as I tried to think of another option. I wasn't going to let this opportunity pass me by. Then I came up with a bright idea. "Maybe I can run to the store and buy him some!"

Jim thought that this might be the perfect solution. "Let's go ask Michael!" he exclaimed as I dropped the magazine I had been reading and scurried behind him. Neither of us cared that the phones would be left unattended. Michael was the only person of importance at that moment. I followed Jim into Sandy's office, which was tucked into the farthest corner of our suite in its own alcove. Michael was sitting in a high-back chair in front of Sandy's large desk, wearing his black fedora and a beautiful black-and-purple leather Los Angeles Lakers jacket.

"Michael, Shana doesn't have any makeup, but she can go to the store and get you some," Jim offered.

Michael was mortified. He looked like he wanted to hide behind the potted plant that sat behind Sandy's desk. He obviously wasn't expecting Jim to actually bring me into the office to update him on the makeup situation. "Oh," he stammered nervously. "That's so sweet. You don't have to go get me anything . . . That's OK."

We all laughed awkwardly and I went back to my desk, amused yet again by the unexpected craziness of my job.

The new issue of *LIFE* magazine had come in the mail that same day and Michael was on the cover accompanied by his llama and a few other animals at Neverland. He looked so cute on it—I had been drooling over it all day. As he was leaving, he approached my desk to get his parking ticket validated (yes, even he didn't like to pay for parking), and I showed him the magazine cover. "Michael, have you seen yourself on this cover? We just got it today," I said, holding the magazine up for him to see.

"Yes, I've seen it . . . unfortunately."

"What do you mean 'unfortunately'? You look extremely handsome on here."

"I don't agree . . . but thank you," he said as he diverted his gaze away from the magazine. He didn't want to see it again.

I rolled my eyes and shook my head in frustration. How could he not see how great he looked?

Michael became so comfortable at our offices that he sometimes had Gary just drop him off in front of our building. He'd ride up on the elevator alone and casually stroll in. He seemed to enjoy being able to do things on his own. The offices for the tabloid the *National Enquirer* were a couple of floors below us and I was always worried that Michael would get stuck in the elevator with one of their pesky reporters. Luckily, no one ever bothered him.

He also set up the production offices for his Dangerous tour inside of our office. Production managers Sal Bonafede, Jack Nance, Paul Gongaware, and Nelson Hayes all moved in and started plotting out the routing and rehearsal schedule for the upcoming world tour. My coworkers used to tease me about how they would always catch Michael hovering around my desk, flirting with me. By this time, they had nicknamed Michael my "husband" or my "boyfriend." Our attraction to each other was so strong it was impossible to ignore. He and I used to steal glances every time he passed my desk, or if he was anywhere in the vicinity of it. Neither of us could stop staring at the other. Sometimes I would catch him staring from the far end of the hallway or while he walked to the conference room for a meeting. Whenever he saw that I had caught him, he would blush and giggle. I'd giggle too. It was like we were two kids on a schoolyard: too shy to actually tell the other we had a crush. It was all so innocent and simple . . . or so it seemed.

I started hearing from Michael's friends that he *really* liked me. I had befriended one of the assistants at his office—I'll call her Nicole. She told me that Michael always seemed nervous every time he was preparing to come to our office. She said that she suspected he had a crush on me because he didn't usually interact in a personal way with people he worked with. He always kept things strictly professional with his staff. She started referring to Michael as "your honey" whenever we spoke of him. It became our code name for him, so that we could discuss him without anyone knowing whom we were talking about. Nicole had recently gone on a date with Michael's older brother Jermaine and she and I would talk for hours, overanalyzing all of the latest developments in our blossoming relationships with each brother.

Michael always made sure he was on time for all of his meetings at our office. In fact, he was usually early—always beating whomever it was he was going to have a meeting with. The person was always shocked when they arrived and I informed them that Michael was already there. He wasn't your typical spoiled superstar. He was punctual and professional at all times when conducting business.

I loved watching powerful business people become nervous just being in Michael's presence. He commanded a room without ever having to say a word. He didn't need a stage to captivate an audience. The funny thing is, he had never been to his own office at MJJ Productions before, even though it was located just a few blocks west of our office on Sunset Boulevard. Most of his assistants there had never even met him. For some reason, he chose to have all of his business meetings at Gallin Morey. I was happy about this but I did find it odd.

I vividly remember sitting at my desk every day playing Stevie Wonder's song "Too Shy to Say" over and over again. The lyrics fit perfectly with what was going on with Michael and me. "I can't go on this way. Being just too shy to say . . ." Stevie plaintively sung.

And that's exactly how I felt: like I was going to burst from the longing, the not knowing what to say or do. It was clear that we both liked each other. So why couldn't we just get together like normal people? Why couldn't Michael just ask me on a date? This slow burn was driving me crazy. I started to think that maybe I needed to be more aggressive. But at the same time, I didn't want to scare him off. I remembered Sandy's assistant Sheila telling me early on that Michael didn't like aggressive women. I was confused and yearning to experience a real relationship, to know what it was like to be held and loved. I was aching for Michael.

7

All journeys have secret destinations of which the traveler is unaware.

—Martin Buber

I traveled to Tokyo, Japan, on December 9, 1992, to see Michael perform on his Dangerous tour. I knew that Michael wouldn't be coming to the United States on this particular tour, so I figured this would be a great chance to see the show. He was scheduled to play eight sold-out shows at the Tokyo Dome, which was an incredible feat and further evidence of Michael's enormous popularity all over the world. Jim Morey had arranged for me act as his assistant in Tokyo, which meant my travel and accommodations were taken care of, including a luxurious room at the hotel where the rest of Michael's party was staying. This would be my first taste of life on the road and I couldn't wait.

After the twelve-hour plane ride from L.A. to Tokyo, I arrived at Narita International Airport. The flight had felt especially long because back then, smoking was allowed on flights and I had the unfortunate luck of sitting behind a chain-smoker for the entire flight. It was miserable. When I arrived at the airport, in true Michael style, there was a VIP escort service waiting with a sign with my name on it. They greeted me like royalty and were extremely friendly and accommodating. I felt like a queen, as I often did when I was in Michael's world. They escorted me to a chauffeured sedan that transported me to the beautiful New Otani Inn.

My room had a spectacular view of sacred Mount Fuji and an unlimited supply of green tea. When I checked in, the bellman had told me to look out of my window every morning to see if Mount Fuji was visible. If it was, it was considered good luck for the rest of the day. So, of course, I did just that. Every morning, at the crack of dawn, I'd wake up to see if I could see the snowcapped mountain. If I could, I'd meditate in a chair by the window and visualize a day filled with good fortune. The grounds of the hotel featured an exquisite ten-acre Japanese garden that offered peaceful areas for meditation as well. There was a sense of zen throughout the entire property, and I soaked it all in. I settled into my room and poured myself a cup of hot tea as I relaxed under the covers of my warm bed. Tomorrow promised to be a busy day and I wanted to make sure I was well rested. I fell asleep dreaming of the exciting days to come.

The next day I met Jim in the lobby of the hotel and our driver took us to the venue. We were headed there early in time for dress rehearsal, which was scheduled for later that day.

As I walked into the massive stadium, I gazed upon the fifty-five thousand empty seats and the breathtaking stage, which displayed a backdrop of Michael's special lighting gear, specific for this tour. I couldn't believe that I was actually in Japan. It had always seemed so far away and unreachable. Being a part of Michael's inner circle meant having access to things you only dreamt about. Seeing this empty arena and knowing it would be filled with screaming fans in a few hours sent a rush of excitement through my veins. This feeling was one of the things that I loved most about the music industry. To be a part of a production that would make thousands of people happy on the other side of the world filled my heart with pride.

I chose a seat in the front row next to Jim and Bob Jones. Bob told me that he had spotted me earlier and thought I was the opening act. He said I looked so glamorous he didn't recognize me. He was told that I was the receptionist and he responded, "Well, I'll be . . ."

Bob and I became pretty close after that. He appeared a bit intimidating to those who didn't know him, and he had a reputation for being tough and unfriendly. But for some reason, we bonded. Bob had worked with Michael as a public relations manager since the early 1970s in the Motown era and was one of the mainstays in Michael's entourage. He was the keeper of all of the secrets and knew all of the old public relations tricks. I was happy to have him as a new friend. It was difficult to stay afloat in Michael's confusing world without having some well-placed trusted allies to help you maneuver through the madness and give advice along the way. In return, I helped him execute a few publicity stunts that he dreamed up to create a buzz for Michael. Small details such as creating signs for fans to hold at Michael's appearances that read I LOVE YOU MICHAEL or WE LOVE THE KING OF POP were all born out of the mind of Bob Jones, and Michael loved it. I remember scrambling before many of Michael's appearances to pass out these signs to waiting fans. If Michael didn't see an abundance of those signs in the audience, he would be unhappy and we would hear about it the next day.

Jim and Bob had grown tired of waiting for the dress rehearsal to start, so they decided to leave. I told Jim I wanted to stay, and he happily left me there—the only person in the audience among a sea of empty seats.

The lights went dark and the short film *Brace Yourself* started to play on two large screens on the sides of the stage. It was a film used to hype the audience for the show they were about to see. The powerful classical piece *Carmina Burana* was the soundtrack. It played over clips of screaming fans and iconic images of Michael. It was magical. Michael knew just how to drive his audience wild with anticipation.

Michael popped up from underneath the stage from an apparatus he called a toaster and stood in a frozen pose for five minutes. This was how he made his dramatic entrance for the show. Usually, at this point the crowd would be wildly screaming. I was the only one in this audience though, so he just stood there in silence. I wanted to scream, but I definitely did not want to call too much attention to myself. I couldn't believe they were letting me sit there alone in the front row in the first place. I felt like Michael was doing a command performance just for me. What a dream.

In between each song, Michael would pose and pretend that people were screaming. Because it was so quiet, I could hear how hard he breathed in between songs. That was something you didn't hear in concerts because of the loud screaming from the audience. This was surprising to me because, through my rose colored glasses, I had always thought that Michael was in such great shape that he didn't get tired at all.

Every once in a while, someone would mess up and Michael would stop in the middle of the song to tell the person. He was very demanding and didn't hesitate to embarrass anyone who had made the slightest mistake.

When he finished performing "Thriller," he was standing up on a riser with his fedora, getting ready to explode into "Billie Jean." Before he started singing, he yelled out, "Hold it! Hold it!" He then launched into a tirade. "Who's doing the lights? During 'Thriller' the black lights were not on. Why weren't the black lights on? In the middle of 'Thriller' when the skeletons come there's supposed to be a black spot on them."

No one said a word . . . not even the person who was doing the lights.

"Hellooo?" Michael shouted through the microphone, imploring the guilty party to reveal himself. He had a smart and antagonizing tone that would have made anyone afraid to admit to his or her mistakes.

At the beginning of "Man in the Mirror," Michael sang the entire first verse flat. He instantly knew he was off and stopped the music. "Hold it. Let's do that again." He sang the verse again a cappella to figure out the right key. He figured it out immediately and sang the song perfectly as they ran through it again.

He then choreographed the entire ending of the song, telling everyone where and when to bow. He said, "When the house lights come on, that signifies the end—the finale. I'll beckon to you and everyone will come up to this line." He pointed to an imaginary line at the front of the stage and then realized the dancers weren't there. "I need all dancers onstage *now*. Did everybody get that ending? Are you sure?"

He was in control of that entire stage and had not even attended very many rehearsals prior to that day. He knew instinctively how to put on a show and it was amazing to watch. Seeing this side of his personality made him even more attractive in my eyes. He was the boss and everybody feared him. People were walking on eggshells around him.

After the rehearsal was over, I walked to the tunnel entrance to look for one of the tour buses that was to take us back to the hotel. I found one that was empty and boarded it. Alan, one of Michael's longtime staff members, boarded after me and sat in the seat in front of me. I looked out of the window and noticed a small group of fans waiting to get a glimpse of Michael. These fans were not Japanese—they had traveled from Europe. Alan told me that this group of fans followed Michael's entire tour all over the world. This always fascinated me. I wondered how these fans had enough money to travel the world and not have to work. Lucky them.

We sat there for about thirty minutes and the driver still hadn't come, so we decided to share a cab back to the hotel. We hopped into the back of the cab and embarked on our journey through the crowded streets of Tokyo. As I looked out the window, taking in all of the unfamiliar sights, Alan started unloading his true feelings about everything that was going on. Michael usually kept his friends and employees compartmentalized for this very reason—he didn't want us to gossip about him with each other. No single person ever knew everything about him, and that's the way he wanted it. When I first started my job at Gallin Morey, one of Michael's assistants told me to always "keep your ears open and your mouth shut." I remembered this piece of advice as I sat in silence, listening to Alan air his frustrations.

"I hate seeing Michael with those little kids all of the time," Alan said with exasperation filling his voice. "I was so glad when Michael stepped off the airplane and no kids were with him. It would be OK if he didn't let it interfere with his work, but he does," he continued. "Recently on the set of *Jam* in Chicago, Michael ran into a kid who had gone on the Bad tour with him—this kid is about sixteen years old now. Michael asked him if he wanted to go on tour with him again. The kid said, 'No, Michael. I'd rather go to school.' Michael was crushed. He couldn't believe that anyone would turn him down like that." Alan gazed out the window as the bright lights of Tokyo whisked by, shaking his head in frustration.

It seemed everyone was hoping that Michael would stop constantly hanging with little boys, but no one dared express their concerns to his face. I doubt it would've made a difference if they had. Nobody could tell Michael what to do.

To be clear, however, at this point no one was thinking that anything inappropriate was going on with Michael and these boys. It truly all seemed innocent. Michael was a big kid at heart and hanging with children created an escape from the stressful rigors of things like touring. I think we were all just a little annoyed that he was focusing so much energy and attention on these boys and their families instead of his work.

On the night of the first show, I rode in the limo bus to the stadium with the band and singers. I was wearing the only Dangerous tour jacket in existence at that time and the entire bus teased me, asking how I had managed to score one before everyone else. Michael's background singer, Siedah Garrett, jokingly started calling me "Mrs. Jackson." She was sure that the only way I could have that jacket was if Michael had given it to me. Working in management had its perks.

Once we arrived at the Tokyo Dome, we pulled into a steep ramp at the loading dock that took us to the backstage entrance. Although it was a cold winter day outside, fans were still waiting by the bus drop-off area hoping to catch a glimpse of any familiar faces. It felt so great to now be on the inside looking out.

Every night before each show, we had a delicious catered buffet dinner that I always looked forward to. Although I had an all-access backstage pass, I didn't have an actual ticket to sit in a seat at the show. Luckily, Bob found me and gave me VIP tickets for all of the shows for the rest of the week.

The first night's show was OK. Michael's energy wasn't as great as it usually was and, after witnessing the private rehearsal earlier, the actual show was a little boring. I suppose I had become spoiled, because I also didn't really like sitting in the VIP section—it was too far away from the stage, in front of the mixing board. Michael had to be seen up close to appreciate his greatness.

During his performance of "Thriller," Michael's spotlight didn't work through the entire first verse. He couldn't be seen at all. That poor person controlling the lights was sure to be in for a Michael lashing after the show.

On the next show night, Bob set me up to have my picture taken with Michael backstage prior to the show. I was escorted into a VIP room to wait until it was my turn. It was tradition for Michael to have a meet-and-greet prior to all of his shows and have his picture taken with his guests. No matter how famous he became, he always kept that tradition going. He loved meeting his guests as well as his fans. He was not one of those untouchable, unreachable stars. He liked staying as close as possible to the outside world.

As I waited in the VIP room, a group of Japanese VIPs eagerly bounded in. I saw them looking and pointing at me. Finally, someone from the group came over to me and said, "You are very beautiful. Can we take a picture with you?" I had no idea why they would want a picture with me, but I was happy to oblige. Just being associated with Michael made others treat you like a star.

When it was my turn to see Michael, Bob led me to the room where Michael was standing. The room was set up with perfect lighting and a deep-red backdrop that matched the color of Michael's shirt. Sam Emerson, Michael's photographer whom I remembered from the Helmsley Palace in New York, was standing in front with a professional camera snapping pictures. There was a group of Japanese girls in front of me. When they reached Michael, they handed him a present. It was a package of banana snacks that could only be found in Japan. Michael was so excited to receive it, he tore the wrapping off with his teeth and instantly ate one. I had never seen this banana snack before but apparently it was very popular. It looked like a Hostess Twinkie with banana filling inside.

After the Japanese girls left, it was my turn. Michael was standing in front of the red backdrop in a red corduroy shirt with a white undershirt and black slacks—the usual. He looked stunningly handsome. This was the first time I had seen him sporting a five o'clock shadow. He had a light beard and mustache that could only be seen up close. It made him look very sexy and masculine—and his eyes were a lighter brown than I had ever noticed before. The lights were so bright; they enhanced all of his features. He had on his stage makeup, but it didn't appear too heavy. It was perfect. As soon as he spotted me, he started smiling and gave me a hug. I hadn't told him I was coming, and I wasn't sure if he had seen me at rehearsal.

"I thought that was you!" he said as he bounced up and down in excitement. "I saw you sitting in the audience at rehearsal and I was wondering if it was you." Then he took a step back, as if a sudden realization had come over him. "You came all the way out here just to see me?"

Sam Emerson interrupted and said, "Of course, Michael. Anybody would come this far to see you." Michael blushed. He seemed genuinely surprised that I cared enough to travel that far for him. His humbleness was not an act. I sometimes believed that he didn't feel worthy of having an attractive girl interested in him. He couldn't believe I could possibly like him in that way—enough to travel to the other side of the world. For all of the bravado and cockiness he exuded onstage, in real life he was just an insecure young man, unsure of himself and what he might have to offer outside of the spotlight. This quality in him was not only endearing but also surprising.

We posed for a few pictures—Sam telling Michael to raise his chin or turn his head a certain way. I was hoping he would direct me on how to look my best too, but he didn't—he only focused on Michael.

"What about me, Sam? How should I pose?" I asked.

"You'll look good at any angle," Michael said, never missing an opportunity to flirt.

As I was leaving, I said to him, "Have a great show!"

He said, "OK."

And he did. That night's show was much better than the first. He seemed to have more energy and was in a better mood. Or maybe it was me who was in a better mood. Seeing Michael had made everything better, including the show.

In total, the Tokyo shows received great reviews and were a huge success. The Japanese audiences were noticeably different from American and European ones. At the end of the concerts, they waited patiently in their seats to be dismissed row by row. I had never seen such an orderly exit from a stadium in my life.

Christmas decorations filled the streets of Tokyo as the eight-show run reached its end. I packed my bags and headed back to the airport. Life on the road had been fun, but I think we were all ready to get back to L.A.

8

> [He] looked at [her] . . . in a way that every young girl wants to be looked at some time.
>
> —F. Scott Fitzgerald, *The Great Gatsby*

"I just wrote this song that the record company has been begging me to finish. If I dictate it to you, can you type it up and give it to Sandy?"

It was shortly after the first leg of the Dangerous tour ended when Michael called me with this unusual request. I was sitting at my desk reading a magazine when the phone had rung.

"Hi. This is Michael. Is this Shana?"

Every time I heard his voice say my name, waves of butterflies fluttered in my stomach. Usually, we would just exchange pleasantries, giggle, and then I would transfer him to Sandy. On this day, however, he had a highly unusual request. I wasn't an assistant; I was just the receptionist. I answered the phones—that's it. The assistants were the ones to type things. I thought that perhaps he was mistaking me for someone else, so I asked if he wanted one of Sandy's assistants to type it instead.

"No, I really want you to do it." He spoke with a firm assuredness. One thing about Michael—he always knew exactly what he wanted and wasn't afraid to ask for it.

This was completely out of the blue, however. We had been flirting with each other on the phone before this, and every time he came in for a meeting, but still . . . he had never asked me to do something like this.

Soon I realized he had an ulterior motive.

He explained that he had written this song to be the theme song for *The Addams Family Values* movie and that a short film would soon be in the works with horror writer Stephen King attached. The record company had been pressuring him to write it and he kept putting it off. So, according to him, he had finally finished it and needed to get it to Sandy immediately.

We didn't have e-mail back then or the Internet or even personal computers, so dictating things and having them typed on a typewriter was a common way to relay information. Other than faxing (which he could've easily done), this was the only way to send a document to someone quickly.

I scrambled to find the nearest paper and pen and told Michael I was ready. He began slowly reading the lyrics to me—his soft, smooth, soothing voice lingering on every word. If any of the lines were in any way sexual, he repeated them twice. At first, I wasn't sure if he wanted me to write those lines twice. I asked, "Do you sing that line twice?"

He giggled and said, "Oh, no. I was just saying that for you."

Most of the lines weren't sexual at all, but the way he read them made them sound that way. If he said a word that he thought I might not understand, he would spell it out. When he came to the word "Addams," he started spelling it for me. He said, "You spell that A-D . . . hmmm, I don't know how you spell that!"

After each line, he would patiently wait for me to say OK before he started the next one. In between some of the lines, for no reason at all, he would pause for over a minute and not say a word, even if I told him I was ready. I just sat and waited until he spoke again, listening to him breathe. It was strangely exciting.

It was a long song, taking up two pages of the notebook I was writing in. One line in particular that I distinctly remember was, *"I'm hard as nails."* He repeated that one twice for sure. At that point, I was pretty certain what was going on.

At the end of the song, he said breathily, "Can you read it back to me please?"

I paused for a few seconds, not believing what was happening. Then, I decided to go for it—all the way. I gathered up the sexiest voice I could muster, and read that darn thing back to him, just as slowly as he had, repeating the same certain lines twice. I heard him chewing gum loudly and excitedly. I also heard other soft noises and I didn't want to even think what they might be. When I was finished, he was completely quiet, other than the sound of gum chewing and breathing.

"Hello?" I said.

I thought that I had disconnected him or something, or that maybe he hadn't been paying attention to my sexy recital of the lyrics.

"I'm here," he said, his voice almost a whisper. He sounded out of breath.

I was relieved that he was still on the other end of the line but was curious as to what he might have been doing.

He then said, "OK. That was good. Now tell Sandy exactly this—'Michael told me to give these to you.'"

I told him I would. He thanked me and hurried off the phone.

Because my job was to answer all of the phones for our busy office, they had been ringing off the hook while this was happening. I had to ignore them all. Michael was our most important client—it didn't matter if God was trying to get through, Michael took priority over everyone. The funny thing is, for this particular song, Michael told me he had just written it, but I later learned that the real songwriter was actually Bryan Loren, whom Michael sometimes collaborated with. When Michael was under a deadline, or wanted to be Cyrano De Bergerac, he saw nothing wrong with getting a little help from his friends . . . and taking credit for it.

This "song dictation" thing happened a few more times after this. It became our secret—the thing that bonded us. I think it excited Michael that I was at the office while it occurred. He enjoyed toying with the public. Just imagining me participating in these phone sessions while my coworkers strolled by must have made it more thrilling for him. He always asked if he could "dictate a song" and would then ask if I could read it back. He told me that he really liked the sound of my voice. Each song was filled with sexual double entendres and, to my knowledge, none of the songs were ever officially released. I could always hear him breathing heavily as I recited the lyrics back to him. At the end, I'd ask if he wanted me to give these particular "songs" to anyone and he would say no, that he just wanted to hear how they sounded. *The Addams Family* song was the only one he had asked me to give to Sandy. He told me not to tell anyone that he had even called. We never discussed what was actually happening. It was an unspoken understanding.

As I look back, I realize that this was his way of testing me—to see if he could trust me. I suppose he figured if I didn't tell anyone about this, he could push the boundaries with me even further.

Hearing him say those lyrics to me made my stomach tingle with excitement. I had never had any type of relationship at this point, so this was major for me. I was in my twenties and had never even been kissed. I was a very late bloomer, having been painfully shy my entire life. These feelings were all new. My mind was racing and in a daze after each of these sessions. Michael's unpredictable behavior was confusing but that was what excited me and kept me intrigued.

Even though I was having these intimate conversations with him, I still didn't feel like I knew what his motivation was. For some reason, I was afraid to ask questions that were too deep, afraid of scaring him off. So I just rolled with the punches.

As I counted down the hours, fighting the boredom that usually crept in at about 4 PM every day, the phone rang. It was Michael. His voice had a sense of urgency that it usually didn't have. He asked if I could get away from my desk for a minute and meet him downstairs in the parking lot where his van was parked. My heart felt like it instantly jumped into my throat. What could he possibly want?

My mind started racing, thinking of all of the reasons he might want to see me. Maybe someone had found out about our song dictation sessions and it had gotten back to him? I started rifling through the pages of my mind, trying to recall if I had told anyone. I knew that I hadn't, but now I was getting paranoid. Perhaps he was going to tell me that Sandy had found out and that I would soon be fired. I was really nervous now.

Beads of sweat formed above my lip and my heart started racing faster. I closed my eyes and took deep breaths to calm myself as the busy phones continued to ring. I was now faced with the task of slipping away from my desk without being noticed. I looked to my right and spotted our floater, Ken, who always covered for me when I had to be away from my desk for lunch. I motioned for him to come my way and asked if he could answer the phones while I "went to get something from my car." He was always more than happy to cover for me and would usually brag about all of the celebrities whose calls I missed while I was away.

I glanced in the mirror and reapplied my red lipstick as I walked to the elevator, which was directly in front of my desk. I wanted to look good for Michael.

My hands were shaking as I pressed the elevator button marked G1. Whenever I knew I was going to see Michael, I always felt like I was going to have a panic attack. I spotted his black van sitting in front of our parking garage, in a space on the side of Sunset. The mere sight of that van always gave me goose bumps. It wasn't just any old black van. This van had been Michael Jacksonized. It was all black with extremely black tinted windows and special chrome rims on the tires, and it seemed to sit lower to the ground than most vans of that type. It was completely pimped out, as they say. This was Michael's main mode of transportation around Los Angeles. He much preferred this van to a limo because it was more incognito.

The windows were tinted so dark I couldn't see if anyone was in the van when I approached it. As I walked closer, I heard the lock on the door unlatch and the door slowly slid open. Michael motioned for me to get in.

As I stepped into the luxurious van, the first thing that hit me was Michael's signature scent, Bal à Versailles, which filled the entire interior. I always knew that Michael was nearby when I smelled that scent. It reminded me of baby powder mixed with a soft, musky, sweet, spicy smell. It would linger in the air for hours after he had left a room, and if he hugged you, his scent would stay on your clothes all day, serving as a reminder of the moments you had shared with him. It was a women's perfume, which Michael preferred over men's cologne. I never asked why, but I always figured he wanted to smell nonthreatening, not too masculine, so as to be acceptable to everyone.

I sat in the plush black leather seat next to him and tried to appear calm, even though it felt like my heart was about to pound right out of my chest. The inside of the van was even more impressive than the outside. There were two rows of black leather seats, with two separate seats in each row. In between the two front seats was a television and a Sony PlayStation. There was also a complete entertainment center that consisted of a CD player, a VCR, a DAT (digital audio tape) player, earphones, and incredible speakers. There was also a thing I had never seen before next to the driver's seat—a navigation system. These were not common at that time and I was fascinated by it. Michael was a technology junkie and was always the first person to have any new invention.

Michael smiled as his eyes scanned my entire body. He always looked at me in a way that made me feel wanted and special. That's one of the things I miss most about him.

He told me that he just wanted to be able to talk to me without anyone listening. He said he was worried his phones were bugged. He asked how my day was going and if Sandy was in the office. Even though I was nervous, hearing his soft voice always had a calming effect on me. I could just sit and listen to him talk for hours. He mentioned that he had been busy preparing to start rehearsals for the second leg of his Dangerous tour and that, although he hated touring, he was excited to visit some of the international cities on the schedule. He would be visiting some cities he had never performed in before.

He then abruptly changed the subject and asked if I had told anyone about any of our phone conversations.

Oh gosh, is this what he wanted to talk to me about? Had someone found out? I told him that I hadn't told anyone.

"Thank you. You really shouldn't trust anyone, especially nobody in your office or my office. You promise not to ever tell anyone, right?"

I told him, "Of course."

Thinking that Michael knew some secret inside information about the people in our offices, I became paranoid of everyone from that point forward, not knowing whom to trust. To this day, my relationships are still affected by this paranoia that Michael instilled in me.

"Where's Gary?" I asked, wondering where his driver was.

"Oh, I sent him to Book Soup to get some art books for me."

Book Soup, which was just a block away, sat directly across from Tower Records, another of Michael's frequent shopping spots. He would often send Gary to both of those places to purchase books and music while he was in meetings at our office.

Michael looked me directly in the eyes, shyly smiling while he gazed at me. I didn't know how to react, so I started nervously giggling and looked away. He had met his match in the shy department. My extreme shyness seemed to make him more confident.

He was wearing his usual attire of a red shirt (with a white V-neck undershirt underneath), black slacks, and a black fedora. I was happy that he wasn't wearing the surgeon's mask that sometimes completed his uniform. He had a faint trace again of a five o'clock shadow. I could smell the distinct, sweet scent of Bazooka bubble gum on his breath as he leaned in closer.

"You are so beautiful," he said, gently grabbing my hand. "I just love looking at you."

I blushed.

It felt like it was suddenly a hundred degrees inside of that van and I started to feel faint. I noticed that Michael was sweating too. It wasn't very hot outside, but inside there was enough heat to warm even the coldest winter day.

He reached up to his head and took his fedora off, revealing his wavy black hair, tied in a ponytail. He continued gazing as he smiled at me. His big brown eyes had a magnetic twinkle. He was so handsome I could barely look at him. His face was the definition of perfection. He, however, seemed self-conscious of it, habitually putting his hand up to cover his nose, almost like a nervous tick.

He then leaned in even closer and gently kissed me on the lips. He didn't ask for permission—he just did it. And I liked it. It was a sweet, soft kiss. Not passionate, but just right for the moment. I had never been kissed on the lips before in my entire life. I was so taken aback by this, I covered my face and started giggling. He grabbed my hand tighter and smiled, still gazing in my eyes. Clearly, he could tell I was nervous.

"Aww, you are so sweet," he said softly as he chuckled.

"I've never kissed anyone before," I said.

"Ever?"

I nodded.

"I knew you would say that. I can tell that you are very innocent and pure. That's what I like about you. It's rare in this town."

I blushed and looked away. Inside I was dying to kiss him again. His lips felt so soft, like a cozy pillow. I wanted to feel them again. A thousand thoughts raced through my mind and at that moment, I hated myself for being so shy. I simply didn't have the courage to do anything but sit there frozen.

I was in my twenties but severely lacking in any social sophistication. For some reason, my emotional development in terms of relationships had been stunted. I had absolutely no experience. My painful shyness had caused me to steer clear of dating my entire life. I couldn't think of anything more torturous than being alone with a man. I may have looked like a beautiful, sexy woman, but inside I felt twelve. Michael had clearly picked up on these insecurities of mine and it made him feel safe, I think. He *knew* I wouldn't try to kiss him again . . . or do anything else. He was the aggressor and that's the way he liked it.

I don't know what prompted this behavior, but I was glad he finally decided to make a move. I started wondering if his shyness was just an act. He seemed to be able to turn it off and on at will. I learned that he actually wasn't a naturally shy person. Some public situations made him uncomfortable and he would appear shy in those moments, but if he felt safe, he was not shy at all.

He wrapped me in his arms and issued one last warning to make me feel more paranoid, "Please don't tell anybody about this, OK? Do you swear?"

I assured him I wouldn't.

"OK, I'm trusting you," he said, looking me deep in the eyes.

It was a good thing he made me promise, because in my mind I was already thinking of everyone who I couldn't wait to tell. I wanted to scream it to the world—*Michael Jackson just kissed me!* How could I not tell anyone? It was going to be difficult, but I resigned myself to keeping it a secret. The last thing I wanted was to ruin this in any way. He then told me that Gary would be back any minute and that I should probably go back upstairs to work.

It was almost a relief when I slid the van door open and stepped back into the cool breeze on Sunset Boulevard. The scent of Bal à Versailles lingered on my clothes for the rest of the day, constantly reminding me of the secret I couldn't share. I replayed every moment in my mind in a constant loop and kept kicking myself for acting so immature—dreaming up lines of dialogue that I should have said, imagining things that I should have done. I started thinking that I had blown the one moment I had been looking forward to for years. *He probably won't want to see me again*, I thought. Maybe I really was too young and inexperienced for him.

I don't know how I made it through the rest of that day. The phones were ringing but I couldn't hear them. People were coming in for meetings but I couldn't see them. My mind was in a hazy daze. All I could think about was Michael.

9

> To be a star, you must shine your own light, follow your own path, and don't worry about the darkness, for that is when stars shine brightest.
>
> —Unknown

It was August 1993 and day one of filming Michael's multimillion dollar short film *Is This Scary,* which was to promote the theme song for the upcoming movie *Addams Family Values.* I was standing on a black-and-white checkered tile floor on the set of "Michael's house," a perfect replica of a creepy, haunted ballroom filled with fog and dusty antique furniture. My role in the film was to play a townsperson in a small, normal town.

To be in a Michael Jackson video had been a lifelong dream. But so was my whole existence at this point. Everything I had ever hoped for with Michael was happening—slowly but surely. I was floating on air and just knew that Michael and I would soon be an official couple. In my mind, he was already my boyfriend.

Michael and the director, Mick Garris (who worked with Stephen King), had come into our office the week before to meet about the project. Sandy's assistant Sheila had urged me to ask Michael if I could be in the video. After all, this would be the short film of that first song Michael had "dictated" to me, called, "Family Thing."

As Michael and Mick were standing in front of my desk waiting for the elevator, I said to Michael, "I would sure love to be a part of this short film. It sounds like it's going to be amazing."

He perked up, as if a lightbulb suddenly popped into his head. "Mick, is there a part that Shana could play? Maybe one of the townspeople?"

Mick, who was extremely nice and not about to say no to Michael said, "Sure!"

And just that easily—without having to audition—I was now a part of the cast for a sure-to-be-classic Michael Jackson short film.

We were filming at CBS/Radford Studios in Studio City, which is an upscale area of the San Fernando Valley, right off of Ventura Boulevard. I was very familiar with this bustling lot because I had spent a considerable amount of time here in recent years taping the NBC sitcom *A Different World,* on which I was a featured extra for a couple seasons. The classic sitcom *Seinfeld* was also currently being taped here next door to our soundstage.

After our catered lunch that day, Michael was brought onto the set for the first time. He made quite an entrance. He was in costume, wearing a scary mask and a long black cape. He didn't fool me though: I could recognize his body and large hands anywhere. Underneath the cape, he was wearing his familiar Michael stage attire—a crisp white shirt with ruffles and black high-water slacks with white socks. His face was completely clean-shaven and covered in heavy pale makeup. It looked so perfect it appeared almost otherworldly. His hair was styled in long, dangling, wavy curls. I had gotten used to seeing him in real life with minimal makeup and a five o'clock shadow, so this less masculine look was a bit jarring.

He spotted me and made a beeline to say hi. He was always kind and welcoming—that was one quality that never changed about him, no matter what was going on in his life. The other actors were afraid to speak to him, so I became the only member of the cast he actually talked to. There were always rumors about superstars like Michael not wanting to be spoken to or even looked at on sets, so none of the cast wanted to be fired on the first day for daring to do anything like that. I was placed right next to him in the scene and he seemed relieved that he had someone nearby who he could feel comfortable with. Right before the cameras were about to roll, he leaned over and whispered in my ear, "When am I supposed to turn around?"

I had been present for a rehearsal prior to Michael's arrival with a stand-in playing Michael's role, so I was familiar with what was supposed to happen in the scene. "The director is going to say your name," I whispered back to him, "and then you turn around."

He thought about it for a second and bent down to my ear to whisper again. "So, he's gonna say 'Michael' and then I turn?"

What other name could it be? I thought to myself.

He had a habit of whispering in people's ears so that no one else could hear his conversations—and I loved it. Hearing his soothing voice and feeling his soft lips graze against my ear sent shivers down my spine, giving me flashbacks of kissing him in the van. It also made everyone else think that we were discussing something really secret and important.

Mick yelled "Action!" and we switched into character. All of us townspeople had to shout, "Come out where we can see you! Come out where we can see you!" over and over as angrily as we could. Earlier that day, we had stormed "Michael's house" with blazing torches and pitchforks to force him out of hiding and confront him about scaring our children. We felt he was too weird, therefore he must be doing something harmful to them. The concept of this short film was Michael's message to the world that just because someone doesn't fit in with the crowd, it doesn't mean he's a bad person. Unfortunately, life would soon imitate art in the worst way, but I didn't know it yet.

As we continued shouting for him to come out, Michael magically appeared in the middle of us with his scary mask and flowing black cape. He was instructed to then drop the mask to reveal his face and recite the line, "Here I am." After that the townspeople were to scatter away, cowering in fear of "scary" Michael. He wasn't wearing scary makeup or anything out of the ordinary. "Scary" Michael was simply Michael Jackson. We were afraid of him because he was *different*—he didn't fit in with us normal folks. We had to do that scene at least ten times, shooting it from various angles. I was directed to stand close to Michael, hiding him until his reveal. I couldn't think of anything to say as we waited, so we stood quietly for a while. He then broke the awkward silence. "How did they let you off from work to do this?"

I told him that I had informed Sandy and Jim that I was cast in the video and they were happy for me. He didn't seem to realize that he was their prized client and they would've done anything to make him happy. We chatted about some other random topics and I felt like I was gossiping with an old friend. He had a way of making me feel instantly comfortable whenever we talked. He was so open and understanding.

Michael's hands were always the first thing I looked at whenever I saw him. They were one of his most recognizable features and were always an indication of any health problems he may be going through. In later years, sometimes his hands appeared swollen and his nails were long and discolored, which was never a good sign. On this day, his hands were heavily covered with white pancake makeup. But one thing the makeup couldn't cover were small brown spots (like liver spots) near his wrists. I figured that this was proof of the vitiligo he had mentioned on his interview with Oprah the year before. At that time, I felt so sorry for him, thinking about how horrible it must have been to deal with such a terrible skin disease.

As we were standing waiting for the next shot, the kids from the video started showing off, dancing in front of us. Michael hit me on the hand and told me to look at this one little boy who was really funny. We chuckled as he attempted to imitate all of Michael's famous dance moves. Then that same boy, who was about nine years old and African American, looked up at Michael with big, innocent brown eyes and said, "Michael . . ." Michael bent down to the little boy's level and looked him straight in the eyes. This small, sweet gesture told me so much about Michael. He wanted to be on the same level as the boy so as not to be intimidating—to make him feel comfortable enough to ask him anything. I felt that he was the most perfect and amazing man in the world at that moment. The boy continued, "Michael, when you were little you had *real big* hair and now it's straight. How did you do that?" Michael turned to me and widened his eyes in amused disbelief, searching for an answer in my face. I looked at him widening my eyes too and we both burst out laughing.

"Don't look at me," I said. "I can't wait to hear your answer for this one!"

Michael, still laughing, stuttered trying to figure out what to say. Finally, he came up with, "It's a different hairstyle." He couldn't stop laughing and also couldn't think of anything else to say. He spotted Karen Faye, his longtime hair and makeup artist. "Go ask that girl over there," he told the little boy as he motioned for Karen to come over.

Karen, a tall, attractive blonde, walked over to where we were standing and the little boy repeated the question to her. Always ready with a serious answer to all questions, Karen said matter-of-factly, "Well that was an Afro."

Michael chimed in, "Yeah, it was an Afro!" The little boy was satisfied with that and walked back to his place in the scene.

A little later, we were standing waiting for the lights to be set for the next scene and I remembered the song he had dictated to me, which was supposed to be for this short film. I found it odd that I had not heard it yet and it hadn't been played here on the set. "Did you ever finish the song for this?" I asked as a stagehand placed a small piece of black tape on the floor to indicate Michael's mark.

Michael looked down at the floor and a wave of guilt covered his face. He whispered, "No, I haven't even recorded it yet." A sly glint came across his eyes as he looked at me with a mischievous grin. He knew he should've recorded that song a long time ago. His look told me he was purposely waiting until the last minute to simply frustrate the record company. He could be rebellious that way.

Michael was placed on his mark to shoot close-ups. A few of us townspeople had to stand by the camera so that he could have someone to say his lines to. We reacted to them as if we were on camera to make it easier for Michael to maintain his character and emotions. We all had to yell names at him like "freak" and "weirdo." It was so strange having to call him these things to his face. The tabloids had been calling him "Wacko Jacko" for years and he hated it. After we yelled these names at him, Michael was directed to look upset and say, "Why? What have I done?" He always looked at me when he said that line. I felt so guilty yelling those awful names at him. In my mind I was thinking, *You know I'm just acting, right? I like you.*

He then had to bend down and ask the main child star of the video, who was a ten-year-old redheaded boy, "Son, do I scare you?" The little boy responded, shaking his head no. The boy's father in the video, who was also the mayor of our small town, corrected the little boy, shaking his head emphatically yes for him.

"Yes, you do scare him. You're scaring all of our children!" the father retorted in anger.

Michael started getting angrier and said, "Oh, so you think I'm scary, huh? Well, how about this . . . is this scary?" He started making funny faces that were not scary at all—the camera right up on his face. We all laughed. And then he screamed, *"Is this scary?"* And he truly became scary. With the magic of special effects, he opened his mouth wide with his hands and ripped his entire face off, throwing it at us. It was a frightening scene, even without the special effects added in. Every time he screamed that line, it really scared us because we weren't expecting Michael to have such a big, loud voice. He got into the character so much I saw him physically shaking in anger at the end of the scene. He even ad-libbed a curse word in one of his exchanges: "*Goddamit*!"

Every time he finished a take, we all clapped. He'd just stand there with his hand on his chin and smile. His acting was truly impressive. I had never seen him let loose like that before. He was intense, as if he had been waiting for a moment like this to let go of all of his frustrations and anger. Those emotions were coming from a place deep inside.

When we weren't filming, I kept seeing Michael glance over at me to see what I was doing. I felt like I was always being watched, which I didn't mind at all, of course. I suppose I was watching him too, or else I wouldn't have noticed him watching me.

The little redheaded boy kept telling me to do this dance step where you move your neck from side to side. Michael had made this move famous in a couple of his past music videos. Begrudgingly, I did it. But unbeknownst to me he had told Michael to look at me while I was doing it. When I finished, I looked at Michael and he was dying with laughter. The little boy was happy to have embarrassed me.

At one point, after I had filmed a scene standing in the group of townspeople, Michael walked over and whispered that he had been looking at the monitor while we were shooting the scene, and he couldn't see me. He instructed me on where to stand so that I could get better camera time. He was always doing little things like that to look out for me—such a gentleman.

After that first day of filming, everyone on set had fallen in love with Michael. He had been friendly, outgoing, and approachable to every single person on the crew, no matter what their position was. I know that the public saw him as being quiet and reclusive but that really wasn't the case at all. He had a public persona and a private one, which were complete opposites of each other. He was actually a people person who loved to talk and meet new friends from all walks of life. He made everyone whom he came into contact with feel special, asking them questions and being genuinely interested in whatever it was they had to say. This was the magic of Michael.

Once Michael left for the day, the other townspeople started asking me if I knew him. They were all shocked that he had talked to me and no one else. People were asking, "So what was he whispering in your ear?" "I saw him talking to you. Do you know him?" I was proud to finally be able to say that yes, I did know him.

Being on that set with him the first day was like heaven. To be able to work with Michael on an amazing project like this was better than any dream I could imagine. And to think, we had thirteen more days scheduled to work together. I figured that every day would be like the first. But sadly, fate had other ideas.

The next day, the townspeople sat for ten hours and did absolutely nothing. Apparently, Michael wanted to do his close-ups alone and it took longer than expected. I didn't even get to see him. The next day, the same thing happened—that was Thursday.

By this time, Michael was starting to get sick. The crew members told me they noticed his energy level was down and it looked like something was bothering him. "The eagle has landed," was the phrase they had used among themselves to inform each other when Michael actually showed up.

The next day, which ironically was Friday the thirteenth, Michael called in sick. We townspeople had to do all of our scenes without him. The child stars of *The Addams Family* movie, including Christina Ricci, were on the set that weekend and were featured in several scenes. There were also live animals, including an armadillo. That thing scared me to death when it accidentally crawled over my feet.

It was difficult to film without our star, but we were all trying to remain positive and figured that he would be back when he felt better. On Saturday, Michael worked a half day and he did all of his scenes alone once again. He didn't show up at all on Sunday, and we did our best to shoot around him. Monday was our first day off, which we all needed. The past week had been grueling.

Tuesday, August 17, would be the last time I'd see Michael for a while. He didn't show up on that day until 8 PM. We townspeople had already finished our shots for the day, shooting around him as usual. I changed back into my street clothes and went back to the set to see him. I hadn't laid my eyes on him since that first day and I was starting to get worried. It wasn't like Michael to be that irresponsible, not showing up for work. His motto had always been "The show must go on," and usually he would show up even if he were sick. I had a feeling that something was going on that I wasn't aware of.

I spotted Michael's driver, Gary, and stand-in, Darrick. They were my two set buddies whom I hung with if Michael was busy. Michael's dermatologist, Dr. Arnold Klein, was also there. I had become familiar with Dr. Klein because he was Sandy Gallin and Elizabeth Taylor's doctor too. He was a doctor to the stars who was known to be liberal when passing out prescription medication. Despite that reputation, he was highly respected and lauded for his numerous breakthroughs in skin treatment. He was also one of Michael's closest confidants.

I asked Dr. Klein if Michael was OK. He told me that he was doing fine now and that he was "in a good mood today." I was very relieved to hear that, thinking that this meant he would be well enough to complete the rest of the scenes we had. The fact that he was in a good mood was also nice to hear. As I had learned, he could be very moody and his behavior unpredictable. A happy Michael meant that everyone around him was happy too. If he wasn't in a good mood, on the other hand, he could make your life miserable.

I spotted Michael and walked over to him to say hi. He was kind and friendly but it was clear something was wrong. He wasn't his usual happy-go-lucky self. He wasn't all there. His eyes, normally sparkling and bright, were like steel—almost as though there were no soul behind them. There was a sadness there that I had never seen before. He had always been hyper and full of energy but now he seemed subdued and dazed, as if he were walking through a fog.

That night, he was supposed to watch the dancers rehearse and film more close-ups. The crew set up all of the lights and set the scene for Michael's shots. I was told he had gone to his trailer to get dressed for his scenes. I walked over to the stage where the dancers were and watched them run through their choreography—for a song that wasn't even recorded yet. The dancers hadn't met or worked with Michael yet, so they were all getting nervous in anticipation of his arrival. Not long after that, I turned around and saw him strolling onto the stage. He was wearing his black fedora and a surgeon's mask—and was accompanied by eleven-year-old Brett Barnes. Brett had accompanied Michael on the first leg of the Dangerous tour and had been constantly photographed with him, wearing miniature versions of all of the outfits Michael wore. They seemed to be inseparable.

I was so mad. I couldn't believe that Michael would come to meet these young dancers for the first time in a surgeon's mask, and I also couldn't believe he would have a little boy with him. I imagined every dancer going home and telling their friends how weird Michael was. Every time it seemed he was acting normal and like a regular man—someone I could see myself having a real relationship with—he would revert back to this mask-wearing dude with a little boy by his side. It was difficult to understand. The Michael I knew wasn't weird, and I didn't want everyone else thinking he was. I had grown to feel protective of him. I wanted everyone to see him as I did. I was sick of people calling him strange. He was just a regular person in my eyes—an extremely nice, normal guy. Why couldn't he see or care about how he was being perceived?

I admit, as funny as it sounds, I was slightly jealous of Brett. I wanted Michael to spend his free time with *me*. Prior to this, I had thought we were on our way to getting closer, but now it seemed like he was more interested in hanging out with this boy—almost using him as a crutch. I was so upset I avoided Michael the rest of the night and went home.

I learned that after I left, he only watched the dancers for twenty minutes even though he was supposed to learn some of the choreography with them. He also decided he didn't want to film his close-ups. He abruptly left and went home right after I did. Everything was so strange. I knew something was fishy, because Dr. Klein had told me that Michael was feeling fine that day.

The next day, he didn't show up again. Millions of dollars had already been wasted because of his absences. No one knew day to day if he would show up or not. I didn't know what could be wrong. It was not in Michael's character to flake out on a major production like this—one that he had been extremely excited about.

The day after that, word came from Dr. Klein that Michael had a 103-degree temperature. He had written a note that stated Michael wouldn't be able to work again until Saturday, August 21. I thought that perhaps he was too stressed over his upcoming world tour on top of filming this short film. The tour was scheduled to start in Bangkok on August 24, which was only a few days away. How was he going to be able to do it? He was looking frail and not well enough to be onstage performing every night for two hours. If he couldn't show up to our set, which was local, there was no way he would be able to embark on a world tour. I also remembered him telling me in the van that he hated touring.

Then I received word that he was so sick he had decided to cancel his entire tour. I was secretly happy when I heard this, because I thought that meant he wanted to focus on finishing this short film, which was very important to him. There was so much depending on the completion of it—the entire *Addams Family Values* marketing campaign was centered around it. It was also two million dollars overbudget because of Michael's absences.

I was told that Michael's publicist, Lee Solters, was preparing a statement to the press announcing the cancelation of the tour. Back at Gallin Morey, I heard that things were crazy. Marcel Avrum, the tour promoter, was about to literally kill himself from the stress. Kenneth Choi, a Korean promoter for the tour, threatened to kill Michael, Jim Morey, and Bob Jones because of the cancelation. He also threatened to hold a press conference and accuse Michael of horrible things if he canceled the tour. All of this happened on Friday, August 20. In the course of one day, everybody's world had been turned upside down, and it would only get worse—much, much worse.

The next day, Saturday, August 21, I went back to the set and continued to shoot scenes with the townspeople. We did everything we possibly could without Michael. The director, Mick, always had a sweet, optimistic attitude, which made things a lot easier. I learned later that on the day before—that crazy Friday—Michael had gone out looking for mansions in Beverly Hills with Brett. While people feared for their lives because of death threats for a canceled tour and we were scrambling to film his multimillion-dollar short film without him, he was *looking at houses.*

On that Saturday, even though the tour was supposedly canceled and Michael was apparently very, very sick, he abruptly left for Bangkok, shocking everyone. Suddenly, the tour wasn't canceled after all. And he had left a day ahead of schedule.

Sunday was the day we wrapped *Is This Scary*, but we were still missing Michael's crucial scenes—specifically the singing and dancing parts. To my knowledge, he still hadn't recorded the song. There were talks that they would fly the entire set to one of the cities on his tour and he could finish it there.

Even though things had been crazy, I was sad to leave that creepy set. It had been a fun and interesting two weeks. I was anxious to get back to Gallin Morey though, to find out what was *really* going on.

That next day, Monday, August 23, 1993, was the day all hell broke loose. I didn't know it then, but the events of the next few days would change the trajectory of all of our lives.

10

> I love him to heaven and back, to hell and back,
> and have and do and will.
>
> —Sylvia Plath

At 4:50 PM on Monday, August 23, 1993, my friend Nancy called to inform me that coming up on the five o'clock evening news there was going to be a report about a criminal investigation regarding Michael. My mind was reeling. My first thought was that maybe he had illegal animals at the ranch. Surely it couldn't be anything more serious than that.

Everyone at work gathered in offices to watch the news report. None of us knew what was coming. My stomach was tied in knots as I nervously checked the clock every minute. When five o'clock finally arrived, the newscaster announced that the Los Angeles and Santa Barbara Police Departments had raided Michael's Neverland Ranch and Century City condo and that a child was involved.

Although the news report was vague, I instantly suspected what it must be about. The thing that everyone had been whispering about for months was coming true. Then, on the six o'clock news, they revealed that Michael was being investigated for child abuse.

Everything changed from that day forward. Not only was Michael's world turned upside down, but mine was as well. Michael's downward spiral started right at that moment—a swift fall from which he would never recover.

As the hours and days went on, it was announced that the child's name was Jordan Chandler, whom Michael had met just a few months prior.

Jordan Chandler was a thirteen-year-old boy who had become inseparable from Michael. The tabloids had pegged the Chandlers as Michael's "secret family." Jordan sat on his lap at the World Music Awards in Monaco, and I remember thinking it looked odd. I had suspected something was amiss because after Michael met this family, he disappeared. No one could find him. He wouldn't return anyone's calls and canceled important business meetings that we had scheduled for him, claiming he was sick. He was missing for an entire month. I had called Michael's office every morning during that month and left a message for him to call Sandy, and he didn't call back for several weeks. Since meeting the Chandlers, he had become irresponsible. His work took a backseat to hanging out with them.

The closer his friendship with Jordan became, the less I heard from him as well. I had kept a calendar and diary documenting all of the days I had seen or spoken to Michael. I compared it with the time line the press was reporting regarding his relationship with Jordan. That seemingly out-of-the-blue encounter we had in the van had occurred in the middle of the drama he was having with that family. It's no wonder he was worried that his phones were being tapped and that he wanted to make sure I remained loyal to him. Everything was slowly starting to make sense.

The first couple days of the scandal were overwhelming. Every channel, every hour, every day some shocking new revelation was reported. I was glued to the TV. I couldn't eat or sleep.

To make matters worse and even more surreal, on Wednesday, two days after the story broke, I had to go back to the set of *Is This Scary* to reshoot some scenes. The scene we had to film was the one where the townspeople were shouting names at Michael like "freak" and "weirdo." Michael wasn't there, but it was just too close to real life. It was eerie. It was almost like he had put this scenario into the universe through this video and it had come true. I couldn't imagine them ever releasing it at that point. How could they?

I could hardly go on that day. I felt like I had been living in hell for the past week. The cast members were all whispering with each other wondering what was wrong with me. I was sad and in a shock-filled daze. The social services report had been leaked saying that Jordan had accused Michael of performing oral sex on him. This was too much.

Michael, understandably, wasn't doing so well either. He had canceled most of the shows in Bangkok because of "exhaustion" and had collapsed backstage from "migraines." The news showed him waving out of his hotel window looking tired. I was worried that he might try to commit suicide. It was *bad*.

Things got so bad that Elizabeth Taylor flew out to be with him. Everyone at the office was worried about me also. I must have looked like a wounded bird. Jim Morey called from the tour and I asked how "my husband" Michael was doing. He said, "He's borderline."

Dr. Deepak Chopra also called to ask how I was holding up. I told him it was like walking through a nightmare. He sounded shell-shocked and sad too. I could always depend on Deepak for wise words. He said, "Just remember—everything has a beginning, a middle, and an end—and this will as well." At that moment, though, it felt like this madness would last forever.

Deepak was Michael's close friend and spiritual guru and had also become my good friend. He had arranged for me to take transcendental meditation classes with a top teacher who had also taught Michael. The teacher came to my office every day for two weeks to give me private instruction. Deepak sent me books and tapes on spirituality and called every day to make sure I had meditated for at least twenty minutes. He felt that nothing was more important than meditating daily. He was a wonderful calming spirit and I was fortunate to have him as a friend during this trying time.

I fielded calls from the press all day. Connie Chung and Barbara Walters both called, personally requesting interviews with Michael.

It had all happened so fast. It felt like the entire world was spinning out of control. I wanted so much to talk to Michael and tell him he had my support but he hadn't called in a week.

That felt like a lifetime, since I had been hearing from him every day prior to this.

And then, on Wednesday, September 8, he finally called. "Hi, this is Michael. Who's this?" His voice sounded hoarse, scratchy, and weak.

"Hi, Michael! It's me—Shana."

"Hi, Shana. How are you?"

I told him that I was OK and then I blurted out, "Michael, I just want to tell you that I love you." The words just came tumbling out. It was the first time I had uttered them to him and I was a little worried about how he might react, but one thing this madness had taught me was that you never know what tomorrow may bring. I had received reports that he was so emotionally fragile it wasn't guaranteed that he would make it through the nights. There was no way I was going to let this moment pass without telling him how I felt.

He did not hesitate. "I love you too," he replied, sounding genuinely touched and sincere.

"Everything is going to be OK, Michael. I promise." My voice started to quiver as I said those words. Deep in my heart, I wasn't sure if everything would be OK at all. At this moment, the chances of everything being OK were slim. Hearing the sound of his voice though, was breaking my heart. He sounded so *weak*, like he was barely holding on. So many awful stories were being told in the press about him. I am sure he was relieved to know he still had me in his corner.

"Oh, you're so sweet. Thank you," he said, his voice quivering too. He then changed the subject and his mood, suddenly sounding like the happiest person in the world. "Wasn't that video we did fun?"

"Yeah, it was." I said, changing my voice to be more upbeat as well.

Michael continued, "Remember when I kept saying 'Is this scary? Is this scary?' and the little boy shook his head no but his father shook his head for him, saying yes? Wasn't that funny?"

It was funny then but it really wasn't now. Now that this exact scene had played out in real life and Michael could get arrested because of it . . . I found it hard to think of it as funny. I felt that this was Michael's way of telling me what was happening with the real-life accusations that were swirling—that Jordan's father was forcing him to make these awful allegations. How life had imitated art so closely was unbelievable.

Michael then kept going and going—talking so much I couldn't get a word in. "I had so much fun doing that video. I just love doing stuff like that," he rambled on.

I agreed with him and said, "Me too. I wish I could do that kind of stuff all the time."

"I know," Michael said sympathetically. Then he started laughing and continued going on and on about the *Is This Scary* video, recounting every line in every scene we had filmed that one day. All of the lines were eerily similar to what was currently happening, with the public ridiculing and judging him. At that moment it hit me that maybe for Michael all of life was simply a movie—all of us actors on a stage.

And then, as if he suddenly snapped back to reality, he said, "But we didn't get to finish it . . ."

"I know. I was so sad about that," I replied, feeling even more depressed about everything. I then changed the subject back to a happy topic. "Where are you today?"

He started laughing. "I'm in Japan."

"Japan? You sound so close—like you're next door."

"I know," he said.

"What time is it there?"

"Early in the morning. *Too* early." It was actually 10:30 AM there.

He now sounded abnormally happy—the happiest I had ever heard him—as if he didn't have a care in the world. In a split second his entire mood had changed. He was extremely talkative and funny. We went on for a while longer and I actually had to ask if he needed to speak to anyone else at the office in order to get him off the phone. The phones had been ringing off the hook and I was worried I was missing important calls. He told me that he would call back later.

Since I knew what a difficult time he was going through, the whole thing seemed odd. But I was happy I had been able to change his mood from sad to excited and joyful. I also suspected he might be on some sort of medication. His speech was slurred and his happy demeanor seemed like a facade. In any case, I was relieved. I felt that Michael just might be able to pull through these trying times. And after speaking to him, there was no doubt in my mind that he was innocent of all of the allegations of child abuse. His voice was so sweet and comforting. And he was so nice. I was convinced that there was no way anyone with such a kind heart and sweet voice could do any of the awful things they were accusing him of. I hung up that phone more in love than ever.

Many of my coworkers at Gallin Morey started throwing out the idea that Michael and I should get married. Everyone felt that it would be the best thing for him. It had become obvious to everyone that we both liked each other, so that would be the only logical step to rectify the bad publicity. Jim told me to make sure my passport was up to date. They wanted to send me overseas to meet up with Michael and be his "girlfriend" for some of his tour dates. If we were caught in photos, even better. "We just have to convince Michael," Jim said. I was extremely excited. What had started out as a sad time had turned into an exhilarating roller coaster ride. Every day held new twists and turns.

The tour cities came and went and I still wasn't flown out to see him. My hope for that ever happening started to dwindle.

Michael had good days and bad days—unpredictably canceling shows at the last minute. It was becoming increasingly difficult for him to perform with all of the lurid allegations continuing to swirl around him. I felt so sorry for him, but I didn't know what to do.

Every day a new awful story was printed. He was on the cover of every tabloid, every single week—with each story getting progressively worse and more shocking. The TV show *Hard Copy* had paid Michael's own maids and bodyguards to tell negative stories about him.

I'm not sure why, but I received death threats from a few crazy so-called fans just because they knew I was close to the situation and Michael. The only threat that truly scared me, however, came when I was answering Sandy's phones one day. It was the middle of the day and a man with a heavy New York Italian accent asked to be transferred to me from the front desk. The receptionist who was filling in for me transferred the man to Sandy's office. I answered, "Sandy Gallin's office."

The man nicely asked, "May I speak to Shana, please?"

"This is she," I said.

Then the man's voice turned menacing. "If you breathe a word of anything you know, I'm going to blow your fucking head off."

I was stunned.

The man hung up without saying another word. I started shaking uncontrollably. *Why me?* I thought. What threat did I pose to anyone? I was Michael's biggest supporter and friend. Why would anyone think I would turn on him? And just what was it that they were afraid I knew?

I admit, after this incident I started doubting Michael's innocence a bit. *If he were completely innocent*, I thought, *why would someone go to this extreme to keep me quiet?* I supposed our steamy phone calls may not have made him appear so innocent if I had spoken out about those, but on the other hand, I was an adult female—surely that could only help him.

It was at this time I started hearing clicks and noises on my office and home phones. I became convinced that Michael, or someone connected to him, was bugging my phones. He had made me so paranoid—telling me not to trust anyone—that I was now not trusting *him*. I searched my entire apartment for possible bugging devices—looking through potted plants, behind bookshelves, combing through clothes in my closet . . .

I had received a huge bouquet of tall sunflowers at work from a secret admirer and even those seemed menacing. The card that came with the flowers wasn't signed by anyone, so I became suspicious. It just said, "I love you." I thought they might be from Michael, but I couldn't be sure. With their bright-yellow petals and big brown centers, it felt like these imposing flowers were watching over me at my desk. I could feel their presence hovering next to me all day like an evil clown. I inspected the brown centers of the flowers closer and discovered hundreds of tiny seeds. That was so creepy I threw the entire beautiful arrangement in the trash. I had become afraid of *flowers*. Yeah, I was paranoid, to say the least.

On my way home from work every night, I was constantly looking in my rearview mirror to make sure I wasn't being followed. I took a different route home every night so as not to become predictable. At night, I found it difficult to sleep, worried that I was being watched.

I decided I couldn't take it anymore and hopped in my car. I drove to a place on Sunset called The Spy Store. I had heard that Michael liked to visit there himself, which was part of the reason I was suspicious of him. The store contained all kinds of devices that you could purchase to spy on people, or to find out if you were being spied on. Video cameras hidden in teddy bears, recording devices concealed in just about anything you could think of . . . I purchased a device that could be connected to your phone and would tell you if it was bugged. It was almost $100, but I didn't care. It would be worth it to have peace of mind.

I raced back home and installed it to the mouthpiece on my phone's receiver. According to the device, my phone was not bugged. The instructions said that the device was not 100 percent foolproof, however, and I was still convinced I was being watched or recorded somehow.

After thinking about it, I started suspecting that this threat had come from Anthony Pellicano, the controversial private detective Michael had hired, and not Michael himself. Allegedly he had made violent threats to people and was known to help his clients prove their innocence by any means necessary. He was also accused of wiretapping people's phones to get information to help his clients, which he was eventually sentenced to jail for. I don't know why I didn't report this death threat to the authorities. There was so much craziness going on that week, I didn't have the emotional capacity to pursue it any further than telling my bosses. I was at my wit's end. Looking back, I think the only way I maintained my sanity was by knowing that Michael was going through much worse, and he was somehow managing to survive.

We were all in the eye of the storm with no end in sight. I was told that Michael's mother traveled to visit him on the road and she became concerned when she spotted the IVs he was hooked up to. His doctor had explained to her that Michael was refusing to eat so they had to feed him nutrients intravenously. He was teetering on the edge and I was a nervous wreck not being able to see him.

It was about noon in the middle of one of these crazy days when Michael called from Chile. I heard his voice and it instantly brought tears to my eyes. Every ounce of emotional pain he was going through could be heard in his usually beautiful voice. A voice that used to sound so smooth, soothing, and full of energy, was now rough, broken, and dejected. He sounded as if his entire soul had been ripped out of him.

"Hi, this is Michael. Is this Shana?"

I told him that it was me and he asked how I was doing. I couldn't believe that with all he was going through—the absolute worst time in his life thus far—he was asking how I was doing. This made me even sadder.

"I miss you so much, Michael," was all I could say.

"I miss you too," he replied, his voice cracking.

We sat in silence for a few long seconds, neither of us knowing what to say. He sounded as if he had been crying. All I wanted at that moment was to hold him in my arms again and never let him go. A sensitive soul like his was not meant for this cruel world, I thought.

"I can't wait to see you again. And when I do I'm going to give you a big hug and kiss," I said trying to lighten the mood.

He giggled and said, "OK. Can't wait." His words were slow and deliberate, lingering longer than they should. It was devastating to hear him sound this way.

The next day was supposed to be a show day in Chile. At about 11 AM, he called for Sandy. Then, ten minutes later, he called again. He sounded happy but I knew something was wrong. He never called on show days. I later learned that if Michael called on the day of any show, that show wasn't going to happen.

Sure enough, Michael called again saying he was "in pain." He had started saying he was "in pain" whenever he wanted to get out of a show. This particular time he said he had pulled a muscle and simply was in too much pain to perform that night.

Michael calling in sick to work was not like if any of us called in for a day off. Him canceling even one show meant millions of dollars would be lost and the entire tour would have to be rerouted. This tour was now in shambles. Michael was definitely in pain, but it wasn't physical.

The fans in Chile were rightfully upset that the show had been canceled at the last minute and some of the more belligerent ones picketed his hotel with signs that read NIGGER GO HOME. Michael abruptly left and flew to Mexico City. It would end up being the last city on the Dangerous tour.

At this same time, we were trying to get Michael to approve the home video release of the videos for the *Dangerous* album in time for Christmas. He was giving everyone at the record company a hard time. Every time they would have it finished, Michael would find something new that he didn't like—petty stuff—anything to be difficult. When the record company finally thought they had it perfect for him, all of a sudden he decided he didn't like the mix of the song "Gone Too Soon." Of course, it was the same exact mix that was on the album—the only mix—the mix he had loved until now. The higher-ups at Sony wanted to strangle him and everyone at my office was concerned he was losing his mind. I figured it was just him being rebellious again.

Rebellion was the excuse I made for him as well when, in Tel Aviv, he started traveling with two young boys, the Cascio brothers. He was flaunting the fact that they were with him. It was like he wanted to show people that he didn't care what anyone thought. If he wanted to hang with little boys, he would. Instead of flying me to be with him, he chose them. I couldn't believe it. He was his own worst enemy.

Back in Mexico City, things were about to get even worse. Michael played his first two shows on October 29 and 31. They went fine other than the fact that he was still not doing six whole songs that he had dropped spontaneously on the first show of the tour in Bangkok. Everyone involved was a nervous wreck. It was our office at Gallin Morey that had to smooth things over whenever Michael canceled a show.

On November 2, Michael called for Sandy. I knew something was wrong because, once again, it was a show day. His voice sounded terrible. It was rough like a frog and his words were slow. "I'm in pain," he complained. I knew what that meant. *Here we go again,* I thought. Another show was about to be canceled. He stated that he had a toothache and was in too much pain to perform. Sandy's assistant said to me, "Michael is losing it. He's going crazy." I told her that I suspected he was on some sort of drugs. I knew what his voice sounded like when he was sober and this wasn't it.

The next day, I received a call from Michael's trusted plastic surgeon, Dr. Steven Hoefflin. He said that Michael had called him late the night before and begged him to come to Mexico City as soon as possible and said it was an emergency. The next show was scheduled for November 6. Dr. Hoefflin asked me to find some flights for him from L.A. to Mexico City. I wondered why Michael would need a plastic surgeon so suddenly. Then we received word that Michael would have to have emergency dental surgery because of that toothache and, of course, more shows would have to be postponed. He was getting creative with excuses for these show cancelations.

On Monday, November 8, there was a huge meeting at Gallin Morey. Michael's entire team was there—his lawyers Howard Weitzman and Bert Fields, the private detective Anthony Pellicano, Steve Chabre (who was the head of MJJ Productions), Jim, and Sandy. They met for two hours. I knew that whatever was being discussed had to be major. When it was over, everyone walked out of the conference room with weary looks on their faces as if they had just survived a war.

Jim came over to me and said in jest, "Why don't you go take care of Michael?"

"He's not feeling so well?" I asked.

Jim said sadly, "No, he's not doing so well."

On that same day, Michael gave a videotaped deposition in a copyright infringement case. The tape was shown on the news that night and he appeared to be under the influence of something. He could barely keep his eyes open during his testimony.

The next day, at our weekly company staff meeting, Sandy announced, "Some shit is about to come down on Michael on Friday. If anyone calls, please refer it to the lawyer's office." This sounded ominous. We all wondered what it could be. I knew that it had to have something to do with that big meeting they had.

Whatever the case, it was clear that everything that was happening now was being carefully orchestrated by some of the best damage-control people in the business. This experience taught me that if a star is in trouble, you should always be skeptical of any statements or actions coming out of that star's camp. You would be better off reading the tabloids for true information.

On that same day, November 9, Michael performed another concert. Although the reviews weren't that great for the show, at least he was onstage.

The next city on the tour was supposed to be San Juan in Puerto Rico, the first city of the tour that was actually in the United States. We were all worried Michael might get arrested if he set foot on US soil. He had purposely left to start the tour early so that he would be safely out of the country when trouble was starting.

But he had one more show left to do in Mexico City on Thursday, November 11. On that day, CNN reported that the rest of the tour would be canceled. I thought perhaps that was the big mysterious news that would be coming on Friday. But I just knew there had to be more to it than that.

To say that Friday, November 12, was the craziest day ever would be an understatement. It was pure madness from the moment I arrived at 9 AM. I was sitting in the very center of the storm.

Sandy's assistant Sheila told me that if anyone called—and they would surely start calling—to tell them I didn't know anything and to refer them to Michael's lawyer Bert Fields. I was thinking, *What am I not supposed to know?* Everyone was running around like chickens with their heads cut off. I kept hearing something about a tape. I was wondering what could be so important about this tape?

The phone never stopped ringing that day. I was dying of curiosity. I knew that something big was about to happen but I had no idea what it might be. The press kept calling saying that they had heard the rest of the tour had been canceled and asking if I could make a comment. I referred them to Bert Fields. If only they knew—I was just as clueless as they were. I did know, however, there was much more to this than a canceled tour.

Nicole from Michael's office called me. Her first words were, "What the heck is going on?"

I said, "I don't know, but something sure is." They had done a good job of keeping us all in the dark. She told me that things were crazy at her office too.

Then Jim called. It was so nice to finally be able to talk to someone who actually knew what was happening. "This is the craziest day in the history of Gallin Morey," I said, exhausted yet excited by all of the drama.

"Has Michael called?" Jim asked.

"No, but everyone else has."

"It's unbelievable, isn't it?" Jim sounded sad and tired.

I was thinking, *What's unbelievable?* I guess he thought I already knew what the big secret was. But I didn't.

Sheila raced to my desk and handed me three envelopes with a tape in each. "You have to stay here tonight until Pellicano and Weitzman pick up their tapes."

I wanted to scream, *What is so important about this tape?*

I left the office a little after 7 PM and rushed home—racing over Laurel Canyon in record time. I didn't want to miss any of the breaking news that was sure to transpire that night. I bolted through the door of my small apartment and turned on the TV. Just a few minutes later, a special "Breaking News" report interrupted the program I was watching. I knew this had to be it. Finally, I would know what all of this craziness was about.

The newscaster in his most serious tone read, "This just in—pop superstar Michael Jackson has announced that he is canceling his world tour to seek treatment for an addiction to painkillers."

I screamed so loud I'm sure my neighbors heard me. I had never been so shocked in my life. So that's what all of this madness had been about. I couldn't believe it. I couldn't believe I had been so right about his drug problem. I knew he had to be on something—his behavior had become so erratic and his speech was slurred during most of our conversations. He had been sounding out of it for the past few months. I had told a couple of my friends that I suspected Michael was on drugs, and they didn't believe me. I thought the problem had probably started quite a while before these allegations were even made.

In the past, sometimes he would call and would barely be able to talk, sounding like an old man. The pieces were slowly falling into place.

Then the news announced that they had a *tape* of Michael making a statement regarding his drug addiction. Michael had recorded an audio tape stating that he would have to end his tour to check into rehab for his addiction problem. Everything finally made sense.

After that night, Michael disappeared from Mexico City and entered a secret drug rehab, the location of which was unknown at the time. It sparked an international "Where's Michael?" search. This kicked the press into even more of a frenzy.

Elton John had started calling the office a lot in recent weeks. It was Elton, at the behest of Elizabeth Taylor, who had referred his drug rehab doctor to Michael. Elizabeth had flown with her husband, Larry Fortensky, to meet Michael in Mexico City and had escorted him to the private rehab facility.

Michael's mother was upset that he was turning to Elizabeth instead of her. Norma, Michael's longtime assistant, had called Mrs. Jackson on Friday, just hours before the big announcement, to break the news to her. Michael didn't want her learning about it on the news like the rest of us. Norma told her that she couldn't tell her where he was and to please not try to reach him. Mrs. Jackson was shocked. She had no idea her son was on drugs. She was upset that no one had told her before then and that he didn't have the guts to call her himself.

I heard that Elizabeth called Mrs. Jackson the next day to tell her personally about Michael's addiction problem. She told his mother the whole sad story.

I was also given the gory details from one of Michael's friends. I sat in shock as I listened to revelations I never dreamed I would hear. They told me that Michael would constantly complain until he got the drugs he wanted. He went to a whole bunch of different doctors who didn't know what the others were prescribing. He would lie to them about being in pain to get medication. All of the unnecessary plastic surgeries and injuries were just elaborate excuses to obtain drugs. He wasn't addicted to surgery like most had thought—*he was addicted to the pain medication that came with the surgeries.* He started mixing all kinds of drugs together, which could be disastrous. His life was in extreme danger. That's why Elizabeth had to convince him to go to rehab. She had gone several times herself for various addictions, so she was able to speak to him from experience. He didn't want to go at all, of course. He fought it the entire way.

His drugs of choice were morphine, Percocet, and Demerol. It had gotten so bad that one time he was on an important business call and in the middle of the conversation he just stopped responding to the person he was speaking to. He had fallen asleep. He had canceled all of those shows on tour because of his addiction problem, not because of any of the illnesses he claimed he was suffering from. And he had started surrounding himself with sleazy underworld types and no one could understand why.

Michael was now being referred to in the press as a drug addict accused of child molestation. How did it all come to this? He had always been known as drug-free, clean, innocent, and pure.

As I was hearing all of these horrible revelations, my world crumbled around me. I felt like I didn't know what was real anymore. I thought I had known Michael. And now I was realizing I didn't know him at all.

Nicole, from Michael's office, and I drove to San Diego to film an infomercial for Dr. Chopra that weekend. He had asked us to participate and we were happy to accept. We both needed to get away from the familiar surroundings of L.A. It's a three-hour drive down to San Diego. On the 405 freeway, with the Pacific Ocean on our side, we were lost in a world of our own, trying to make sense of how everything had spiraled so wildly out of control. She and I had both been fans of Michael's growing up and we never dreamed it would ever come to this.

I played the song "One Day I'll Fly Away" by Randy Crawford in a constant loop. The lyrics hit me so hard; I broke down in tears.

I thought back on that summer of '93 when dreams of hope were still alive. Looking back, I see it as one of those gilded moments in time that would never come again. I spoke to Michael almost every day then and the feelings of falling in love made each day feel like a wondrous dream. Now, I didn't know if I would ever see him again—and if I did, how could it ever be the same?

When I spoke to Dr. Chopra, he asked how I was doing. I told him that I was trying to hang in there. He said sadly, "It's true you know—about the drugs. If Michael would only get off of those drugs, everything would be OK."

Hearing his own doctor and friends talk about Michael's problems with drugs was very difficult. Although I had suspected something was wrong for some time, to hear others say it made me very sad. Usually in these situations, friends and family would try to hide what's really going on. In this case, everyone was trying to convince each other that the problem was real.

On that Sunday, November 14, I think my life reached a turning point. Never again could I look at the world and life so naively. Illusions and childish dreams disappeared on that day. The cold hard facts had slapped me in the face.

On Friday, November 19, Michael's longtime loyal assistant Norma quit. The police wanted to question her but she had somehow eluded them and moved to Greece. This only made Michael look guiltier.

Harvey Levin, who was an investigative reporter for Channel 2 News Los Angeles back then, called the office and asked me if it was true about Norma quitting. I told him that I had no comment and that I didn't know. He said aggressively, "You must know. You work with her." I can see why he became so successful in later years with TMZ. He was always persistent and had the innate ability to sniff out a good story before it happened.

On Wednesday, December 1, there was a huge meeting at Elizabeth's house on Nimes Road in Bel Air that included all of the key members of Michael's team. Michael's public image was in shambles at this point and everyone felt it would be best if another publicist who specialized in crises were hired, as well as a new criminal attorney. Bob Jones suggested Johnnie Cochran. Everyone felt it would be good for Michael's image to have a black lawyer, and Johnnie also had connections in the district attorney's office. Johnnie was hired and took over the case. This was before he became known for the infamous O. J. Simpson trial.

A couple days after that big meeting, Michael finally called me. I hadn't spoken to him since he had gone into hiding and rehab. I was so happy to hear his voice again.

"Hi, it's Michael."

"Hi Michael! How are you?" I said.

"I'm fine. Thank you," he said, his voice sounding strong and clear. He continued, "I spoke to Timmy yesterday. I just wanted to call him to say hi." Timmy was our mutual friend who also happened to be seven years old. Michael had called all of his special child friends to assure them that everything would be OK.

Many parents of young boys had tried to befriend me in the past in hopes that I would introduce their sons to Michael. If I felt the parents and the child were trustworthy, I would make the introduction. Michael almost always called the children immediately and became their friend, inviting them to Neverland. This is how we ended up having mutual child friends in common.

We chatted about some other random topics and I told him I was happy to hear him sounding so good. He said, "I'm really most embarrassed about the drugs stuff. I've always been against them my entire life."

I told him that it was understandable with everything he had to deal with. "I care about you, Michael. Please just stay strong."

"I will, and I care about you too," he said. And for the first time in a long time, I believed he would stay strong and pull through this. His entire demeanor and tone of voice had changed since going to rehab. He was now very serious, not giggling, and talking naturally. His voice was slightly hoarse, but strong. His words were no longer slurring and his thoughts seemed clear. He sounded ready to take on the world and fight for his life. It was as if he had grown up over those weeks, finally able to face reality. I had never heard him sound like he did now. He was a survivor, that was for sure.

On Friday, December 10, after four weeks in seclusion, Michael returned to the United States and Neverland Ranch to face the music. Most people thought that he would never return. He had been out of the country on tour for four months and I was so happy to know he was nearby again.

Unfortunately, he had to face a humiliating strip search upon his arrival. Jordan Chandler had described Michael's genitals to the Santa Barbara district attorney and they wanted to take pictures of those areas to see if Jordan's description matched. Michael called that day sounding more upset and angry than I had ever heard him before. I wasn't aware of what was going on at the time, but I knew that something must be very wrong for him to lose his cool like that. He had impatiently asked me to have Sandy call him and told me that he didn't want to speak to anyone else. Even when he was upset, though, he was always polite. The next day, I found out about the strip search. I couldn't have felt worse for him.

The following week, I attended the annual Gallin Morey Christmas luncheon. Every year, Sandy and Jim took the entire staff out to eat at a nice restaurant for Christmas. That year we went to Le Dome, which was located in the lobby of our office building. I ran into Stevie Wonder on the elevator ride down to the restaurant. I told him how much I loved his song that I used to play constantly, "Too Shy to Say." Encounters like that had become the norm in that elevator.

We were all escorted to a private back room in Le Dome and placed at tables filled with the finest linens and china. I was sitting next to one of Michael's tour staff members. Once the guests had consumed a few bottles of wine, he started unloading his true feelings about everything that had transpired on the ill-fated Dangerous tour.

The tour had been a nightmare, he said, with no one ever knowing if Michael would show up. One time he canceled a show claiming he was sick and that same day he was seen at a toy store buying toys. The tour member confronted Michael about it, and Michael lied and said it wasn't him. Michael said, "You're going to believe the press over me?" He said that Michael's ability to bend the truth was remarkable.

I couldn't believe what I was hearing. I knew that Michael wasn't an angel but to hear these opinions about him was depressing. He had always presented himself as a perfect gentleman to me and that is what I chose to believe. Even after hearing these things, it didn't change my feelings for him. My love for him was unconditional. I didn't care that he wasn't the perfect guy I thought he was. When you're in love, there's not too much someone can tell you to make you fall out of love. Only time—or overwhelming circumstances—can do that.

11

When love is not madness, it is not love.
—Pedro Calderón de la Barca

On August 1, 1994, it was announced that Michael had married Lisa Marie Presley on May 18. There had been rumors for weeks. He kept denying it and told no one. Somehow, though, in my gut, I knew it was true.

Michael and Lisa had met about a year and a half earlier. He wanted to sign her to his record label, MJJ Music. They had a meeting at Sandy's house in Beverly Hills one evening—I remember it was at 7:30 PM. She was also at *The Jackson Family Honors* show secretly in Las Vegas with Michael not long before that. She had accompanied him to Disney World in Orlando during that time as well. That's when I suspected something was going on with the two of them.

Michael wanted everyone to keep "as far away from it as possible" when the story first broke. Now, on this day, he admitted it. The press was automatically dubbing it a publicity stunt because of his recent child molestation allegations, but I wasn't so sure. Michael had always been obsessed with surpassing Elvis in history. Marrying his daughter would be the ultimate win for him. I also knew that Michael could turn on the charm and make anyone fall in love if he wanted, and I am certain Lisa was not immune. I wasn't sure if Michael was truly in love, but I was sure Lisa was.

When I wasn't feeling jealous and angry about the whole situation, I actually felt happy for them. I liked Lisa. We were close in age and I had followed her interesting life since I was a child. I had heard nothing but good things about her from Michael's friends, and I did want him to be happy. She obviously didn't need him for his money or anything else but love. A part of me was hoping it was real and that it worked out.

He called the office on the day of the announcement and I didn't know what to say. I admit, I felt more than a little betrayed. The least he could have done was warn me that this was going to happen. Instead, I had to find out from the press. I knew that something had changed recently because he had been acting more and more distant—like nothing had ever happened between us. It was like all of it had disappeared, and now this new married Michael was here. He had been accused of a horrible crime, been to rehab, had a strip search performed on him—the sweet Michael I used to know was no more, I figured. His world had come crashing down seemingly overnight, and with it, my hopes and dreams for a future with him had vanished as well.

I could hear a difference in his voice but I couldn't really pinpoint what it was. It was like he had grown up. He had been through more in a year than most people will go through in a lifetime. I was just dying to jump through the phone and hug him and kiss him again but . . . he was *married* now.

I didn't know if I should congratulate him or not. I mean, he didn't tell me about it, so why should I say anything? As I sat thinking about everything I had gone through with him, all of the useless feelings I had felt—the endless nights I spent awake just trying to figure out what to say to him, the hope I felt after our first kiss, the phone calls, the songs, the "I love yous," the amount of effort he seemed to put into simply making me fall in love with him—all of that was for nothing. And suddenly I was furious.

A couple days later, Sandy sauntered off of the elevator wearing his usual office attire: a tailored Armani blazer with a Gap T-shirt underneath and jeans. "Are you heartbroken?" he asked sympathetically.

I hesitated for a second, not knowing if I should reveal my true feelings. Come to think of it, I didn't even know what my true feelings were at this point. It had all happened so fast. One thing was for certain though—I was definitely heartbroken. I felt a lump suddenly forming in my throat and tears welling up in my eyes. "Yes," I said, stifling the tears.

I felt stupid and embarrassed. Why should I be heartbroken? Michael didn't care enough about me to tell me this was going to happen. He knew how I felt about him. Why wasn't I the one he married? He had been avoiding me and acting distant and cold ever since his case had been settled and his trouble appeared over. Now I knew why. I felt like a fool. Lisa Marie had millions and I didn't, *and* she was Elvis Presley's daughter, which clearly meant a lot to him. I wasn't rich or famous. How could I have ever thought he would actually marry me or take me seriously at all? I guessed I never stood a chance.

"You're heartbroken? Really?" Sandy said, genuinely concerned.

"Yes," I said, "but I'm happy for him. He needs this."

Sandy said, "Did you say anything to him when he called?"

"I haven't really had a chance to talk to him yet, but I'll say something the next time he calls."

"Are you going to tell him that you're heartbroken?"

"Should I?"

Mischievously, Sandy said, "Of course."

Just a few minutes later, Michael called. It was almost like it was a setup. I picked up the phone and, like music to my ears, there was that voice.

"This is Michael. I'm at the studio. Could you find Sandy and tell him to call me, emergency?"

I said, "OK. And he knows the number there?"

He said, "Yeah."

And we hung up. I wanted to say something but he sounded so hurried, serious, and intimidating. So I said nothing. His demeanor had certainly changed since his marriage. He had become more assertive and demanding, or maybe he had just adopted that attitude with me to discourage me from saying anything to him. Whatever the reason, it worked. I was afraid to broach any personal topics with him. I kept it strictly business. Why he had decided to treat me so coldly was beyond me. He seemed almost embarrassed to be married—like he didn't want to discuss it. I suppose he was just afraid of confrontation, but something needed to be said.

Sandy walked down from his office a few minutes later. He asked if I had said anything to Michael when he called. I told him I had chickened out because Michael sounded too rushed. Just then, Jim waltzed by and, as if on cue, said, "Well, look at it this way. At least now maybe you can be his mistress on the side and you won't have to put up with him every day. Maybe she'll break him in for you."

It had been a running joke at the office that Michael was inexperienced and innocent and that I could help him in that department. Surely it was just a joke, but Michael presented himself to everyone, even his own managers, to be very innocent, so no one really knew what happened behind closed doors with him, and I wasn't about to shatter those illusions that he had so carefully crafted. I knew from our phone calls and the way he kissed me that he wasn't innocent *at all.*

I spoke to a couple of his tour members about the marriage. They were all very happy for Michael. Elizabeth Taylor started calling again too—all of the time. It seemed like all she wanted to do all day was gossip with Sandy about Michael. You would think a legendary movie star of her caliber would have more to do than spend all day talking about someone so much younger. I'd never seen anything like it. Don Cornelius, the iconic host of *Soul Train*, befriended me around this time. He would call me every single day just to gossip about Michael. Even he was curious as to what was really going on. Diane Sawyer started calling daily as well to push for an interview with Michael and Lisa Marie, which they eventually agreed to do.

Michael and Lisa Marie returned from their honeymoon in Budapest on August 9. It seemed like such a PR stunt. The press loved it and photographed them like a happy, loving couple. They had actually traveled to Budapest to film a teaser for Michael's upcoming *HIStory* album. The press dubbed it a honeymoon because it occurred right after their marriage announcement.

I thought that Michael and I would never flirt with each other again, but he was full of surprises. He called the day after they got back from Budapest at about 3 PM from New York.

He said his usual, “Michael for Sandy.”

I said, “Hi, Michael, hold on.”

For some reason I couldn’t transfer him. It wouldn’t work. We had just had a very minor earthquake, so I figured that perhaps it had messed up the lines somehow. Or maybe it was the divine from up above intervening and helping me out because I was definitely too nervous to mention his marriage to him, although I knew that I should.

I was taking a long time to transfer him, so he thought I had disconnected him. He hung up and called right back. “Did you disconnect me?” he asked.

“No, I don’t know what’s wrong but for some reason I can’t transfer your call. We just had a small earthquake, so that’s probably why.”

Michael’s entire tone of voice changed. The topic of earthquakes was fresh on everyone’s minds because we had recently had the major 1994 Northridge shaker, and it had been traumatic, especially for those of us living in the San Fernando Valley. Michael had been staying in the valley too, not far from the epicenter, when it occurred, so he was understandably terrified of them.

“You had an earthquake?” he enthused. “Really? How big was it? Was it big?”

“It was maybe a 4.0. Not too bad.”

“Good!” Michael was so excited. “I am so glad you had one.”

“Good?” I chuckled. “That’s mean of you to say, Michael. Why are you happy about this?”

He started laughing. “I’m sorry. I didn’t mean it like that. It’s because I’ve been telling everyone to get out of L.A. ever since the Northridge earthquake. No one would listen to me. Maybe now they will!”

“I’m sure that most people would leave if they could,” I offered. “I wish I could but it’s not easy to do. I was in the valley for that one and it was the scariest day of my life.”

“Well, you know,” Michael said, “they said that after that big one, we won’t have another major one for another fifty years!”

“Really?” I said, fascinated by the fact that he always knew the most random information.

"Yes, it's true. So you have nothing to worry about. Of course, that's easy for me to say, right? I'm three thousand miles away in New York," he laughed. "When that big one happened, I was there in the valley too and I was scared to death. I swear I packed up as soon as I could and moved to New York. And my father—he is just like me. He tries to act all tough, but he was just as scared as me and moved to Las Vegas. He couldn't take it!" We both laughed. He could be so funny just telling the simplest story.

Michael's whole mood had changed with this news. He was now extremely excited and happy; you would think something good had actually happened. He then realized he was being insensitive and asked if I was OK. "How are you? Are you OK?"

"I'm OK. What can I do? I wish I were like you and could move too. Thank you for the comforting thoughts though."

"From far away, right?" he chuckled.

I laughed and told him that I would have Sandy call him.

He said, "Oh, I'll just call back."

"Where are you? Is there a number where he can call you?"

"I'll just call later," he replied.

"Oh, Sandy will be mad that I didn't put you through."

He said, "Can you walk up to his office and tell him?"

"I could, but I still wouldn't be able to transfer you."

"What's his number? I'll call him back."

"You just called it," I said. "He's here at the office."

"He doesn't have a direct line?" Michael asked. I told him that he didn't.

I figured it was now or never to change the subject and mention his marriage. He sounded like he was in a good mood, which wasn't always the case. I gathered my nerves and my fake happy voice and said, "By the way, congratulations on your marriage!"

He paused for what seemed like the longest five seconds ever, giggled, and said, "Thank you."

"You're welcome," I replied. "Hold on, let me see what I can do about getting your message to Sandy." I felt like a weight had been lifted. Finally, the elephant in the room had been acknowledged.

I managed to call Sandy's office and tell them the problem. They told me to tell Michael they would call him at the Trump Tower in New York because that's where he had been staying since getting married. I got back on the phone with Michael. "Are you home?" I asked. "They're going to call you now.

"But I'm tired. I have to go," he sighed.

Then I heard his other phone ringing. "I bet that's them calling right now," I said.

"Oh, but then I'd have to get up. I don't want to get up."

"I think you should get it, Michael. Go answer that phone."

"OK," he begrudgingly said. "I'll get it."

We hung up. Then about five minutes later, the phone rang again.

"Gallin Morey," I answer.

"Hello," that old familiar voice said.

"Hi, Michael."

"You still can't put the calls through, huh?"

I said, "No, but I can try."

"That's OK."

"No, wait. I'll try." I said, worried that he would get upset that he couldn't get through to his own manager.

"No, I already talked to Sandy," Michael said. "I just wanted to tell him that it was me who was calling him so he didn't need to call me back. He was just returning my call." Or something like that—whatever he said, it didn't make any sense. He was now rambling and slurring his words.

I felt like he was trying to get up the guts to say something, because he didn't seem to really want anything. He didn't want Sandy. He just wanted to talk but obviously didn't know how to go about bringing up the subject that was hanging over our heads like a brick—*his marriage.*

Then Michael blurted, "I just wanted to call you back to thank you for always putting my calls through."

Putting his calls through? Had he lost his mind? That was my job. *Come on, Michael . . . just spit it out.*

Not knowing what else to say, I said, "No problem." I figured just letting him talk would be the best thing right now. Eventually, he would get to the point . . . hopefully.

He continued, "I mean it. I *really* appreciate it. Thank you so much."

I said, "Any time."

At this point his voice had changed to his flirty voice. It got deeper, talking slowly and lingering on every word. It reminded me of how our calls of the past used to start out before they took a turn into the sexy song lyrics. I hadn't heard this particular tone in his voice in such a long time. I was getting excited. I thought that maybe this would turn into one of *those* calls. So much had happened, and I really didn't think we would ever get to this point again. I thought it was over for us. All of my feelings came rushing back like a tidal wave washing ashore.

"You don't know how much I appreciate you," he stammered. "You've always been there for me. Thank you for all of the little projects you've helped me with . . . and all of the other stuff. You've proven your loyalty and I appreciate that too. You always know how to make me smile. I'll never forget it."

"You're welcome," I said, not knowing how else to respond. As happy as I was to hear him say these things, I was baffled. It came straight out of the blue and he seemed too embarrassed to mention anything specific. I interrupted his slurred rambling and changed the subject, telling him that I had seen clips the day before, of him in Budapest on his so-called honeymoon, and that he looked really handsome.

He giggled and said, "Thank you." Then suddenly, he said with conviction, "Promise me you won't believe anything that you see on television, OK? It's just publicity."

That's what I was waiting to hear. I told him that I wouldn't believe anything unless he personally told me.

He sounded relieved and said, "You know that I'll always be your blanket. You can turn to me for anything."

"I know, Michael. I'll always be here for you too. I love you."

"I love you more. Do I have your home number? I might need to talk to you." I gave him my current home number and he read it back to me to be sure he had it correct.

"OK, Shana. I'll be talking to you soon. I'm going to go to sleep now. I love you." He couldn't end a conversation without saying I love you, even if he had already said it.

"I love you too, Michael." I was so touched by his words; I had tears in my eyes as I hung up the phone.

He was good. He always knew just the perfect thing to say at just the perfect time to make me forget about anything negative that might be happening. Suddenly, I didn't care that he was married. I knew that I was on his mind, and that was all that mattered. Once again, I felt like there was hope for us. He had given me a lifeline and I happily grabbed onto it. It didn't take much to keep me hooked and I sensed he knew that.

He sounded dazed throughout the conversation, like he had taken a strong sleeping pill for jet lag. He always sounded like that whenever we had long conversations. I was hoping that he hadn't relapsed back into taking painkillers.

After we hung up, Sandy called me. "What happened? Michael called twice and you couldn't put him through?" I explained to him what happened. He said, "That's interesting."

Sandy's new assistant, Marty, raced down to my desk. He was cute, young, and always hyper. He talked a mile a minute. He blurted out, "Michael's in love with you."

Taken aback I asked, "Why do you say that?"

"I was in the room just now when Sandy and Michael were on the phone. The whole conversation was about you. Michael wanted to know how you were doing and how you felt about his marriage. He was concerned with how you were taking the news."

Then Sandy walked down from his office and joined Marty at my desk. He said, "That's weird that Michael called you back. I told him that you were upset because he got married."

My face dropped. He had told Michael that I was upset? I was so embarrassed. Here I had been trying to act unbothered while playing it cool with Michael, and Sandy had blown my cover. "Well, what did Michael say?" Although my face was red with embarrassment, I was curious about what Michael's response was.

"Nothing. He never says anything about his marriage."

I had a feeling that things were about to get interesting again with Michael and me. Getting the topic of his marriage out of the way appeared to make things normal again. He truly seemed embarrassed by the marriage and wanted me to think it was fake so as not to hurt my feelings. He wanted to appear available and keep me hanging on. I don't think he could bear the thought of me no longer loving him or being upset with him. After this conversation, he was no longer cold toward me. The Michael I used to love was suddenly back.

The newlyweds caused a commotion by opening the MTV Video Music Awards with a kiss not long after they were married. MTV had proposed two options for the opening.

The first option was to have Michael and Lisa Marie walk out onstage. Michael would say, "Welcome to the 1994 MTV Video Music Awards! In case you haven't heard, Lisa Marie and I got married . . . and there's one thing we haven't done yet. Honey!" Lisa Marie would take a bouquet of flowers she'd been concealing, turn her back to the audience, and throw it as far into the house as she could. The couple would then blow kisses to the audience and exit.

The second option—Michael and Lisa Marie walk out to center stage. Michael says, "Welcome to the 1994 MTV Video Awards. And you thought it wouldn't last." The couple would then kiss and walk offstage.

Michael chose the second option. He wanted to kiss his bride on national television so that the whole world could see it was real.

This plan backfired. The public criticized the kiss, saying it lacked passion. He just couldn't win. The press was convinced that the marriage wasn't real, and there was nothing Michael could do to change that perception. Regardless, it did at least create the buzz that he wanted. It was *the* topic of conversation all over the world the next day—another iconic moment was in the history books.

After a year of hell, Michael was getting his life back on track—and his career as well. He was back in the studio recording the *HIStory* album, mostly in New York, at The Hit Factory and in Sherman Oaks, California, at Record One. I was keeping tabs on Michael and his marriage through his friends, looking for any shimmer of hope that it wouldn't last. I learned that he would go weeks without seeing Lisa, preferring to spend time with his young friends. I was baffled that he would choose the company of children over his pretty new wife. Somehow I knew that it was only a matter of time before the marriage completely imploded.

During this time, I attended a business dinner hosted by a high-ranking executive at Lisa Marie's record label. The subject of the marriage came up after a few cocktails had been consumed. The executive knew where I worked and asked my opinion of it.

"What are your thoughts on the marriage?" he asked.

I told him that I was happy for them and that I hoped it worked out. I had learned not to say too much and to let the other person share their own thoughts instead.

"Well, I was talking to Lisa the other day," he continued, "and she says that the marriage is real but it's not normal. She said that they do have sex but Michael uses it to control her. He withholds it to barter for other things he wants. He makes her think that she wants it more than he does and he uses that to his advantage."

Everyone at the dinner table was surprised to hear these interesting musings, but most still didn't believe the part about them having sex. I was happy to hear it, though. Michael being open to having an intimate relationship with someone meant that there was hope for me.

While Michael was in the studio in Sherman Oaks working on the album, I kept getting reports back from our mutual friends that he was always asking about me. I hadn't heard from him much lately, though, so I was surprised I was still on his mind.

One day, at about 5 PM, he called the office. "Michael for Jim Morey."

"Sure, Michael. How are you doing?"

"I'm fine. Thank you," he said coldly. I took that to mean he didn't feel like chatting so I transferred him to Jim. He was good at being cold and unfriendly when he wasn't in the mood to talk.

About five minutes later, Jim called me at my desk. I picked up the phone and Jim announced, "I have the King of Pop for you."

This was a surprise. Jim hung up and Michael was on the line.

"Hello?" I said.

"Hi, Shana. I'm sorry I didn't say hi to you before, but I didn't know it was you."

I told him that it was not a problem.

He was quiet for a second and then said, "I just wanted to tell you that I miss you."

I was speechless. Lisa Marie's birthday would be the following day, so I would've never thought he would be thinking about me. He made me so happy by saying those words.

"I miss you too, Michael. *So much* . . . When am I going to see you again?"

"I'll be seeing you very soon," he said.

"Do you promise?"

"I promise," he said—and I believed him.

"I'm so happy about that. I love you."

"I love you too."

We hadn't physically seen each other in over a year and it hadn't been easy. After we hung up, I asked Jim what had prompted Michael to want to speak to me. Jim said that Michael asked to be transferred back to me after they finished their conversation. Jim told him, "I guess Lisa Marie isn't in the car with you." Michael laughed and said, "I like Shana. She's nice."

It seemed like Michael could sense whenever I might be losing interest. Now that he was married, I had been trying to figure out a way to get over him.

Jordan Knight, from New Kids on the Block, had come into the office a few weeks prior to Michael calling. He was at the height of his fame at this time and was very cute and charming. He started calling me at the office the day after we met and then asked for my home phone number. Eventually, we went on a date—along with his manager, Miguel—to Jerry's Deli in Sherman Oaks. I found him to be very nice, down to earth, and easy to talk to. He had to go back to his home in Boston the next day, so that one dinner date was all we ever had. We chatted on the phone a bit more after that but that was it. He was the only person who could have possibly taken my mind off the King of Pop at that time, but alas, it wasn't meant to be.

Because of my high-profile job, men (and clients) were always hitting on me, but I simply wasn't interested in any of them. I remember that the actor Paul Walker, who was a client at the company and just starting his career, was constantly flirting with me. I'm mad at myself now for not going out on a date with him. He was nice and handsome, with blond hair and blue eyes, and he always greeted me with a big smile. Actors Martin Lawrence and Terrence Howard were also clients who both tried relentlessly to go out with me. They were both very persistent and sometimes showed up at our offices unexpectedly just to beg me for a date. Unfortunately for them, all of my thoughts and focus were totally consumed by one person—Michael. It was tortuous. Just when I thought I was ready and able to let go of him, he always came back. It reminded me of that song by Dolly Parton "Here You Come Again"—"just when I've begun to get myself together . . ."

Yeah, I had it bad. Michael was like a drug that I was addicted to. He gave me just enough to keep me hooked, pulling away before he gave me too much, which only made me crave him more. The poetry of our dance had become familiar and exciting. It was a vicious cycle, but this push and pull was all I knew. Michael's unpredictable behavior and elusive nature is what kept me intrigued. Sadly, this emotional roller coaster would damage me in ways I could have never predicted. To this day, I find myself still drawn to the emotional unavailability and ambiguity I became used to in Michael. Because of this, I have never experienced a real, committed relationship. The few future romantic relationships I did have mirrored the one I had with Michael. I find it difficult to even be attracted to men unless they possess that rare, charismatic, exciting quality that Michael had. Having Michael Jackson as my first love was not only a blessing but also a curse.

12

Beautiful things are naturally elusive. You can never fully have them. They're meant to be shared or experienced, not possessed.

—Rob Hill Sr.

As the recording sessions for the *HIStory* album were wrapping up, Michael decided that he needed one more surefire hit. During one of our conversations, he told me that he wanted to work with hip-hop producer Dr. Dre. He was a fan of Dre's hard-hitting beats and just knew that a collaboration would produce some classic songs. I agreed and got excited just imagining Michael's smooth vocals gliding over Dre's powerful beats. Shortly after my conversation with Michael, I was invited to a party that Dr. Dre was hosting. I just knew that this was my opportunity to make this dream pairing come true.

The party was star-studded, filled with every current hip-hop artist on the charts. My only mission, however, was to meet Dr. Dre and convince him to work with Michael. I didn't think this would be a difficult task. Who wouldn't want to work with Michael?

As soon as I spotted Dre, I walked directly to him and introduced myself. I told him that I was a part of Michael's management team and that Michael would love to work with him. He turned and looked at me with the meanest scowl I had ever seen.

"Michael Jackson?" he grunted. "No, I'm not interested. I only work with new artists."

"Well, can you just call him?" I responded. "I'm sure he would love to discuss it with you. Can I give you his number?" I wasn't going to give up too easily. I knew that this pairing could potentially make Michael's album a classic.

Dre continued to scowl at me and rudely replied, "No."

I was shocked, to say the least. I couldn't believe that anyone would turn down the chance to work with Michael. Dr. Dre seemed upset that I would even ask such a question.

The next day, I had to break the news to Michael. "Was he mean?" he asked. I fibbed a bit and told him that he wasn't mean, he just wanted to work with new artists only. I didn't have the heart to tell him how Dr. Dre had acutally responded.

Michael delivered the *HIStory* album to Sony in the early months of 1995. He also kept his promise to see me soon.

Gallin Morey had recently moved from its original location at 8730 Sunset Boulevard in West Hollywood to a new, fancier spot at 345 North Maple Drive in the heart of Beverly Hills. The office was classy and sophisticated like a museum, with expensive art lining the walls. Sandy's impeccable taste in decorating was displayed everywhere.

On April 20, 1995, Michael came in to meet with the top executives from his label, Epic Records, which was a subsidiary of Sony. They gathered to discuss a marketing plan for the new album.

Walking with a confident swagger, Michael breezed in through the shiny glass doors of our new offices. His driver, Gary, accompanied him as he surveyed the lobby, admiring the new digs. He never traveled with bodyguards in L.A. back then, and no one ever seemed to bother him.

He spotted Polly Anthony, who was standing in front of my desk. Polly was one of the top executives at Epic Records and a key member of Michael's record company team. He gave Polly a warm hug and saw me sitting behind my desk as he hugged her. He smiled and stared at me as he continued their hug. He then strolled behind my desk and enveloped me tightly. It was nice to feel his comforting arms once again.

Several other executives from Epic Records arrived and they all headed to our conference room. Throughout the meeting, Lisa Marie called several times. Each time she asked if I could pull Michael from the meeting to talk to her. I don't know what could've been so important that she needed to interrupt so often. I laughed to myself and imagined that she was asking him to stop by the store on the way home to pick up some groceries or something.

As awkward as it was, I did as she asked—walked into the meeting every time and slipped Michael a note that she was on the line. She was always nice and patient, willing to hold as long as it took for Michael to come to the phone. She also had a speaking voice that sounded eerily similar to her father, Elvis. I got a kick out of that.

In the middle of the meeting, Sandy called me from the conference room and asked if I could make Michael some popcorn. I had just popped some microwave popcorn for myself and I figured he had probably smelled it. It's hard to smell that buttery aroma and not crave some.

I made the popcorn and interrupted the meeting once again to give it to Michael. I had barged in on that meeting at least five times at this point—I don't know how they got any work done. As I was placing the glass bowl of fragrant, hot popcorn next to Michael, he whispered to me, "Can you show me where the bathroom is?"

I had gotten used to Michael's constant trips to the bathroom from his prior meetings. He would usually go no less than ten times throughout the course of three hours. I'm not sure what he was doing in there but the bathroom was always his first stop whenever he arrived for a meeting.

I told Michael to follow me as we left the large conference room, which was filled with record executives wearing stuffy, conservative suits and sitting at a long table. He closed the door behind us and finally we were all alone in the hallway.

"Thank you for saving me from that meeting," he chuckled.

"Of course. I'm always happy to help." I smiled. "How's everything going?"

"Everything's good. Just getting ready to release this album."

"Yes, *HIStory*," I said. "I've heard so many good things about it!"

"You have?" he asked, genuinely surprised. "What have you heard?"

I wasn't expecting such a direct question from him and had no idea how to answer it. Thinking quickly, I stuttered, "Well, there's a great buzz about it on the streets."

"A buzz, huh?" He sounded like he didn't believe me. This was going to be his first album since the terrible molestation allegations and he was worried about what the public reception might be—especially in the United States. I assured him that the songs I'd heard were amazing and sure to be hits. He still seemed unsure. He then spotted an empty office and asked if we could go in it for a second. We ducked in and closed the door.

"I just needed to get away from that meeting for a minute to breathe," he sighed.

I hadn't seen him since that last day on the set of *Is This Scary,* back in that crazy summer of 1993. A lot had happened since then, but he was still here standing stronger than ever and looking very good. I was proud of him. Instinctively, I gave him another hug.

"I'm so happy to see you again," I said as I held him—all of the tumultuous drama of the past year floating through my mind. There was a time when I thought I'd never see this man again.

"I'm happy to see you too," he said as we held our embrace. "It's been too long." He kissed my forehead as we let go of each other. Shivers exploded all over my body.

"I can't believe you got married on me," I said, teasing. "I was so mad at you when I heard the news."

"Aww, I know. I'm sorry. Please don't hate me."

"I guess I can forgive you this time." I smiled.

Embarrassed, he giggled and looked down at the floor. "Thank you."

This was the Michael I knew and loved. All of the crazy tabloid stories and revelations from the past year seemed irrelevant at that moment. In my mind, I was wondering how I could have ever believed any of them in the first place. This beautiful, sweet soul couldn't harm a fly.

I escorted him to the bathroom and waited until he finished. We held hands as I walked him back to the conference room. Like a magician, he had drawn me back under his spell. Butterflies tingled in my stomach for hours after he left.

There was one problem though—he was still married. And, judging from the number of calls from her that day, his wife seemed to be just as in love with him as I was.

Michael and Lisa Marie filmed a video for the R. Kelly–penned ballad "You Are Not Alone" a few months after the *HIStory* album was released. I was called into the conference room to screen a rough cut of it. Sandy, Jim, and the executives at Sony wanted my opinion. I was the only person in our office who was a self-proclaimed Michael Jackson fan. In addition, I was young and black—the key demographic that Michael was worried he was losing. They dimmed the lights, turned the sound up as loud as it could go, and started the video.

I sat in disbelief for the entire five minutes. Michael and Lisa were nearly naked, prancing around in loincloths. One scene actually showed Lisa topless and her bare breasts were caught on camera. In another scene, Michael was naked except for a small cloth covering his front private area, his bare butt fully exposed—he was wearing angel wings. The film looked like it had been color corrected to make his skin look smoother and whiter than ever before. He looked exactly like a baby cherub. His face was heavily covered in makeup, with long fake eyelashes, what appeared to be red lipstick, and a new short black wig. He looked more feminine than Lisa. I was in absolute shock.

When it was over, I hopped on a conference call with the president of Epic Records, Dave Glew, along with Sandy, Jim, and Polly Anthony, to tell them how I felt. They asked specific questions—"What did you think of the color of his skin?" "As an African American how does it make you feel to see his skin that white?" "What do you think of his new hairdo?" "Do you like the scene with the angel wings?" "Is there any scene you would take out?"

I was still in shock from what I had seen, so I had to take a second to formulate my thoughts. I was afraid to be too critical because I wasn't sure what the record company's opinion of it was. I also wasn't sure if Michael was on the call listening. I've never been good at sugarcoating things, though, so I just told them my true feelings. "I think he needs to have a little more color. He looks too pale. I also don't like the angel wings. People are going to say he looks feminine and that's exactly what we don't want. The angel wings will make people laugh at him and not take the rest of the video seriously. I would also love to see more of Lisa Marie and the two of them interacting. She looks beautiful—although I think her topless scene will be too much for TV."

They were satisfied with my opinions and agreed with me about all of them. I was told after the call that Michael was demanding to keep the angel wings part in—he loved it. He was also fighting to keep Lisa's bare-breasted scene in—he loved that part too. Sony was worried this video would ruin Michael's career if they kept all of those scenes in. Luckily, the final version was a compromise of everyone's opinions, and it turned out to be a big hit—albeit controversial. There is a rare director's cut available somewhere that has all of the scenes included that Michael wanted.

Watching the uncut dailies of the "You Are Not Alone" video became our favorite pastime at the office. Sandy's assistants and I would go into a private office and watch that footage over and over again whenever we had free time. It was like watching a pornographic tape starring Michael and Lisa. Lisa only had a small strip covering her private area below. Other than that, she appeared to be completely naked, covering her breasts with her hands most of the time. Michael seemed unfazed by her nudity and was not shy to be walking around nearly naked himself. Lisa briefly kissed him a couple of times on the lips, but there was absolutely no passion on his part. It was a fascinating video to watch, to say the least. One thing was for sure: they were comfortable being naked in front of each other.

Despite what Michael had said and their lack of on-screen chemistry, I started believing the marriage was real—or as real as it could get with him. Lisa was certainly trying to make him happy, but I got the sense that Michael was just used to being free. He didn't want to have to answer to anyone, including his wife. He did what he wanted to do, when he wanted to do it. If he wanted to take a trip to Euro Disney with his young male friends without telling her, that's what he was going to do. And that's exactly what he did. The marriage was doomed from that day forward.

On January 18, 1996, Lisa Marie filed for divorce, citing irreconcilable differences. I was not surprised at all.

Although I was a little sad it didn't work out for them, I was excited at the thought of perhaps picking up where we had left off. I couldn't wait to see Michael again. I suppose he couldn't wait to see on of the never-finished three years before. This

e filming was scheduled also vent some frustra-

wered the phone at my

I was so happy to hear ad heard from him. wasn't telling the truth. ded angry and agitated. ed by his tone of voice. n I knew he wasn't. So vell was alarming.

he's going to be repre- age and intensity that I that I heard him angry, . He had a surprisingly ive if you did something d done, but Michael was

aid, stunned by the rev-

t—but I don't trust your ease don't tell anyone I n us, OK?"

"OK. We have to talk in person."

"I'm available whenever you are. Just let me know," I responded. I was not only curious but also concerned about what could possibly be so secret and critical.

"You know, we're gonna start filming a new video in a couple of weeks. Remember the one we didn't finish in 1993 . . . *Is This Scary*? Well, we're redoing it with a whole new cast. The children who were in it before have grown up now, so we can't use them. I was wondering if maybe you would like to be in this one too? I would love to have you. I was watching the footage we shot and you looked really good. You're the only one I'm asking to come back . . ."

"Oh wow, thank you! I would love to! Are you kidding? When does it start?" I was so happy. This man was full of surprises.

"We're gonna start next week. We'll probably be filming for about a month."

"That's great! I'll be there. I can't wait!"

"Oh good. I can't wait either. I want to make this better and scarier than *Thriller*."

"This is so exciting. You are so sweet. Thank you, again."

"Oh, of course. So we'll talk when I see you. I'll have the casting people call you. And don't forget—please don't tell anybody about the Sandy stuff. It will be our secret, OK?"

"I won't, Michael. I promise. I love you."

"I love you too. I'll see you soon."

He never failed to amaze me. Although I was worried about what had made Michael so angry, I was thrilled at the prospect of spending a whole month with him.

Things were about to heat up again.

13

> Dancing can reveal all the mystery that music conceals.
>
> —Charles Baudelaire

The bright California sun was rising in the distance as I eagerly drove down Sherman Way looking for the entrance to Van Nuys Airport. Even though it was 6 AM, I was wide awake. This would be the first day of shooting *2Bad*, which would later be called *Ghosts*, Michael's multimillion-dollar short film, and I was excited—to say the least.

The airport was located deep in the San Fernando Valley, right in the middle of the lower-income sprawl of small suburban houses that filled the streets nearby. It was an unbearably hot April that year—1996—and this part of town always seemed dusty and miserable. But I wasn't complaining. I was about to spend a month with Michael—away from the office, the press, the public, and the constant distractions that had plagued us in the past. Not only that, but we were finally about to complete the project that Michael and I had started filming three years prior, before his world came crashing down. I couldn't have been happier.

I had been given instructions to look for a hangar far away from the runways and airplanes. I drove around until I spotted signs marked 2BAD directing me to a dirt parking lot and a large hangar. I checked in with a production assistant who then ushered me onto the set.

I couldn't believe my eyes. This plain airport hangar had been transformed into a scary haunted mansion. The floor was tiled with black and white squares and fake cobwebs covered antique furniture. It was as if the Haunted Mansion ride at Disneyland had come to life. There was also a fog machine constantly pumping smoke onto the set to make it appear even creepier. It was all very much déjà vu because the exact setting had been used for the *Is This Scary* short film we had made in 1993.

I was introduced to Stan Winston, the director, who had won numerous Academy Awards for his amazing special makeup effects on such films as *Jurassic Park* and *Aliens*. He was very kind and affable, and I quickly understood why Michael chose him to direct this passion project. He had a childlike wonderment and fun attitude, which Michael always liked in people.

Michael had cast me as a townsperson again—a member of a group of people in the small town of Normal Valley, USA. We were a group of very normal people who didn't like the fact that the "weirdo" named Maestro had moved into our quiet, boring town. Michael was to play Maestro, along with five other characters in the film. Led by the mayor (also played by Michael), we townspeople were on a mission to kick Maestro out of our town. The mayor felt that Maestro was just too weird and scary to be around our children.

The story was obviously based on Michael's real-life recent battle with the district attorney of Santa Barbara, Tom Sneddon. Mr. Sneddon had been the one leading the pack against Michael for the alleged child molestation accusations by Jordan Chandler. It was because of those allegations, and the public crucifixion that followed, that *Is This Scary* had not been finished. Michael was determined to finish it now, no matter what—to defiantly prove to Tom Sneddon that he was still standing strong.

I always suspected the character of the mayor to also be the manifestation of Michael's own mind. The mayor shouts nasty names at Michael like "weirdo," "freaky-boy," and "circus freak," among others. It's hard to explain, but it was as if Michael's private insecurities were spilling out and he was finally able to verbalize the incomprehensible inner hate he had for himself. *Ghosts* is by far the most personal work Michael has ever created, and one of his proudest accomplishments. There was a message hidden deep within the art and Michael hoped the public would understand it. At almost forty minutes in length, *Ghosts* is an epic masterpiece, and one that

Michael was involved in every step of the way. He was even in the editing room making sure that every shot was to his liking. It's an amazing study of the complex mind of Michael Jackson.

It was probably ninety degrees outside of the Van Nuys set and not much cooler inside. We weren't able to have the air conditioning system on while filming because it made too much noise. There was one huge, portable oscillating fan directed at the set, but it could only be turned on between scenes.

As I stood waiting with the townspeople, trying to stay cool, Michael strolled onto the set. He was dressed as his Maestro character, which was just his usual Michael Jackson attire—black slacks, white ruffled shirt, and loafers. His hair was long and wavy. His face was pristinely made up, making it appear almost porcelain. He looked good—*really* good. He'd gained a little weight, which looked great on him. I could always tell when he had gained weight because I could see it in his butt. His butt was always the first thing that got bigger.

He spotted me immediately and waved. As our eyes met, I felt everybody else's eyes on me suddenly. I'm sure they were wondering how Michael could possibly know a mere townsperson.

Standing and watching Michael work was one of my favorite things to do. It was like watching Da Vinci create a work of art. I was honored to be able to study his brilliance up close. He was one of those rare performers who was even better in person than on video. He had a powerful presence that can never be duplicated. If he walked into a room, you could feel him, even if you hadn't seen him. The entire energy would change.

Witnessing Michael dance was like a religious experience. Just before we started the scene, he was standing next to me and we were giggling and joking about something. Then Stan told Michael to go to his mark. Michael walked over to a very small piece of tape that was on the floor. They turned the wind and smoke machines on. Stan yelled "Playback!"

The song "2Bad" started booming out of the large speakers that were on either side of the set. And right before my eyes, Michael transformed. Just a few minutes before, he had been just Michael, joking and laughing with me. But now, the wind was blowing through his hair, the lights were just right, the music was blasting, the cameras were rolling . . . and he became *Michael Jackson.* At once, he raised his eyebrows and had a certain glint in his eyes that he didn't have before. The man and the myth merged seamlessly. In the blink of an eye, he turned on the magic, like a carefully constructed character he had been practicing all of his life.

A haze of smoke engulfed the air. Dancers dressed as ghouls filled in behind Michael. After a few beats, he and the dancers burst into the most spellbinding choreography I had ever seen. He was like a puppet on a string, bouncing up and down so smoothly it took my breath away. I was standing just a few feet away and he did not mess up ever. He did it perfectly on the first take. After it was over, he went to the playback screen to view what they had just filmed. Although he was perfect, he found the most minuscule things that he felt were wrong. For instance, he didn't like the way one of the dancer's socks looked. So they did the scene again and again until the socks were just right and every other imagined imperfection had been corrected. He was a detail-oriented perfectionist and that's what made him great. Things that most people would never notice, he did notice.

During each break from dancing, he'd look over at me and smile the biggest smile, as if searching for my approval. I would smile back, sometimes giving a thumbs up. After all of these years he had grown to expect my glowing praise following all of his performances.

Although he was extremely confident in his talent, he was insecure about most other aspects of himself. Being in the spotlight is where he felt most comfortable. It was where he could be the cool, self-assured guy he wished he could be in real life. Dancing and performing in front of thousands of people came naturally for him. Having a one-on-one relationship with a girl did not. As I stood there spellbound, watching him seamlessly execute some of the most intricate choreography ever created, there was no doubt in my mind—I was still in love. I could only hope he felt the same way.

While Michael was standing waiting for the music to start again, he walked toward me. "Let me ask you a question," he said with a serious tone. " Do they know that you're working on this? Sandy and Jim?"

I told him that I had told Jim Morey and that he was kind of shocked.

"Don't they know you did the first one?"

I said, "Yeah, they know."

I didn't fully understand the undercurrent of paranoia that I was seeing with Michael. He had grown distrustful of not only his record company Sony but Sandy and Jim as well. I had the feeling that part of the reason he wanted me in this short film was to stick it to them that their receptionist was allowed on the set and they weren't. He could be calculating and spiteful like that. Prior to the first day of filming, he had distributed a list to his entire team of everyone who was *not* allowed on the set for the entirety of the *Ghosts* shoot. This list contained everyone from Sony Records, Gallin Morey, as well as his own office, MJJ Productions, including longtime loyal entourage members Bob Jones and Bill Bray. Pretty much his entire team, unless the person was directly involved with the production. He didn't want to be watched or spied on by anyone. He wanted to feel free.

As he walked back to his position, he yelled back to me, "Be careful—the speakers there are really loud. I don't want it to hurt your ears."

I was standing right by these huge speakers and Michael insisted on his music being played as loud as possible. Sometimes I wondered if he had a slight hearing problem. The music was so loud at times it was unbearable. But he wanted to *feel* the music. He said the louder the music, the more inspired he became. The bass was so strong on this track I was sure it could be heard from miles away.

Always a gentleman, every day he would tell me to be careful if there was some sort of hazard on the set. He would say, "Watch your step. Don't trip on that piece of wood." Or, "Is there too much smoke in here? Are you able to breathe OK?" He was like a mother hen, always worried and always making sure that conditions were perfect and safe.

Michael would usually sit next to the big oscillating fan between takes to get some relief from the stifling heat on the set. When he was in his mayor fat suit and costume, he would be especially hot. If I were standing beside him chatting, he'd always turn the heavy fan to me—sacrificing his own air. He was always more concerned about my comfort than his own. He was the most famous man on earth yet he was making sure I was being treated like a princess on his set. He made me feel pampered and special. This guy was too good to be true.

He summoned his personal assistant, House, over to meet me. "Shana, this is House. House, this is Shana. House is going to take real good care of you on this set. Aren't you, House?"

"I sure will," House said flirtatiously.

"Hey, be nice, OK?" Michael jokingly reprimanded him.

"I'm always on my best behavior. You know that, Michael," House teased.

They had a playful rapport that was refreshing. Most people treated Michael like a fragile child. Not House, though. He constantly teased Michael and was not afraid to embarrass him whenever he had a chance. Michael seemed to love that about him and he teased House relentlessly as well.

Michael and House were the extreme opposites of each other in looks but they always joked with each other about getting girls. Short, stout, and Jewish, House was a huge flirt. He was no bathing beauty, but he compensated for that by always being extremely funny.

Michael wanted House and I to be friends, so I tried to take his constant flirtations in stride. He seemed harmless and I knew Michael would put his foot down if he became too obnoxious. He kept the vibe on the set light and fun with his constant jokes, so he was fun to have around. Most important, he made Michael laugh, which made the entire shoot enjoyable.

From that point forward, House was not only Michael's personal assistant but mine too. I felt pretty special because I was considered an extra yet I was being treated as an equal to Michael. I'm sure the rest of the extras must've wondered why I was receiving such special treatment. I was the only one allowed to stay on set to watch Michael film the scenes that the extras weren't involved in. They had to stay in a holding area in another hangar when they weren't being used. A couple of them eventually asked Michael and I if we were related. They couldn't figure out our relationship. We just looked at each other and smiled.

If House brought Michael an orange Gatorade while we were waiting for a scene to start, he would bring me a bottle of water. He could always be seen on the side of the set with Michael's Gatorade in one hand and my bottle of water in the other. If he brought Michael a towel, he would bring me one too. After a while, Michael and I would habitually look over at House at the same time when a scene had ended. Our look was all he needed to bring us our Gatorade and water. It was pretty funny. Sometimes Michael would start laughing and say to me, "Look at him standing over there." Just looking at him made us laugh. Michael also got a kick out of watching him wait on me hand and foot. He would just shake his head.

"You told me to take care of her, Michael," House would say.

Toward the end of that first week, Michael was outfitted with a fat suit and full facial prosthetics to become the mayor. He looked exactly like an old white man in a suit with a bulging stomach, eyeglasses, and a huge butt. He was unrecognizable. I could tell he was enjoying being someone other than Michael Jackson. He fully embraced this other character, even walking differently. He changed his voice to play the mayor character as well. It was deep, which was a lot closer to his real voice than the high, soft voice he put on in public. I much preferred his natural, deeper voice. It was sexy. I don't know why he insisted on using the childlike one for public appearances or around people he didn't know.

The next day, he excitedly told me that after he had left the set the day before, he had gone to his childhood home in Encino, on Hayvenhurst Avenue, where his mother still lived. Encino was just a few miles from our set in Van Nuys. Michael had grown up in this area of the valley, back when Moon Unit Zappa made it cool by singing about being a valley girl and hanging out at the Sherman Oaks Galleria. Michael was an authentic valley boy.

He had gone to the Hayvenhurst house dressed in the mayor costume, and his mother didn't recognize him at all. He pretended he was someone else and kept the joke going as long as he could. He told me that he loved dressing up like other people because it was the only time people treated him like a regular person. "I don't like being treated like a star," he said. And the cool thing about him is that he also didn't act like a star. He liked blending in and just being one of us.

When he was dressed as the mayor, I found myself treating him differently as well. I had always found Michael's eyes to be hypnotizing. They were big and bright and had a certain magic that sparkled through them. He had a way of looking so deep into my eyes I felt like he was literally gazing into my soul. All of my hopes, dreams, and desires were right there for him to discover. Staring pensively into my eyes, he always spoke to me without ever looking away, as if he were trying to see inside of me. This was another indication that he was not as shy as he wanted people to think. I was painfully shy, however, and this deep eye contact would sometimes make me uncomfortable. It could be intimidating. The mayor costume made Michael's face not as visible and, in turn, it was easy to forget that those eyes belonged to him. I found it a lot easier to have conversations because of that.

The next day, he had to dance a few feet in front of me to film a solo dance. This performance would serve as a guide for the special effects engineers to create a digital Michael Jackson skeleton in postproduction. Michael was dressed in his everyday clothes—an opened, untucked red shirt with a white T-shirt underneath, black slacks, a fedora, and loafers. His hair was long and tied in a ponytail. Everything about him was perfectly imperfect. He wasn't wearing his stage costume or any makeup and he was cuter than I'd ever seen him. He didn't need layers of makeup or flashy costumes. He was naturally handsome and exuded charisma in his street clothes.

Before he started dancing, I saw him going over in his mind what he was going to do. He acted out a few of his dance moves without the music and grabbed his crotch. The woman standing next to me, who was an actress in the video, yelled out, "He's grabbing his balls!"

Of course, Michael heard this and said, "Oooh, who said that?"

We all pointed to the woman. He was very amused.

Like a child putting the blame on someone else for his naughtiness, he insisted, "It's the skeleton doing it, not me." Then, still laughing, he turned around to Stan Winston and said incredulously, "Did you hear what she just said?"

Seconds later, the music to the song "2Bad" was cued and started blasting out of the speakers. Michael burst into a solo dance that was not choreographed, just pure improvisation. I was mesmerized. He did all of his trademark moves, including the moonwalk.

He, of course, grabbed himself again a few times. I, and a few of the other actors, were standing just a few feet away and he was not embarrassed to dance provocatively in front of us at all. He loved having all eyes on him.

When he finished, we all clapped. He took off his fedora and bowed. And with that, he exited and left for the day. It was Friday evening, and as with a soap opera cliff-hanger, I was left to mull over this amazing week with Michael the entire weekend. He had left quite an impression on me. In fact, I don't think it was possible to be more in love. The more time I spent with him, the deeper I fell.

That weekend, every time my phone rang, I was praying it was Michael. I felt like I couldn't go another minute without seeing him again. I had gotten so used to spending every day with him that past week it was hard to be without him, if only for two days. I had his phone number but I was always apprehensive to call. I figured I would let him make the move.

We returned to the set after the weekend and it was back to the fun and laughs. That morning, Michael was sitting in his director's chair, which had MICHAEL JACKSON stitched into the back of it, watching the playback of a scene on a video monitor. I walked right in front of the monitor wearing some tight black jeans. After I walked past, I looked back to see if he was looking, which was always my test to know if men were interested in me. He was staring at my butt. He got so embarrassed that I caught him he started smiling. I just smiled and gave him a knowing look. He was like a naughty teenager.

Michael was dressed as the maestro that week, which was his "Michael" character. He looked like himself—no fat suit or mayor costume, just his trademark Michael Jackson look, which was actually also a character . . . one he had been perfecting all of his life. He wore a white ruffled shirt, black trousers, and loafers. His hair was perfectly coifed in long, flowing curls and his face was made up to perfection. After every break in action, his hairstylist, Janet Zeitoun, (whom he sometimes jokingly called Janet Cartoon) would walk over and spray his curls to keep them shiny. His makeup artist, Karen Faye, also doted on him during every break, powdering his pristinely made up face or wiping his forehead of sweat.

Michael was one of those touchy-feely types of people. He liked to hold hands and made any excuse to touch or hug you. Every time Karen or Janet came to him between scenes he would try to pull down their shirts, which were usually loose or low-cut. His mission was to make their bra straps show. When they walked away, he would squeeze their waist or touch their necklaces on their chests. They could never be too careful around him. If any other boss did something like that, it probably would have been considered sexual harassment. But with Michael it was just cute and funny. It's no wonder most girls around him developed crushes on him, even if they were married, and no matter their age. He was magnetic. It was nearly impossible to resist his charms.

One time, between scenes, Janet Zeitoun was sitting in her folding chair with a cup of water and Michael said, "You look like you're just sitting back sipping on some lemonade in the shade at a barbeque." He was extremely observant and his mind was always in daydream mode. And he was always funny.

After one of the scenes, Michael sat down in his chair in front of the monitors to watch the playback of what he had just filmed. I was already standing right behind his chair and I stepped back a little so that I wouldn't get in the way. He turned around and reached out for my hand, pulling me closer—letting me know it was OK to stay there next to him. I had learned, early on, to let Michael come to me. I made a point to never be the aggressor and to match his moods. This was the trick to making him feel comfortable—it brought him out of his shell. He had a way of making me feel like I was the only one in the room. His excitement to see me always made me feel special.

Later, House came over to chat with me. He wanted to play a joke on Michael. "Go over to Michael and whisper in his ear, 'Don't you think House is cute?'"

At first, I was afraid to do it. Michael appeared to be busy watching the playback of the scenes on the monitor. House walked over to Wayne Nagin, who was Michael's longtime head of security, and told him about the joke. I asked Wayne if I should do it and he said, "Yes, please do." These guys were always looking for ways to play jokes on Michael and make him laugh. I'm sure that's part of the reason he liked having them around.

I walked up behind Michael, who was sitting in his director's chair, and bent down, putting my mouth next to his ear. I grabbed his arm and squeezed it, right on his firm bicep. I whispered, "Don't you think House is cute?"

Michael jumped up out of his seat and turned around in shock. Then he burst out laughing when he saw that I was the one who had whispered in his ear. He looked behind me and saw House and Wayne dying with laughter.

Michael said, "This is a setup. Look at House! Look at how red he is!"

House was completely red with embarrassment.

Michael kept laughing, "I knew this was a setup because Shana wouldn't say something like that. It's not her personality." It made me feel good to know that he knew me so well. He knew that I was shy and normally would not do something like that, which made it even funnier.

A little while later, Karen Faye and Janet Zeitoun sat next to Michael in their chairs. They started talking and it seemed like they were discussing something very important and serious. They were engrossed in what appeared to be deep conversation. I was standing nearby. I heard Michael say, "Let's ask her."

Michael turned around and said, "Shana, come here." Hearing him say my name always made my heart skip.

I was so happy he wanted to include me in this important discussion. I walked over to them. Michael said, "Shana, this is Karen and this is Janet. You know them, don't you?" He was the most polite person I had ever met.

Karen turned to me and began to speak. Her tone and demeanor were so serious, I was sure she was going to ask the most important question ever. "Don't you think the shirt Michael is wearing is sexy?" she said. "Don't you think ruffles are sexy on a man?"

Surprised by the question, I burst out laughing. I didn't know if she was being serious or not. I thought they were going to ask me something really important but no, it was all about the sexiness of ruffles . . . and Michael wanted my opinion. My laughter made him laugh too, but Karen was serious; she really wanted to know what I thought.

Through my giggles, I finally said, "Yes, it is sexy. But everything is sexy on Michael." Karen and Janet looked at him and smiled. Michael blushed. He got embarrassed easily, which made him even cuter.

Michael was really dedicated to making this the best and scariest video he had ever created. He was always on time—sometimes early, usually arriving at 5:30 AM or earlier. On most days, I didn't have to get there until 8:30 AM. The cast of actors and crew had a twelve-hour turnaround, so if we worked until 8:30 PM the night before, by law, we were not allowed to work again until twelve hours later. Michael, being the star and one of the producers, didn't have to worry about these restrictions. He was working hard and it was great to see him back in a healthy mindset. He was alert, focused, and happy.

The next day, when we were getting ready to shoot our scene, Michael, dressed as the mayor, asked me, "Who is taking your place at work?" He seemed fascinated by the fact that I was able to be off from work for so long and had asked me about it several times. "Are you happy not to be there?"

"Yes, thank God," I replied. "I have one of our runners taking my place. Have you spoken to Jim or Sandy lately?"

"Yes, Sandy actually called me today and I saw him last night." He looked at me with sad eyes. "I hope it works out."

"Me too. I would miss you if you left us," I said, equally sad.

"I'd miss you too. I told Sandy I was taking good care of you here. He said that I should've married you instead of Lisa Marie," he giggled.

"I agree!" I laughed.

We still hadn't talked about whatever it was that had made him angry with Sandy. I figured I would let him bring it up when he was ready. He had been in a good and carefree mood thus far, and I definitely didn't want that to change.

House devised another joke for me to play on Michael. He told me to walk over to Michael and say, "Michael, please give me some freedom."

House let Wayne and Michael's other bodyguard, Yannick, in on the plan. They both couldn't wait to watch me make a fool of myself. I had no idea what "give me freedom" was supposed to mean, but I decided to go for it. It felt good to be one of the guys and included in on all of these practical jokes. I figured there weren't too many things that the word *freedom* could mean, so I didn't feel too apprehensive about asking Michael for it.

I waited for a break in the scene and walked over to Michael, who was surrounded by dancers dressed as ghouls. I glanced over at House and Wayne and gave them a nod, indicating that I was about to put their plan into action. They smiled with mischievous glee as I approached Michael. "Michael, will you please give me some freedom?"

I had caught him off guard. He paused for a moment. With a confused look, he widened his eyes, "What?"

I repeated it, asking innocently, "Will you please give me some freedom?"

He started giggling. "House put you up to this, didn't he?"

I nodded my head yes, still not sure what any of this meant.

Intensely, he looked me in the eyes, holding back his laughter, "Do you know what *freedom* means?"

"Umm . . . not really," I said. Now I was worried. What had I gotten myself into?

Michael, never missing an opportunity to be dramatic, grabbed my hand and said, "Come with me."

Hand in hand, we walked to the other side of the set. We stepped over the fake cobwebs, maneuvered around the antique furniture, and waded through the smoke that filled the air. I looked over my shoulder and spotted House, Wayne, and Yannick doubled over in laughter. I shot them an *I'm gonna kill you* look. Michael led me to the farthest, darkest corner he could find, out of earshot of everyone.

"Are you sure you *really* want to know what freedom means? It's really bad."

At this point I was dying to know. "Yes, please tell me."

"I don't know if I should . . ." he teased.

"Michael," I pleaded. "You have to tell me. *Please*, I need to know."

He started laughing. "OK," he took a dramatic pause, "it means to pass gas."

My mouth hit the floor. I almost died from embarrassment. Standing there speechless, I laughed, not knowing how else to react. Never had I imagined that "freedom" would mean *that.* The joke was obviously on me. Thank you, House.

Michael said smiling, "Aren't you sorry he told you to say that?"

"Yes," I said, my face red with embarrassment. "I'm going to kill him."

Then suddenly, it was as if he turned into a child about to be scolded. He became defensive, "I didn't make it up."

"I bet you did," I said, teasing him.

Now serious, he protested, "No, I didn't. I swear."

I felt like I was now dealing with a teenager trying to plead his way out of punishment for misbehavior. "Well, who made it up then?" I asked, not believing him at all.

"The kids," he said. "Remember when I was in New York? They made it up then, when we were at the Trump Tower."

By kids he meant his friends who were kids. He didn't have actual children at this time. Although I was twelve years younger than Michael, I definitely felt like the more mature one. He was wiser and more experienced in life, but I was more mature. Interacting with him was sometimes like dealing with a fourteen-year-old boy—and it wasn't an act. This is who he was. It was like he had stopped maturing emotionally the moment massive fame snatched away his childhood. He was very levelheaded and smart in his business life and with his creative endeavors, but outside of that, he was stuck at age fourteen. He liked hanging around boys of that age because they were his peers. They liked to do what he liked to do—play video games, talk about girls, and listen to music. The more time I spent with him, the more I wondered if our relationship would ever make it past the stage where we were. Was he even capable of having a real, adult relationship?

Often when I was standing next to Michael waiting for a scene to start I'd think, *This is the most famous man in the world?* The realization that fame was nothing more than an illusion—manufactured hype—had never been more evident than now. Michael was just a human being with enormous talent. A person with feelings, hopes, insecurities, desires, and dreams. The public and press had made him into this almost mythical, otherworldly character, and he wasn't that at all. I had worked on movie sets before with major stars as well as with other artists that Gallin Morey represented, and Michael was the most down-to-earth of them all. I had to keep reminding myself that this was the man worshipped by millions . . . the man all of the outrageous tabloid stories had been written about . . . the mysterious icon speculated about since the age of ten. But he was just a human being trying to navigate his way through life, just like the rest of us.

On this shoot, he didn't demand any preferential treatment. He didn't even have special food brought in for him or a private chef cooking him gourmet meals. He ate what the rest of us ate. We had a catered lunch every day that always consisted of either fish or chicken, green salad, some simple side dishes like pasta or potatoes, and ice cream for dessert. He wasn't picky with his food choices at all, or anything else for that matter. He was one of us.

When I arrived on set the next morning, Michael was already in a playful mood. I gulped down a weak cup of coffee that I had grabbed from my favorite place—the craft services table—and searched for the small piece of tape on the floor that would indicate my mark. The gaffers and stagehands adjusted the lighting in anticipation of the first scene of the day. Once those were adjusted, we had to stand and wait for the dry ice, which was masquerading as fog, to fill the scene. This was a ritual that occurred prior to every scene. The fog consistency had to be just right to create the creepy atmosphere before the cameras rolled.

I stood with my fellow townspeople, with Michael leading the pack as the mayor. There were about fifteen of us, a variety of ages and races. We must have looked like a ragtag bunch, dressed in plain dresses and ill-fitting suits that the wardrobe department had purchased at secondhand stores. My costume consisted of a blue plaid skirt that hit just below my knees, white bobby socks, flat brown shoes that were always covered in dust from the dirt on the set, a white V-neck T-shirt, and a white sweater that buttoned in the front. I looked like your typical young girl from the smallest town in America.

Michael scoped me out in the crowd and walked over to me with concern and worry. "Sandy just called and he's looking for you!" Those were his first words to me that morning. Usually he would greet me with "Good morning" or ask how I was doing, but not this time. A wave of nervousness shot through my body. *Why would Sandy be looking for me? Had I done something wrong? Oh gosh, would I have to leave and go back to work because of an emergency?* I couldn't think of any scenario where this could be good news.

"You're kidding," I replied over the din of random conversations amongst the other townspeople. My voice was rife with worry as I looked at Michael with angst.

"Yeah, I am kidding," he said sheepishly. I stared at him with daggers in my eyes. He had gotten me again. It wasn't even 8 AM and he had already started with the jokes.

After the scene was over, Michael looked in my direction and started laughing. I walked over to where he was standing amongst the group of extras and punched him on the arm. "You're bad," I scolded him.

"Oh, you thought it was real, didn't you?" he laughed.

"Yes, I did. I don't want to see Sandy or work anytime soon."

"You've had your share, right?" He always had the knack of knowing just how I was feeling.

Don't get me wrong. I loved Sandy and my job, but being there on set made everything else pale in comparison. I never wanted to go back into the real world again. I was perfectly content under those lights, amid the fog, creepy furniture, and dancers dressed as ghouls. I even had a team of people doing my hair and makeup every morning. What could be better than that? Sitting behind a desk again for eight hours a day seemed like a land far, far away that I never wanted to return to.

Trying to ease ourselves out of the stifling heat that encompassed the dusty hangar, Michael and I sat in our usual spot in front of the big portable fan. As the murky, hot air recycled back into our faces, Michael spotted House on the other side of the set. "Once he sees us, he's going to walk over here . . . watch," Michael whispered. He could always accurately predict someone's behavior. "He's always jealous when he sees me talking to you. He won't let this go on for long without him trying to join in."

Sure enough, less than one minute later, House started making his way over through the haze of smoke that still lingered in the air. He was wearing a simple blue cotton shirt that had a few buttons opened at the top. Michael looked at him with a serious face and scolded him, "Look at that. That looks really bad. You shouldn't walk around like that."

House had no idea what he was talking about.

Michael then turned to me and asked, "Doesn't that look bad?"

"What?" I asked, unable to figure out what he was referring to.

"The hair on his chest!" Michael exclaimed.

I turned to House and, sure enough, he had thick, curly hair peeking out from under his shirt. I would've never even noticed it if Michael hadn't pointed it out. He always noticed *everything*.

"Yeah, it looks like a gorilla actually," I agreed as I chuckled.

Michael started laughing hysterically. "A gorilla! Did you hear that, House? She said you look like a gorilla! That looks awful. You need to always have your shirts buttoned up." Then he proudly proclaimed, "I don't have that. I don't have any hair on *my* chest."

"I know," I said as I seductively ran my hand over Michael's chest. "Michael is so sexy. His chest is perfection." We were laying it on thick.

To rub it in even more, Michael purred out, "Oooh." He and I had now teamed up to thoroughly embarrass House. Michael continued to laugh loudly and teased, "You know, Arnold Schwarzenegger has a smooth chest too. Even he knows it looks better that way."

House had turned a whole new shade of red from embarrassment. Michael, however, was relentless. He lifted up House's pant leg to see if he was hairy there too. He was. "Look at that leg! You ought to be ashamed of yourself, House." Michael turned to me and smiled as he shook his head in feigned disgust.

We then started talking about the other cast members in the film. The hodgepodge group of townspeople was gathered on set waiting for the cameras to be set up. We were standing at a distance on the dark edge of the set. I noticed Michael staring at Kendall, the adorable ten-year-old blond boy who was the main star of the video.

I said to Michael, "He is so cute."

Michael did not say a word. He just gazed off into the distance with a faraway look. He suddenly seemed sad. I lightened the mood and told him that one of the little girl cast members was only thirteen years old. She was really big for her age and looked at least sixteen. Michael didn't believe me. "She's not thirteen. No, she's not. That one?" He pointed at her. House told him not to point—that it was rude. I assured Michael that she was indeed thirteen.

"Well, girls mature faster than boys," Michael stated.

"That's true, because you're still not mature," House teased.

I had to agree with him on that.

Michael, House, and I were talking and laughing so loud that Stan Winston angrily stormed over to us and kicked us off of the set. "We're trying to get some work done here, guys," he chided. We had gotten so lost in our laughter we had forgotten there were even other people around. Embarrassed, the three of us dutifully slinked off of the set and found an area further from the action to continue our fun. Even though Michael was the star of the film, he didn't protest at all. I think he was enjoying being treated like a regular person.

House pretended to blame me for getting us kicked off the set and started tickling my stomach as punishment. Michael, always in protective mode, scolded him. "House! Look at you feeling all on her. Getting your feels in."

I laughed and said, "That's right, Michael. Thank you for being my bodyguard."

Once again, he had made House turn red with embarrassment. We laughed even louder. Michael's humor was like a horny teenaged boy's. No matter what the situation, he always managed to turn it into something dirty and funny. He was a natural comedian, yet another of his many talents.

Michael told me that House's original nickname was Outhouse. I asked Michael where he got that name. With a wicked grin, he said, "Don't you know? Have him tell you." House was right there and Michael said, "House, tell her how you got your nickname, but make sure you say it right *here*." Michael pinched my nose.

House launched into the story. "My real name is Scott. When I first met Michael, he told me my breath smelled like outhouse doo-doo. And from that moment on, he started calling me 'House.'

Michael paid for me to get all of my teeth fixed, though, so I don't have that problem anymore."

Michael laughed loudly as House finished the story and I joined in with a shocked giggle. I thought it was pretty cruel and insulting, to be honest. But House seemed to be proud of his new teeth and new breath, so I suppose that counts for something.

Michael's mother, Katherine, came to the set often to make sure her son left early enough to get a good night's sleep. He had been working until the wee hours of the morning every day, coming right back a few hours later for a 6 AM call. Just like any mother, she was concerned that he wasn't getting enough rest.

As we were standing around waiting for the next scene to begin, Michael spontaneously grabbed my hand and walked me over to his mother. "I want you to meet someone!" He led me to where she was sitting. "Mother, this is Shana. She's one of the townspeople and also works for my manager," he enthused.

Mrs. Jackson smiled graciously and shook my hand. I felt honored to finally meet the woman who produced this amazing man. I was also ecstatic that Michael felt the need to introduce me to her.

Mrs. Jackson regularly sat quietly on the sidelines in a director's chair to observe her son. Always dressed in a classy two-piece pantsuit, she was beautiful, with a calming and gentle aura. It was clear where Michael had inherited his kindness. It was also obvious he wanted to impress her and make her proud.

All throughout the day, Michael and I would look at each other as soon as a scene ended and giggle—as if laughing about a secret joke, in a world of our own. I don't think either of us knew what we were giggling about. I think we were just giddy to finally be able to stare at each other all day. There was such an attraction between us, like a magnet. When I looked into his eyes, all I felt was pure electricity. It was so strong sometimes I felt like I was going to explode from the longing. I could tell he was trying to fight his feelings too. For some reason he seemed scared. I always felt that Michael didn't feel worthy enough to have a pretty girl want him in that way. Whatever had happened in his childhood had screwed him up in a major way, causing him to have low self-esteem. We had been doing this flirtation stuff for almost five years—surely he should feel secure in my feelings for him by now.

A few times that day, Michael got the giggles right in the middle of the scene, thus ruining the entire thing. He was trying hard not to laugh, but he couldn't stop. Little things just kept giving him the giggles. For instance, he filmed a scene with the dancers who were dressed as ghouls. They all had been covered in dust by the makeup department, so when they made a move, the camera would show dust flying off of them. This was to intensify the point that these ghosts had risen after a long slumber in their graves. For some reason, every time the dust flew, Michael would start giggling. This was supposed to be a very serious scene that would turn into a huge dance routine. Michael just couldn't contain his laughter and they had to do take after take until he could keep a straight face. He kept saying, "It's not my fault!" But, as usual, it was. He was so cute when he laughed. Every time he smiled, two big veins popped out on his forehead and a knot would appear. This was so endearing, seeing it on his otherwise pristine face.

He loved dirty jokes too. And if they weren't dirty to begin with, he would make them that way. One of the actresses said nonchalantly that she would like to ride the camera. She meant that she wanted to sit in the chair attached to the camera and ride around on it. It was one of those moving cameras. Of course, Michael's dirty mind went straight to the gutter and thought of it in a very different way. He couldn't stop laughing. He didn't even have to say anything. All he had to do was give me a look and I knew exactly what he was thinking. "Stop it, Michael," was all I could say. His laugh was so infectious I started laughing too. The actress had no idea what we were snickering about. Of course, we never told her.

Another day one of the female extras did a funny little dance for Michael. House walked over to him and said, "I wonder what she would look like doing that naked?" Michael burst into laughter. I felt like I was back in junior high with these guys. I shouldn't have been surprised though—one of Michael's favorite comedians was Benny Hill. He loved watching his classic TV show, *The Benny Hill Show,* which was filled with raunchy British humor.

One day while we were bored, Michael decided to teach the kid actors sign language. He slowly signed with his hands as the three preteen boys watched in awe. He repeated the gestures until the boys learned how to do it perfectly. He then taught them the same phrase in two other languages. They asked him what it meant and he told them it was something bad and to not do it again after they left the set. They begged him to tell them what it meant and he said, "It's something you should only do when you're mad." They were satisfied with that answer, but I wasn't. I had learned the sign language right along with them and I wanted to know too.

I pulled Michael aside. "OK, you can tell me . . . What does this sign language really mean?"

He leaned into my ear and whispered, "It means 'fuck you.'"

I looked at him in disbelief.

He explained that he had learned it for a music video he filmed called "They Don't Care About Us" that Spike Lee directed. I remembered that video well. It had been banned from the United States, and one of the reasons was because of that sign language part. We had to deal with that controversy at the office when it was released. His record company was not happy about it at all.

Michael continued, "Sometimes I do sign language onstage, not knowing that I'm saying bad things. A lot of times it's something bad in a different language and I have no idea." He was a detail-oriented perfectionist, so I'm not sure if I believed that. And furthermore, he definitely knew what this particular sign meant. Then, as if a sudden epiphany had just come over him, he mused, "These kids are learning all of these bad things on this video."

The bemused look on my face had probably helped him come to this realization. I said, "Yeah, and you're the one who's teaching them."

He looked off into the distance. "You're right. I'm teaching them." He sounded as if he was suddenly ashamed of his own behavior.

I began to see that Michael didn't really know how to place boundaries between himself and kids. Although he acted like a teenager most of the time, he was actually a thirty-seven-year-old man. He didn't seem to realize that kids were not adults and could not just do whatever they wanted without rules. Many things that Michael talked or joked about with them would fly right over their heads because they weren't mature enough to understand, which I suppose was a good thing. And he simply wasn't aware that there were some things that weren't appropriate for kids. I believe that the problems Michael ended up having with kids all stemmed from this naïveté that I saw on display. He truly felt there was nothing wrong with letting kids break rules and he was happy to join in and encourage them to do so. However, it wasn't coming from a predatory place—Michael was on their level. He was their peer. He had such a rigid childhood during which he was working all of the time, with nothing but rules, responsibilities, and commitments. So now, his whole attitude was that childhood shouldn't be that way. Kids should be able to be free. And kids loved being around him because of that. He had a different way of thinking, an entirely different perspective on things—and he wasn't hiding any of this so-called bad behavior, because he thought it was perfectly normal. He had been a superstar since the age of ten. None of us will ever be able to fully understand how that affected him. In my opinion, he would never purposely do anything to harm a child or to ruin another person's childhood. In fact, it was just the opposite—he wanted kids to be kids and to have the best childhoods possible, because he felt his own was robbed from him. I know it's difficult for most people to understand, but if you met Michael and spent some time with him, you would get it.

At one point, Stan Winston walked over to me while Michael and I were chatting and told me that he had watched some of the scenes we had filmed the day before and that I was a good actress. That was a great compliment coming from Stan, whom I admired greatly. It's not every day an Academy Award winner compliments you on your acting. Sadly, Stan would pass away shortly before Michael, in 2008. He was a delight to work with.

The next day, the three boys who were the stars of the video were eating Popsicles and walked over to us. They were contrasts in personality and appearance. Kendall was small and adorable, with thick blond hair; Seth was a redheaded firecracker with a constant scowl and an edge of mischief etched on his face; and Loren was a sweet African American boy who was very polite and kind. I found myself hanging with them more than the adults because they knew how to have fun. A trailer sat outside that had been transformed into a schoolroom for them. The only female child actor in the video was a pretty African American thirteen-year-old extra named

teen years old in my hometown of Washington, , wishing I was in California. I have my *Thriller*-era chael buttons pinned to my jean jacket.

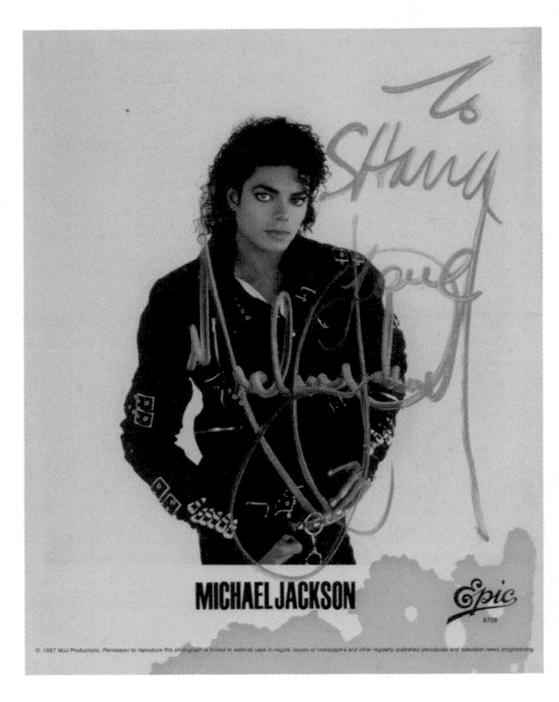

Michael's autograph from the first night I met him at the Helmsley Palace in New York, 1988.

Eighteen years old on my first day in Hollywood. This was my first stop.

Smiling at my desk in the center of the storm at Gallin Morey Associates on Sunset Boulevard in West Hollywood. My coworkers used to tease me that Michael could always be seen hovering here.

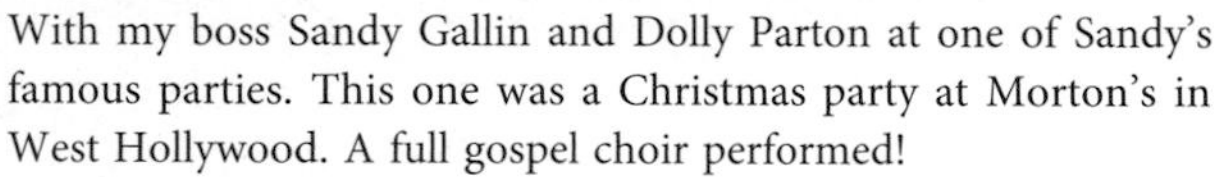

With my boss Sandy Gallin and Dolly Parton at one of Sandy's famous parties. This one was a Christmas party at Morton's in West Hollywood. A full gospel choir performed!

With my boss Jim Morey on our way to Micha
rehearsal at the Tokyo Dome in Japan, 19

Photo I snapped of the elaborate *Dangerous* album display on Tower Records on Sunset the day it was unveiled. It was on not only the side wall but the roof as well. It was covered in lights and lit up at night. Sony spared no expense on promotion for this album.

With Michael shortly before he took the stage in Tokyo on the Dangerous tour in December 1992. He performed eight sold-out shows at the Tokyo Dome that month. This was the last city of the first leg of the tour. My T-shirt says WHY BE NORMAL (it's upside down). *Sam Emerson*

Fooling around on the drums during a break in rehearsals for the Dangerous tour in Tokyo, Japan, 1992.

Outside during a break on the set of *Is This Scary* with Michael's stand-in, Darrick Morgan

With the ragtag cast of extras for Michael's never-finished short film *Is This Scary* on the Studio City set, August 1993.

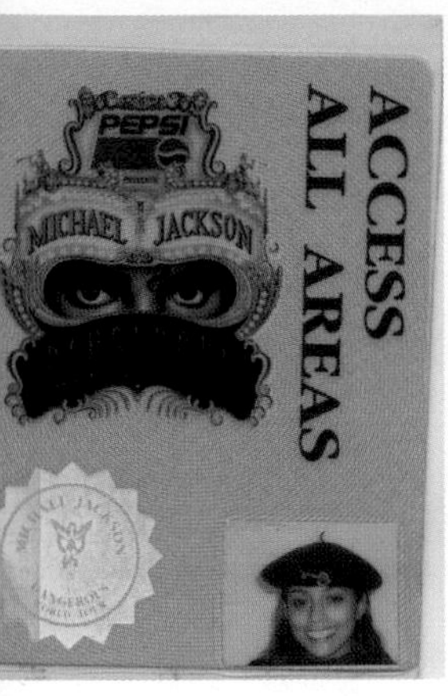

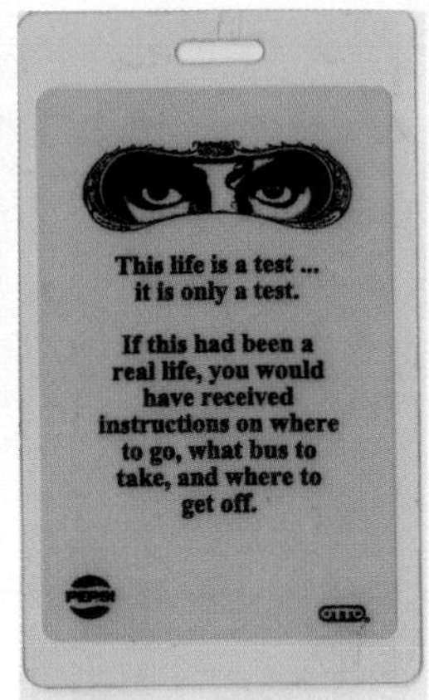

Backstage and rehearsal passes for the Dangerous tour and my ID badges for *Is This Scary* and *2 Bad* (later to be called *Ghosts*).

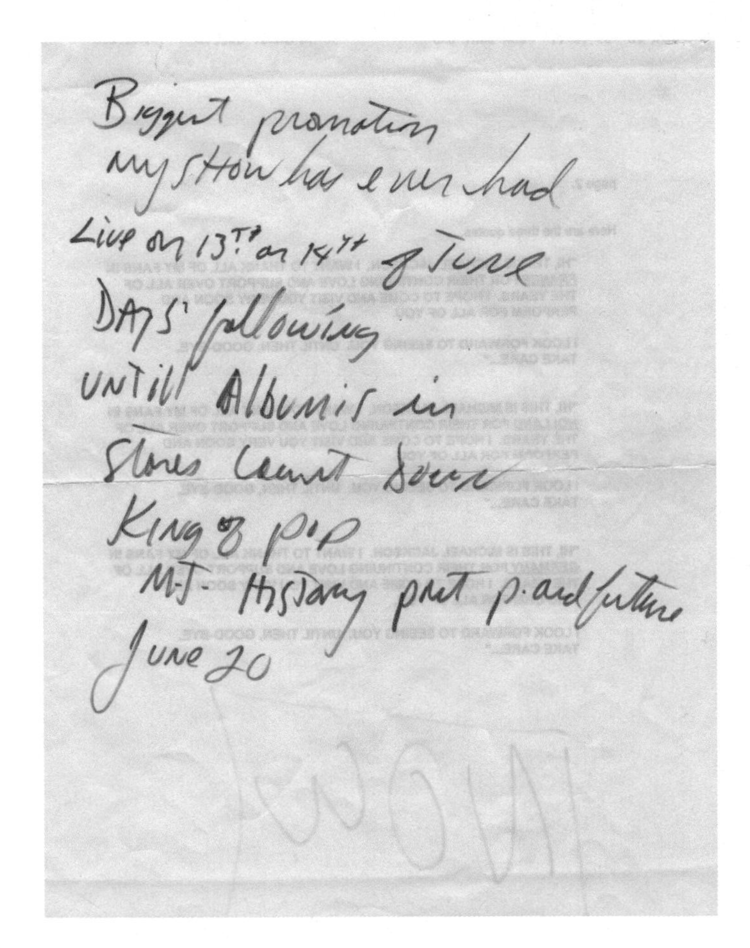
Biggest promotion
my story has ever had
Live on 13th or 14th of June
Days following
until Album is in
Stores count down
King of Pop
M.J. History past p. and future
June 20
NOW

Handwritten notes given to me by Michael. He wrote these on April 20, 1995, during a marketing meeting for the launch of the *HIStory* album. As always, he wanted the promotion for the album to be the biggest and best ever.

Michael dressed in costume as Mayor and Scott "House" Shaffe the set of *Ghosts*. Michael is drin his orange Gatorade. He had to straw because his lips were atta to facial prosthetics. He fooled own mother with this disg April 1996. *Used with permission the personal collection of Scott Sh*

In my costume from *Ghosts*. Michael told me it reminded him of Ola Ray's in *Thriller*.

Hanging with my buddies, the cast of kids from *Ghosts*, in their schoolroom trailer.

Headed in to Michael's forty-fifth birthday party at Neverland Valley Ranch, September 2003.

With my former boss and friend Earvin "Magic" Johnson.

With my friend Shemar Moore
on the set of *Soul Train*.

Michael, in all of his glory. *William Stevens/Gamma-Rapho/Getty Images*

Keisha. Being a sensitive and observant girl, she instantly noticed the chemistry between Michael and me and made it her mission to get us together. I felt like I was back in junior high school whispering with my girlfriend about a crush I had on a boy. It was fun hanging with these kids. They had endless energy and no hidden agendas, which was refreshing. Keisha decided she would be my spy to find out how Michael really felt about me. Every day it was exciting to receive new intel from her and her teenage investigations.

As they licked their Popsicles, which were threatening to drip colorful liquid all over their clean costumes, the boys asked Michael if they could come to his trailer to play Sony PlayStation. They had gone the day before at lunch to play for the first time. "Sure," Michael said. "You can come whenever you want. I get lonely in my trailer and I don't have anyone to play with." He looked at me after he said that. I had the distinct feeling he was hinting that he wanted me to join him in his trailer sometime too.

He and the kids had played Mortal Kombat the day before. Kendall said, "You let me win yesterday, didn't you?"

Dramatic Michael assured him that this wasn't the case. "I swear on my mother and all of the children of the world that I didn't."

I wasn't too well versed or even interested in video games, but I offered my contribution to the conversation by telling him that I had a Sega Genesis at home, which I mainly used to play Super Mario Bros. Michael insisted that I should switch to Sony PlayStation, which was much better, according to him.

And then he said it: "You should come to my trailer sometime. We can play together."

Since I knew Michael was always making jokes about naughty things, I was hoping he meant more than playing video games. I smiled and said, "I would love to."

Up to this point, I had resigned myself to the fact that being just friends with Michael would be the fate I would have to get used to. After all, wouldn't he have made a move by now? There was really nothing stopping him. He was divorced and single now, so the marriage issue was no longer a problem. All of our romantic dalliances had happened years before. I started second-guessing myself. Perhaps it was my own actions that were preventing things from moving forward. Should I force myself to be more aggressive?

He was sending me mixed signals and it was frustrating. On set, he was flirtatious and everyone was telling me he had a crush on me. Not to mention he had personally cast me in this video, obviously wanting me to be close to him for this long shoot. But he had my phone number. He could've easily called me on the weekends to hang out. I was so confused. We had been talking almost daily and flirting for five years, yet somehow he remained elusive—so close and yet so far away. After all of these years, I still couldn't figure him out.

The next afternoon, we had a long wait in between scenes, which was not unusual. Every time the crew had to break down a scene and reset the lights, it could take an hour or more. This meant we had to sit around and wait. The extras would usually go to their holding area and play cards, read books, eat snacks—anything to pass the hours away. Contrary to popular belief, life on a movie set was not glamorous at all. Sometimes Michael would sit on the side of the set and take a nap. On this day, however, I saw him leave to go back to his trailer. I took this as my cue to follow.

14

Love is a friendship caught on fire.

—Unknown

I slipped out of the hangar door praying no one else was planning on joining Michael. He had told the child actors in the film that they were welcome in his trailer anytime. With an open invitation, they often showed up unannounced. He was so down to earth, kind, and welcoming; the kids felt comfortable around him. It was difficult for Michael to say no to anyone—especially children.

As I climbed the three small stairs that led to his white trailer door, thinking of every possible thing that could go wrong, my knees felt weak and my legs buckled. *It's now or never,* I told myself. I knew this might be my only chance to be alone with him. I was so confused about everything that was happening between us, and I couldn't go another day not knowing where I stood—where we stood. I needed to know if I meant as much to him as he did to me.

My heart was pounding as I knocked on the door. The blinds opened slightly on the side window and two eyes peered discreetly out the crack. Within a moment the lock turned and the door opened.

Thank God, I thought. It was Michael—and he was alone.

He seemed surprised but happy to see me. I walked through the door into the cool breeze of an air conditioner. The entire room smelled like the perfume he was wearing, Bal à Versailles—and it was a mess. Videotapes of cartoons and movies were scattered around with faxes, documents, and packages—obviously sent from his office, mostly unopened. I noticed a plain, half-eaten bagel on a plate, which I assumed was his breakfast. Bazooka bubble gum wrappers were everywhere. He'd often chew three or four wads of it at a time. "The flavor leaves too quickly when I only chew one," he once told me.

He also had an unlimited supply of Tic Tacs. These little mints had become a member of the cast. Michael always kept a pocketful—throwing them at members of the crew when he was bored. The orange flavor was his favorite. "Can I have one?" I once asked.

"Reach into my pocket and get it," he had said with a flirtatious smile.

I was happy to oblige.

He showed me his video games and Sony PlayStation, which were sitting next to a television, and asked if I wanted to play.

"Sure . . ." I lied. The last thing I wanted to do was play video games, but if it meant spending time with him, I would become a video game junkie. I stood awkwardly before him—too nervous to make myself comfortable.

"Please sit down," he said. "Would you like something to drink?"

"Yes." I chose a glass bottle of Martinelli's apple juice, which was in the shape of an apple. He grabbed an orange Gatorade, then sat down beside me on a small sofa and launched into a story about how he no longer drank Evian water because he read that it allegedly wasn't as pure as they claimed. With childlike glee, he also told me about a Japanese company that was coming to the set to discuss turning *Ghosts* into a video game.

He was still wearing his costume from the video—the white ruffled top and black slacks. He unbuttoned his shirt, revealing a white V-neck undershirt, and scooted closer to me. He was finally able to relax. His call time had been 5:45 AM that morning. It had been a long day—but it wasn't even half over.

He asked if I was enjoying filming the video. I told him I was. We gossiped about a married couple we both knew. I told him that the husband tried hitting on me.

"You must get that a lot," he said, staring admiringly.

He was the master of flirting. He could turn any conversation into something flirtatious and it would usually come out of left field. For some reason, I always felt the need to gossip with Michael. He was so easy to talk to and always had an interesting take on every subject or person mentioned. He was a great listener and never failed to offer the perfect assessment or advice. He had the innate ability to understand and sympathize with whatever it was you were going through. He was thirty-seven years old with the wisdom of someone who'd lived a thousand lives.

"Do you like doing this kind of stuff—being an actress?" he asked.

I told him I loved it.

"I can tell you love it," he said. "Your facial expressions are really great in all of our scenes. Is this what you want to do—more than anything?"

"Definitely," I gushed. "I don't want to go back to work, that's for sure. It's going to be difficult."

"I bet," he replied. "I really love doing this too. This is what I want to focus on—doing film. I have to go on tour in September and I don't want to. The record company is always pushing me to do stuff. Did you know that they refused to pay for this short film? I had to pay for it myself! I really don't trust them anymore. And Sandy is friends with Tommy Mottola, so I'm not sure about him either."

He straightened up, as if struck by a sudden revelation and blurted, "I think I'm going to fire Sandy. There's been some stuff going on and I just can't trust him. Shana, please swear that you won't tell a single soul any of what I am telling you."

I told him that I wouldn't, of course, and then I assured him that Sandy and Jim were not the bad guys. He had become so paranoid for some reason. It all started when Sony refused to pay for *Ghosts*.

"I've been wanting to talk to you about this for a while," he continued. "You're there with them every day, so please give me your honest opinion. Let me tell you something—I own the Beatles song catalog and Sony wants to steal it from me so bad. All that stuff that happened to me before was all a conspiracy to try to take me down. They thought I would be forced to sell the catalog to them. That's how these record companies try to control us. They keep you in debt so that you'll do anything they say—like touring. I hate going on tour but it's the only way to make money without them taking it."

He sighed and shook his head, "I fear for my life, Shana. I really do. There's some bad people in this business."

I sat in stunned silence as I listened to him unload his feelings—feelings that had obviously been building up for quite some time.

"I always knew I would finish this film no matter what," he continued. "Remember when we started on it the first time? And we couldn't finish?"

I was hoping he wouldn't start thinking back to that awful time in his life. He expressed a stubborn determination to finish this film even though, as he said, the record company didn't want him to. He was already largely indebted to them, and this would put him further in the hole—with no way out. I had heard he was $300 million in debt to Sony. And the budget for *Ghosts* was $7.5 million, so it was understandable that Sony didn't want to pay for it. Michael's own accountant, Marshall Gelfand, had told him that he couldn't personally afford to pay for it either. But Michael was a visionary, a dreamer, and he did as he pleased.

I felt uncomfortable hearing him talk about such things. Although my loyalty was firmly with him, my bosses, who paid my bills, were now seemingly the enemy, simply because they were friendly with Sony, or more specifically, Tommy Mottola. I didn't understand how this had happened. I thought Michael was being overly paranoid. I told him I was certain that Sandy and Jim were good guys and that they loved him.

"There's absolutely no way they're in cahoots with Sony to take your Beatles catalog," I assured him. I'd been with them for over five years at this time—they were like family to me. I would know if something shady was going on.

His fears and paranoia weren't the ramblings of someone out of his mind. He was fully present and sober and he truly believed the conspiracy was real. Despite his worries, he was in a good place—a healthy space—and I was happy his mind was sharp. It was refreshing.

Thankfully, he changed the subject. "You know, I was looking at you, and I was thinking that you could have been in the *Thriller* video. You look like you could have been and your outfit looks just like the one in the video. Remember, with the bobby socks?"

"How can I forget?" I gushed. "I watched that video a million times in a row. I remember running home from school just to catch the premiere on MTV. I dreamed I was the girl in that video. What happened to her?"

"Ola Ray? I don't know."

"I heard she's not doing well now." Here I was gossiping again.

"I heard that too. Where did you hear it?"

Michael should've been a lawyer—he was the king of asking direct questions and putting you on the spot. "*Hard Copy*," I admitted, reluctantly. It was a popular tabloid show that had pursued negative stories about Michael in the past.

"Oh, they're terrible. They pay people to lie," he said.

"I know, but they actually interviewed her and she said she was broke, or something. What about Tatiana, from 'The Way You Make Me Feel' video? Whatever happened to her?"

"Tatiana," he sighed. "I don't know. She was gorgeous. Everyone loved her. She had a presence. I don't know what happened to her." He gazed off into the distance and anger emerged in his voice, "I gave them both the perfect opportunity to make something out of it. Look what they did with it . . . nothing."

His moods were mercurial. One minute, he was laughing and joking like a teenager, and the next he appeared angry and defiant. Sometimes on set, I'd see him drift off as if in deep thought. He'd stare at the children in the cast and suddenly become quiet and sullen. I always felt that he was thinking back on the hell he'd gone through with the Chandler allegations. Children were his lifelines—his key to happiness. Without them, he always said, he wouldn't want to live.

But, at this moment, I was just hoping to get back to the subject of us. He turned to me with a sly smile, "Do you remember when I used to call you and dictate those songs?" He was referring to our steamy phone calls.

"How could I forget?" I giggled, embarrassed at the memory.

"Do you still promise that you're not going to tell anybody about that?"

I told him I hadn't told anyone anything after all of these years, and I wouldn't.

"Do you swear?"

"Yes, I swear."

These words had become a script that he repeated constantly as if it were a mantra. He was always asking me to "swear I wouldn't tell a single soul," like preteens making a pact before getting into trouble. I always went along with it, of course, but I felt he was just being dramatic most of the time.

He leaned in closer. My heart starting pounding so fast I thought it would jump out of my chest. I could smell the orange Tic Tacs on his breath. The baby powder scent of his perfume engulfed the air between us. Then his lips parted and he kissed me.

The feel of his soft mouth pressing against mine felt like an old, familiar pillow—warm and inviting. He gently grabbed the back of my head with one hand and stroked my hair as we continued. He kissed me more passionately than before and I felt shockwaves pulsating all over my body. My arms filled with goose bumps as I rubbed my hand on his muscular thigh. Years of pent-up frustration and longing radiated between us. From this moment forward, I would never be the same. *I am his forever*, I thought. No one and nothing could ever change these feelings I had. Visibly shaking—he wrapped me into his arms and held me.

"Do you like it when I kiss you like that?" he whispered.

"Yes I do," I muttered.

"I'm sorry if I keep staring at you, but you're so beautiful," he gushed.

There was a loud knock on the door. "Michael, we're back on set in twenty minutes," a production assistant shouted.

Michael closed his eyes and sighed. "They'll probably be coming to get me soon to get me ready."

Still trembling, I agreed and told him I would go back to the set. He held my hand as he helped me up from the couch. He opened the blinds and peered out of the window to make sure no one was around, then opened the door for me.

We never did get to play those video games.

I walked into the beaming sunlight as the valley heat seared into my skin. After thirty minutes alone with Michael, the sun looked brighter and the sky seemed bluer than I remembered . . . and everything inside of me felt different too.

"Ladies and gentleman, that's a wrap for Michael Jackson!" Stan Winston made the announcement that always followed the star's last scene of a production. Everyone clapped wildly for Michael. I was standing next to him as the cameras stopped rolling, ending our month in paradise. He turned to everyone and smiled.

I looked at him with sadness in my eyes and said, "Goodbye."

He wrapped his arms around me in a tight hug.

"I'm going to miss you," I said as I squeezed him close. With Michael, I never knew when I would see him again.

"Oh, you'll be around," he said with certainty.

"You better call me," I told him.

"I will."

Always mannerly, he walked around and shook everyone else's hands, thanking them for their hard work. It was 12:45 AM and we all were exhausted. But no matter how tired we were, it was always a sad moment after the final shot of a long production. We had all spent hours together, day after day, and now we had to say goodbye. Before we left, I gave Michael an autographed picture of myself to remember me by. I wrote on it, "To Michael. I love you, Shana."

It had been a sixteen-hour workday for me, with my call time being 8:30 AM. Michael had arrived at 4:45 that morning and had spent twenty hours on set. The days were long but they always went by surprisingly fast because of the fun we had.

After spending every day of the past month with Michael, for over twelve hours a day, I had a completely different feeling for him. I had been infatuated with him before, but I felt that there was always so much distance between us. In the past, he managed to distance himself whenever we were getting close. But for this past month, it had been impossible to do that. We had to be with each other every day and I felt secure knowing he wouldn't just disappear without warning. I think that distance had caused me to romanticize him as this perfect guy and what I was actually in love with was the *idea* of him as opposed to the real Michael. Now, after spending so much time with him, all I could see was Michael the man. The love I now had for him was much deeper and different.

Michael dubbed the last day of filming "prank day." He sent House to his favorite magic shop on Hollywood Boulevard to pick up any cheap prank or magic trick he could find. House came back with a brown paper bag full of classic dollar pranks like stink bombs, fake spiders, and handshake buzzers. There was also a cigarette lighter that shocked your whole hand and arm when you flicked the switch. The kids loved that one. I was afraid to try it, fearing it would really shock my hand, but Michael kept encouraging me to do it. "It's not that bad. Try it!" The behind-the-scenes cameras even filmed us shocking each other with this lighter. There's footage out there somewhere of it all.

These pranks had brought back childhood memories for Michael. "Remember when they used to have cards that would have ladies on the front? You touched it and all of their clothes would come off?" Michael asked me.

"Of course not. I would never look at something like that," I joked.

He continued, "My father used to do that to us. There would be cards and when you pulled one, all of the clothes would come off. Me and my brothers would be so excited to see a naked lady."

Although he seemed to resent his father now for exposing him to things only an adult should see, it appeared that he had picked up this same bad trait when around children without even realizing it. He was a lot like his father in many ways. He had the sweet, gentle personality of his mother and, in business and other areas, the ruthless cold streak of his father.

I told him that I remembered the pens that had ladies in bathing suits and when you turned them upside down, the clothes would come off. He said that he remembered those too. Leave it to his mind to take the gigantic leap from a cigarette lighter buzzer to cards with naked ladies.

Even though he was always mentioning sexual stuff, when he did it, it was cute and not offensive, for some reason. He managed to maintain an air of innocence even when talking about dirty things. He was a walking contradiction.

A little later he asked if I ever watched the Three Stooges. With the excitement of a starstruck fan, he proudly pointed to the side of the set where a few people were sitting in director's chairs. "Do you see that lady sitting over there?" He pointed to an older woman who was probably in her seventies. "That's Moe's daughter, Joan. She wrote a book about her uncle Curly back in the eighties and I wrote the foreword for it. I love the Three Stooges so much," he gushed. I had learned to always look on the sideline of the set to see who was watching us. He always had interesting visitors.

As the end of the day grew nearer, the kids went to Michael's trailer to give him going-away presents. My thirteen-year-old friend Keisha had joined the boys as well. As soon as they left his trailer, all four of the kids bounced over to me smiling, as if they knew something I didn't.

"What are you guys smiling about?" I asked, suspicious of the private joke they were obviously sharing.

Kendall, who was ten years old and the star of our film said, "Somebody likes you."

Keisha excitedly told me what happened. She was so anxious to tell me the words came spilling out. She said that they were all sitting there in the trailer with Michael, wanting to have fun, and out of the blue he said, "So what do you guys think of Shana?"

All of the kids told him that I was pretty and Keisha said that I was really pretty and nice.

Then Michael started spilling his guts, gushing to the kids, "I just think she's so beautiful. She's the most beautiful girl I've ever seen! She is so sweet. She works at my manager's office. I talk to her on the phone every single day. Did you know that she was in the original video of this? We had a lot of kids in it, but Shana was the only one I brought back."

One of the kids told him that House had a big crush on me. Exasperated, Michael said, "I know."

My ally Keisha wanted to make it clear to Michael that he was the one I liked. "She doesn't like House like that, though. She just thinks he's really sweet. I bet if you asked her out, she would go."

She said they wanted to play video games, but he just went on and on about me. The young boys tried to change the subject to talk about the video games, but Michael kept going back to the subject of me, saying how beautiful I was. Boys that age don't like girls yet, so the subject of me was not one they were interested in. They were really too young to understand these adult feelings from Michael. Keisha, being the oldest, understood and knew I would be happy to hear these revelations.

The boys just stood there looking at me with confused smiles as she recounted the story. They didn't know how to react. My reaction couldn't be denied, however. I was over the moon hearing these things. I felt that Michael had been fantasizing about me all of those years, just as I had with him. He even exaggerated to them that he spoke to me every day. There were periods when we did speak several times, every day, but after he got married those calls were fewer and further between. It made me sad to think that he had been daydreaming about me for so long and yet had waited this long to attempt to make those fantasies come true. So much time had been wasted. I started realizing that he preferred to live his life in a fantasy world, where he couldn't be hurt. He would rather talk and fantasize about a girl he liked than actually be in a real relationship. It was obvious he was trying, and he had mustered up the courage to make some moves, but most guys would've made things happen at a much faster rate. I don't know why, but I started feeling sorry for him after this. It was as if he hid behind this magical Michael Jackson persona, but underneath he was still a scared, insecure little boy dreaming that he could just be normal.

I saw a clip of Michael at the World Music Awards a few weeks later, when he performed "Earth Song." The staging of the song made him appear almost Jesus-like. He was bathed in white light, surrounded by young children as the celebrity-filled audience watched with their mouths agape. It was a breathtaking performance that only he could've pulled off. Fans mobbed him. It was weird to see him in those situations. I found it strange to see people screaming for him now. When I was with him, I tried so hard to remember the excitement that people felt for this King of Pop. Tried to remember all of the hype, all of the hoopla. I tried to remember how I felt when I would've done anything just to meet him. The way I felt when he was onstage back then or when I watched his videos was amazing—and I couldn't imagine ever feeling that way again. When I saw him now, all I could see was Michael, not the image I obsessed over as a teen. It was sad because that feeling of excitement you get when you're completely naive is a great feeling. It's a safe and warm place to dwell . . . a place where your idols are perfect and untouchable . . . a place where you can mold them into your perfect fantasy. All I could see now was the man whom I had fallen in love with—who was sometimes silly, enjoyed practical jokes, liked Bazooka bubble gum and orange Tic Tacs, and was a great kisser. But above all, he was not perfect . . . he was *real* . . . and so were my feelings.

15

> The raging fire which urged us on was scorching us; it would have burned us had we tried to restrain it.
>
> —Giacomo Casanova

The scorching heat of the summer of 1996 felt like an inferno inside of my small North Hollywood apartment on Hesby Street as I rifled through my closet searching for the perfect outfit. Michael had just called and he wanted to see me. I felt a panic attack coming on.

I hadn't seen or heard from him since our last day on the *Ghosts* set. It had been a few weeks, and I was missing him badly. He was very good at disappearing for weeks, sometimes months, at a time, so I was pleasantly surprised when I actually heard his voice on the other end of the phone.

It was late one Sunday evening when he called. We spoke just long enough for him to ask if I was available to stop by the hotel where he was staying, the Universal Hilton. Luckily, I lived three miles and a few minutes from the hotel, which was also located in the North Hollywood area, on the Universal Studios lot. I knew that lot extremely well, having worked as a tour guide there when I first landed in Hollywood. I had no idea what Michael might want to see me about, but I wanted to look my best.

I tried on what seemed like a hundred outfits until I settled on one—a black-and-white plaid miniskirt and open-toe wedge heels, with a plain black T-shirt. My entire closet was now strewn across my bed.

"Can you be here in an hour?" Michael had asked after giving me exact instructions on how to get up to his room.

"Sure." I said. But an hour was not enough time. I felt like I needed at least an entire day to prepare, but I knew if I didn't seize this opportunity, it might never come again.

I quickly showered, fixed my hair and makeup, and bolted out the door. Michael, of course, didn't want anyone to know I was coming to see him—"Be careful when you're walking through the lobby," he said. I felt like I was a Bond girl on an undercover mission. A very nervous Bond girl . . .

I was so nervous when I pulled up to the imposing high-rise hotel, which sat high atop a hill overlooking Universal Studios, that I couldn't find the entrance to the parking garage. I drove up and down the incredibly steep hill, failing to see the entrance several times. Finally, after the fifth time, I spotted the sign that directed me to valet parking. I imagined Michael in his room waiting for me and I got even more nervous.

I pulled up to the valet and handed my keys to the young attendant after he opened my door. Strolling quickly through the bustling lobby filled with tourists, I started thinking that perhaps this was another one of Michael's practical jokes. I expected to open the door of his room and be doused with buckets of water or something.

In search of the elevators, I passed by the front desk and a crowded bar where businessmen in suits were mingling. My heart started beating faster when I spotted the elevators that would take me to Michael's floor. I took deep breaths and tried to remember everything I had been taught in meditation class to calm myself. Was I on an episode of *Candid Camera* perhaps? This surely had to be a joke of some sort.

The elevator quickly rose to the top floor and I walked down the dimly lit carpeted hallway to find the suite number he had given me. I composed myself one last time before placing my trembling hand on the door to knock. I was so scared that I was tempted to turn around and forget the whole thing. I stood there for at least a minute before I heard the lock on the door turning. And there he was—*Michael*. He smiled when he saw me. The biggest smile I had ever seen.

He was wearing blue pajama bottoms, red socks, a white V-neck undershirt, and a fedora, which was strange since he was at home.

His loose black curls were dangling, and he wasn't wearing much makeup.

He still seemed self-conscious about his nose. He kept automatically putting his hand up to it and then when he realized that his hand was there, he would put it down. He didn't know what to do with his hands, it seemed. And, although he wore a small piece of white tape that covered the center of the nose, it looked just fine. He had no reason to be self-conscious at all. He was handsome. I stopped noticing the piece of tape after the first few minutes. His hands and arms had a few brown spots, like age spots, on them, while the rest of his skin—what was visible—was pale white, with no color at all. How he had achieved this consistent white skin was beyond me. At first I thought it was makeup, but no, this was really his skin color.

He led me into the suite. It was a mess—a bigger version of how his trailer had looked. There was a lobby in the suite and a bedroom to the side. It was large, fit for a king. There were papers and faxes everywhere and unopened packages, just like in his trailer. It was safe to say he was a pack rat. Loud classical music that sounded like the soundtrack to a Disney movie filled the air.

We walked to the living room area, where there was a standard hotel sofa with a large TV in front of it. There was a Sony PlayStation attached to it and games on the coffee table in front of us. For some reason, seeing Michael made me calmer than I thought I would be. I had been much more nervous getting ready at home. Now that I was in his presence, everything seemed right again, as if this was where I was meant to be. He always had a calming effect on me.

Still, I felt like I was on a date with a teenage boy. The Disney music and video games aside, he got excited talking about cartoons and had a boyish enthusiasm when speaking about the *Ghosts* film we had just completed. He turned off the classical music and turned on a movie, *Baraka,* which was a beautifully shot film filled with images from around the world. He asked if I had seen it before and told me that he loved it. It was a movie showcasing the interconnectedness of the entire world through beautiful clips, of scenery across the universe. It reminded me of the song and video called "Earth Song" that he had recorded. I also noticed the kids' movie *Blank Check* lying on the table in front of us.

He got up and went to the kitchen area, offering me a glass of white wine. This surprised me because although I knew Michael had his issues with prescription drugs in the past, I never knew he drank alcohol. He brought back the bottle and two hotel glasses, poured the wine, and took a few sips. I had the feeling that he had been drinking before I arrived, because he seemed to get tipsy immediately. I hadn't even had two sips yet. He also brought over some popcorn and assorted candy from the kitchen area. I noticed an empty box of Kentucky Fried Chicken hot wings on the kitchen bar and packets of hot sauce next to it. He asked if I was hungry. I lied and told him I had already eaten. Although it was after 8 PM, I had actually been too nervous to eat dinner. The popcorn would have to suffice.

This was the most comfortable I had ever seen Michael. Although he was still wearing his fedora, he was relaxed. Gone was the giggling man-child that I had encountered in some of my earlier meetings with him. I was, by far, the shy one here. I was hoping the wine would help loosen me up a bit.

It flashed in my mind that Michael was twelve years older than I was. I suddenly felt like an inexperienced little girl sitting next to him. Visions of Michael's exciting and worldly life as a superstar rushed through my brain. All at once, he seemed like a mature man with a wealth of life experiences, and I felt like a child, unsure of what might happen next.

As the wine started to take effect, beads of sweat started forming on my forehead. We had polished off the entire bottle and I felt a little woozy, which was a good thing. I was finally feeling relaxed. As we watched the movie, he made small talk—asking me more about Sandy and Jim and telling me of his continued suspicions and frustration with Sony, his record label. Their lack of support for *Ghosts* was really bothering him. I'm not sure what he wanted me to tell him, but I insisted that he shouldn't worry about Sandy and Jim, at least. He had been contemplating firing them as his managers, and I think he just wanted reassurance that he shouldn't. After all, he was on the eve of starting another big world tour, and the last thing he needed was to be without management during that time.

He told me that he personally cast me in *Ghosts* because "white directors always cast unattractive black girls in movies. I had to make sure I had a pretty black girl in my video."

I pretended to watch the movie, but I could not focus on anything but the man sitting next to me. The wine had made the room appear as if it were enveloped in a foggy haze. Since I hadn't eaten, I was feeling the effects intensely.

He asked if he should open another bottle and I told him yes, yes, he should. That second bottle disappeared quickly and all we could do was giggle. Every scene in this *Baraka* movie suddenly seemed funny. I was more than tipsy at this point . . . I was drunk. The high of sitting so close to Michael, mixed with the wine, had created a euphoric feeling that was indescribable.

It also made me bold. I suddenly had the overwhelming need to touch him. I rubbed my hand on his thigh, remembering how muscular it had felt when we were in his trailer. His thighs were one of my favorite body parts on him. He had a dancer's body. Lean but filled with tight muscles, especially in his legs. He squeezed my hand and held it tight. The lights were already dimmed, but he turned off the one that was closest to us as he took off his hat.

"I've been waiting to be alone with you for so long," he said, his large hand rubbing my arm.

"It's been a really long time." My words were slurring.

"Years, right?" he chuckled. "Are you seeing anybody right now?"

That seemed like such an absurd question at this moment. How could I ever see anyone when all I could think about was him?

"No, Michael . . . of course not. All I want is you." The wine had fully taken over by this time, and words were coming out of my mouth that I would never have the courage to say otherwise.

As he leaned closer, I could have sworn I could hear his heart beating, although it was probably my own, since it was pounding out of my chest. I could smell the familiar Bal à Versailles as he looked me directly in the eyes, gently pinching my left ear with his long fingers. "You are so pretty. Your face is like a work of art."

The calmness I thought I had went away at that moment, and I had to fight myself from shaking. His presence was overwhelming—and his eyes were hypnotizing. Michael's words were slurring too, so I knew he was just as tipsy as I was. He must have felt me shaking, because he reached over and grabbed a blue cotton blanket that was lying on the sofa. As he laid the blanket over both of our legs, he unintentionally brushed his hand against my bare thigh, making me so nervous, I quivered.

He gently held my hand. "You're so shy. I thought I was shy," he laughed.

This only made me shyer, of course. I giggled and looked away. At this point, I didn't consider Michael shy at all. He was looking me straight in the eyes with every word he spoke. His gaze was so intense I kept looking away. His big brown eyes were staring right through me, as if he knew what I was thinking—what I wanted.

As he continued holding my hand, he placed his other under the blanket and stroked my leg. "I just think you're the most beautiful girl in the world," he gushed.

I was quickly melting. I don't think I had said a word in ten minutes. I was tipsy and nervous, unable to fully process what was happening. Although it had taken us years to get here, it felt like it had all happened so fast.

"Do you swear not to tell anybody about any of this?" he whispered, reciting his inevitable, reoccurring script. I told him of course I wouldn't tell anybody and that he should know by now that he could trust me.

"What are you going to say if one of your girlfriends asks about me?" he asked.

"I'll just tell them that you call me at the office and that's it."

"What about if Sandy asks?"

"I'm not going to say anything."

"You swear?"

"Yes, Michael. I swear."

"You really have to promise me, because no one can know about this. No matter what happens in the future, please remember to keep this between us. It's very important."

"I promise, Michael." I wouldn't find out until later why he was so adamant to keep this all a secret.

He cradled my face in one hand and pulled me close to his lips, kissing me softly and gently at first. His soft kisses progressed to passionate ones, and we made out for what seemed like an hour, but it probably was ten minutes. I don't know. I was lost on cloud nine somewhere.

"Have you ever been kissed like this before?" he whispered.

"No, I haven't. Only by you." I was embarrassed to admit it. I was about to turn twenty-six, and still Michael was the only "experience" I'd had.

I don't know whom Michael had kissed in the past but it seemed like he'd had lots of practice. Then again, he had been married for the past year and a half. I kept forgetting that little fact.

It was pitch-dark in the room at this point; the only light was the flickering television. My heart was beating so fast and loud I could hear it louder than anything else. It felt like it was pulsating inside of my throat. I knew where all of this was leading, and although I was scared and nervous, I was ready.

He turned the TV off and put the loud classical music back on. It was so dark now; I couldn't see a thing—which created a needed sense of anonymity. With the lights off, I almost forgot whom I was with. He became just a man I was on a date with. We fumbled around in the dark for a while as the world around us faded. His kisses were so deep and so passionate; my stomach started tingling as I trembled.

He took my hand and softly placed it between his legs, which I had purposely been avoiding. He was clearly excited. I had never felt a man there before and I was overwhelmed. I wanted him so bad at this point, but I didn't know what to do.

He became my teacher, guiding me every step of the way. I still didn't know how far he wanted to go, so I continued to let him make all of the moves.

Then he asked if I had ever kissed anyone "down there" before. I told him I hadn't. "Do you wanna try?" he giggled.

At this point, I was so tipsy and turned on, I was willing to try anything. He guided me down there . . . and I kissed it.

I *really* didn't know what to do now, but I tried. He coached me, telling me exactly how he liked it. I stopped after a few minutes because I felt so awkward and I didn't know what to do next. It was also so dark that I couldn't really see what I was doing.

"Please don't stop," he said, his voice a whisper.

"But I don't know what to do," I sighed, frustrated with myself.

"It's OK. Just have confidence. You're doing great." He sounded like he was coaching me to win a football game or something.

I continued, as he tenderly explored my body with his hands.

"Do you wanna go all the way?" he asked mischievously.

Even in the midst of all of this, I still felt like I was dealing with a teenager . . . except I was the inexperienced one.

"We don't have to if you're not ready. Only if you want to . . ." he said softly. He was so patient and understanding.

"I'm ready," I managed to utter.

"But you won't be innocent anymore. It'll be gone forever . . ." he said wistfully.

"Well, I have to lose it sometime. I'm already too old," I laughed.

"You can never be too old for innocence," he said with a serious tone. "Maybe we shouldn't . . . I don't know if you'll be able to handle it. I'm gonna be gone soon. The tour that I'm doing is really long . . . I don't want to hurt you. My brothers always did that to girls and I don't want to be like that."

"But we've known each other a long time now, Michael. I know how you are. I'm used to it," I chuckled.

"Are you suuure?"

"Yes, I'm sure. I promise I can handle it," I lied.

"If we do this, you have to swear that you won't tell anybody ever. And no matter what happens, you won't get mad at me."

"Why would I get mad at you?" I asked, genuinely wondering why he was so worried about that.

"If there's something in the press, please don't believe it, OK? That's all I ask. Do you swear?"

"Yes, I swear."

"You're going to end up hating me. I know it."

"I could never hate you, Michael. I love you."

"OK, but if this ever gets back to me, we will no longer be friends. I'm serious."

"You can trust me. You know that."

He wrapped me in his arms and softly kissed my ear. "I love you," he whispered.

My entire body filled with shivers.

"Do you like that?" he asked with his lips still caressing my ear.

"Yes," I said breathlessly. I could no longer take it. I needed him now.

He grabbed my hand and led me into the bedroom, which was also pitch-dark.

We spent the entire night snuggled in each other's arms—years of longing and frustration finally relieved. Neither of us slept. In fact, I felt more awake and alive than ever before—filled with the adrenaline that can only come at the dawning of a new love. My innocence was gone but I had gained so much more. Michael had been so gentle and caring. It was everything I had ever dreamed it would be. He was an amazing man and lover.

As the soft morning light peeked through the curtains, Michael uttered a revelation. "You know . . . I pray to God every night to take my sexual desires away."

Typical Michael—coming up with a zinger straight out of the blue. "Why do you do that?" I asked, not believing him at all.

"I have to channel all of that energy into my art—my music and my dancing. In order for me to be able to create the things I want to give to the world, I have to make that kind of commitment. I have so much inside of me that needs to get out . . . That's why you see so many artists have a good first album, but by the second one there's no more hits. They lose focus and start concentrating on other things. I can't do that."

Oh great, I thought, he was already trying to convince himself that he shouldn't be doing normal things like this. I let him ramble on, with hopes that he would reconsider this outlook once he had some sleep. Although I understood where he was coming from, to me it was just another excuse he could use in case he decided to run away again.

I left as the sun was rising, not wanting to overstay my welcome. He told me I could stay longer, but I had to go to work in a few hours. I needed to go home and pull myself together. The night had been amazing, but I had to go back to my normal existence and figure out a way to pretend that none of this had ever happened.

16

Dreams that do come true can be as unsettling as those that don't.

—Brett Butler

We spent several more nights together that summer. It felt as if we were making up for lost time. Each time he stated that he needed to concentrate on his upcoming tour and that he didn't want to lose his "focus." "I don't want you to get too attached," he said on our last night together. I wasn't sure why he said that, but I didn't want to ask. I figured he was just getting scared, like usual. All I know is, I was already attached and deeply in love—but it seemed that he was already looking for a way out.

Living in the real world after these nights was difficult. I felt like I had suddenly been transported to another dimension where dreams came true and love was the only thing that existed. Anything that impeded upon that world now seemed foreign. I didn't want to live life if Michael wasn't in it. Thoughts of him consumed my every waking moment. I imagined myself quitting my job and going with him on his upcoming tour. *Maybe we would even get married and have children,* I thought. Whatever the case, I wanted to be with him at all times. I was so in love I couldn't see straight.

It was torture not being able to tell anybody what had actually happened, but I did manage to make Michael the topic of conversation with everyone I spoke to. I really didn't care about any other subject. I couldn't hide the fact that I was head over heels in love—everyone around me knew it. I was in a Michael daze. At that moment, I felt that anything was possible and that this feeling would last forever—that *we* would last forever.

Boy, was I wrong.

The glorious summer of 1996 was coming to an end and I hadn't heard from Michael in weeks. He hadn't even called the office. I chalked that up to the fact that he was preparing and rehearsing for his tour, which was set to begin in September. If I ever had something I needed to give Michael during this time, his wonderful driver, Gary, would come to my apartment in North Hollywood and pick it up from me. I had given Michael an autographed picture of myself on the last day of *Ghosts* and Gary had called to excitedly tell me that he had found the picture framed in Michael's bathroom. "You have an admirer," he enthused. He was always so kind and thoughtful. He knew that this information would make the entire rest of my summer a happy one. I felt like I was living inside of a wonderful bubble. *But why hadn't I heard from Michael?*

I had been hearing from everyone but Michael. House started calling me constantly, inviting me on shopping trips to help him "pick out items Michael might like." I thought that this was something Michael had asked him to do, so I happily joined him. Looking back, however, I think that House had developed a crush on me himself and was using this Michael angle to try to hang out with me on his own. I was so confused and too naive to understand any of what was going on. I was just happy to be with someone who could tell me what Michael was up to day to day. Not hearing from him made me cling to any and all forms of information. To this day, I kick myself for going shopping with House at all. Even though Michael was the one who introduced us and encouraged us to be friends, it had to have made him feel insecure after what we had done. I certainly was not interested romantically in House, or anyone else for that matter, but at that time I had no idea that Michael struggled with so many deep insecurities. If he found out you were friends with a guy, suddenly he was convinced you were also sleeping with that guy. He was unreasonably paranoid in every aspect of his life. For a long while, I felt that my innocent shopping excursions with House were the reason certain events transpired in the months to come. My suspicions were realized when Michael confronted me about that very topic a few years later. But for now, hope was still eternal and life was grand.

On Michael's birthday, at the end of August, I wrote him a thoughtful note and included a yellow happy-face mug filled with his favorite candies—mostly Bazooka bubble gum. In the note, I wished him a successful tour, told him I loved him, and asked him to call me. Gary made a special trip to my apartment to pick this gift up from me. He had given me advice on what to give Michael. He told me that although Michael didn't celebrate birthdays, he was sure he would be happy to receive this present from me. He delivered it to Michael—but I never heard from him. Not even a thank-you. The thought that he could be pulling a disappearing act after what we had shared didn't even enter my mind. I was so in love I was blinded. I was also used to this behavior from him. Why should I expect him to suddenly be predictable? I figured that he would appear again when he was ready, just like all of the other times.

As the intense heat of summer dissipated and the breezy days of fall descended upon Los Angeles, Michael left for his world tour. It was aptly named after his last album, *HIStory*. I still hadn't heard from him, but I would occasionally receive word from mutual friends that he had asked about me or wanted them to tell me hi. Somehow these world tours always managed to start just as things were heating up between us. It was almost like he timed it each time, knowing he would be gone for months to come, providing a perfect excuse to run away.

Those months of the past summer when things were perfect were enough to sustain me for the coming weeks, I figured. The spell he had cast upon me was like a white cloud that hovered over me at all times—bathing me with love, light, and magic. It felt impossible to escape . . . and why would I want to? It couldn't get any better than this. The roller coaster we had been riding for years was finally at its peak. And it felt amazing.

Unfortunately, what goes up almost always comes crashing down—especially in Michael's world.

17

Hearts are made to be broken.

—Oscar Wilde

I was still managing to sit for eight and a half hours a day in my role as the receptionist at Gallin Morey. I was now a staple at the company, having been at the front desk for over five years. It had become the perfect job for me because it allowed me the freedom to also go on auditions during the day.

After filming *Ghosts*, the acting bug had hit me hard. One of the junior managers at the company even agreed to represent me and I started booking several small parts on various sitcoms. I also obtained a lawyer who helped me find an agent. I enrolled in acting classes and focused on becoming better at my craft. I wanted to make Michael proud.

It had been a month since Michael had left to start his tour and the days were creeping by like molasses. One evening, as the clock struck exactly 7 PM, I enacted my daily ritual of leaving work and driving back to the valley through the curves of Laurel Canyon. I now had a brand-new sporty black Honda Del Sol with a convertible top. I had always dreamed of having a convertible in L.A. There was nothing better than driving through the streets with the top down, sun on my face, and wind blowing through my hair as the palm trees swayed in the California breeze. Every night when I drove home, I played Michael's song "Give in to Me" on full blast. There was something about that song and his lyrics that made me feel like he was right there in the car with me. "Don't try to understand me . . . Love is a feeling . . ."

That was the side of Michael I knew and loved, and that powerful song encompassed his personality fully. It kept me going on many long, lonely nights that fall.

On this evening, I stopped by Vons, my local grocery store on the corner of Laurel Canyon and Ventura Boulevard. I wasn't in the mood for In-N-Out or McDonald's for dinner, so I decided to pick up some items to cook. Yeah, I was still at the age where I loved fast food and didn't gain an ounce of weight when I ate it. I couldn't have it every night, though, so Vons it was.

I parked my Honda and strolled into the brightly lit food oasis. This was a popular grocery store where I would often see actors from my favorite shows. It was located a short block from where we had filmed *Is This Scary* in Studio City.

I grabbed a squeaky silver cart and made my way past a new display of orange-and-black Halloween decorations and candies—always an indication that summer was definitely over and the holidays were right around the corner. I spotted some stir-fry vegetables and grabbed a pack of chicken breasts, then headed to the long checkout line.

I had gotten into the habit of reading the tabloids while I waited in line. There was usually something about Michael every week, and it was entertaining to read even though I knew most of it wasn't true.

As my eyes scanned the magazine rack, I saw a new *National Enquirer* prominently displayed. I immediately noticed it had a picture of Michael with a blonde woman. I bolted out of my spot in line and grabbed a copy.

The headline read, MICHAEL JACKSON EXPECTING A BABY WITH BLONDE NURSE.

I stood still in disbelief as I read the headline again. Surely I had read it wrong . . .

MICHAEL JACKSON EXPECTING A BABY WITH BLONDE NURSE.

No, I had read it right.

OK, perhaps the title was misleading, as it often was. I rifled through the pages dreading the worst but hoping for the best. I still had faith in Michael. There's no way he would do something like this . . .

I arrived at the story, which included exclusive full color pictures of Michael and the blonde nurse. She looked familiar. I soon realized it was Debbie Rowe, whom Michael had introduced me to on the set of *Ghosts*. She had come a few times to watch us film after her shift at work. She was Dr. Klein's nurse. She lived in a small apartment in Van Nuys, not far from our set, so it was convenient for her to stop by on her way home. I didn't have any reason to think there was something going on between the two of them. Debbie was a biker chick, riding to the set on her Harley most of the time. She had a foul mouth and an unsophisticated personality. They appeared to be close friends, but there was not even a hint of anything more. I could tell she cared about Michael just by the way she looked at him while we were shooting our scenes. Like everyone else, she appeared to have a crush on him. She was nice and harmless, though, and I didn't feel threatened at all. According to the *National Enquirer*, however, I should've felt more than threatened.

Debbie was six months pregnant with Michael's child. The picture used for the cover was one of Michael and Debbie backstage at his concert, her pregnant stomach in plain view. She was glowing. That image hit me like a shot from an assault rifle. In a daze, I left my basket with the chicken breasts and package of frozen vegetables right there in line and walked out of the store. I was no longer hungry.

The next few days and weeks were a blur. Endless tears filled dark, lonely nights. I felt alone and confused. My mind was reeling, trying to put the pieces of this incongruous puzzle together. Six months ago was right around the time Debbie was visiting the *Ghosts* set. While Michael and I were flirting on set and engaging in other activities at the Universal Hilton, she was pregnant. None of it made sense, but it did explain the elusiveness that Michael displayed. Even his disappearing act now made sense. While I had been daydreaming of a future with Michael, he had been planning his own without me. Was I not good enough to have a baby with . . . to be seen with? Perhaps I wasn't blonde enough.

Suddenly, the reasoning behind his intense need to keep everything between us a secret became crystal clear. I felt like I didn't know what was real anymore. I was alone—stuck in this crazy world without a soul to confide in.

I frantically and obsessively called Michael but couldn't get to him. I left messages, did everything I could think of, but still nothing.

He had a habit of changing his cell phone number nearly every week. You could be his best friend one week, and the next his number would be disconnected. He was good at cutting people out of his life without so much as a second thought. Never did I think I would be one of them.

This was like the Lisa Marie marriage all over again, except this felt even worse. A baby had a certain finality to it. And Michael and I were much closer now than we had been then. This was devastating.

I spoke to House and everyone else I knew on the tour to get as much information as I could. I needed answers.

The general consensus was that Debbie was just a friend doing a good deed for another friend. She knew that Michael wanted to be a father and she offered to help him achieve his dream. I was also told that Debbie was allegedly supplying and administering the drugs that Michael needed to sleep while on tour, and that was their main connection. I decided to believe that scenario. It was the only way to make getting through the day bearable. Thinking of it in any other way was too painful.

Finally, late one night, my phone rang. It was Michael. A wave of relief and comfort washed over me as I heard his soft voice.

"Hi, this is Michael. Who's this?"

Even though we had been talking on the phone now for over five years, he always asked if it was me before launching into a conversation and he almost always announced that he was Michael. Didn't he know that he had one of the most recognizable voices in the world?

"Hi, Michael! Where are you?" I asked, unable to hide the excitement in my voice.

"I'm in Bangkok."

Hearing the word *Bangkok* always made me cringe. All I could think about was the last time he had traveled there, on his Dangerous tour, and the madness that ensued thereafter.

He sounded happy, yet I detected a familiar slur in his speech. Something about touring caused him to have to take medication, it seemed. He had been healthy and fine prior to the tour, as far as I could tell. But now he was back to the way he used to sound. Touring was not good for him.

"I just wanted to check in and see how you were doing," Michael said. "I'm sorry I haven't called, but I've been so busy with this tour and everything." He was using his sweetest voice—it had a childlike quality to it. This voice would often appear when he was stressed out. I feel like he used it as a defense mechanism. It was impossible to get mad at him when he was speaking in such a kind, almost ethereal way. Hearing that voice just made me melt.

We chatted about how the tour was going and some other topics, but I knew he wasn't going to bring up any of the recent turn of events unless I did. So I did.

"I read about your baby news. Congratulations."

I didn't know what else to say. I'm sure I sounded phony, and he had to know there was no way I could be happy about such news—but I also couldn't be mad at him after hearing his sweet voice. I've never been the type to explode in anger at someone. Calm, cool, and collected was always my demeanor. Plus, I loved this man. As angry and sad as I had been, hearing his voice sent a cascade of butterflies adrift in my stomach. Just like in the past, hearing his voice was all I needed.

"Oh, thank you," he giggled. "Please remember to not believe anything you read, OK? Especially in the tabloids . . . it's nothing but garbage." And then he continued, "Promise me that you're not mad. I never wanted to hurt you."

"Well, I admit I was really shocked when I heard the news. But I'm OK now that you've called . . . and I want you to be happy. I know that you'll make a great dad." I just didn't have it in me to be mean or even upset now that I was talking to him. I hated that about my personality. I've always been too nice and too loyal. Even though I don't curse, sometimes people deserve to be cursed out. He definitely deserved it at this moment, but I just *couldn't*. He was also smart to let some time pass before he called me. Time will diffuse most difficult conversations.

"When am I going to see you again?" I asked.

"I'll be back in the states in January. I'm playing some dates in Hawaii. You should come!"

He didn't have to ask me twice. Hawaii would be his only US city on the tour and I had already planned on flying there to see him. I had never visited Hawaii and felt this would be the perfect opportunity to not only see Michael's show but also visit the beautiful big island as well. I told him I would definitely be there and that I couldn't wait to see him again.

"I can't wait to see you too," he said.

"I miss you and I love you, Michael. I'm so happy you called."

"Thank you for understanding. I love you too. Always remember that, OK?" Michael's words had now taken on a slow, melancholy tone and they wrapped around me like a warm, crackling fire. At the time, I refused to hear the words that weren't being said.

This seemed like déjà vu. We had almost the exact same conversation after the surprise marriage to Lisa Marie. It was like he had a set script for every situation to get him out of any uncomfortable confrontations. And it worked like a charm.

Hearing from him definitely made me feel much better. I resolved to feel happy for him. I knew that Michael was complicated and by this time I was used to expecting the unexpected. My years of being inside of his world had made me almost numb to feelings most people felt. Looking back, I don't know how I remained sane. I guess when you're living inside of a bubble, you don't realize what a crazy life you're living. It takes time and distance away from that existence to be able to look back and make sense of the madness.

Shortly after our phone conversation, Michael and Debbie got married, which was yet another shock, but that was explained away too. Tarak Ben Ammar, a rich businessman originally from Tunisia, had managed Michael's tour and was now financing him. His religion frowned upon babies born out of wedlock. So Michael married Debbie to please him—or at least that's what I was told.

18

> Life isn't about waiting for the storm to pass . . . It's about learning to dance in the rain.
>
> —Vivian Greene

Ten . . . nine . . . eight . . . seven . . . six . . . five . . . four . . . three . . . two . . .

Dick Clark's voice boomed from my television as that familiar sparkly ball descended into Times Square.

It was now 1997 and I was packing for my first trip to Hawaii. I rummaged through my closet, picking out every outfit I thought Michael might like to see me in. I hadn't seen him since our encounters over the summer and I was as giddy as a schoolgirl. What an amazing way to start the New Year.

Michael was scheduled to perform at Honolulu's Aloha Stadium on January third and fourth. These dates would signify the end of the first leg of his successful HIStory tour. So far, he had played forty shows in twenty-five cities across the world, without any cancelations or major drama . . . other than getting married and having a child on the way, of course. Things had gone relatively smooth so far on this tour and I was happy for Michael. I remembered the difficulties just to get him onstage for the Dangerous tour, so this was a big accomplishment. After Hawaii, a short hiatus was scheduled, and then he'd perform forty more shows across the rest of the world.

Always a gentleman, Michael had arranged for a flight and hotel accommodations for me. I was ecstatic. My excitement was not about seeing the show, however, but about seeing Michael.

As I stepped off the plane at Honolulu International Airport, I was greeted with a colorful lei and a waiting car with a chauffeur. I loved going to visit Michael on tour because he always made sure I was treated like royalty. I also never had to worry about paying for anything. It always felt like a free vacation.

While checking in at the grand front desk of the Hilton Hawaiian Village, I ran into several of Michael's tour staff and band, as well as his personal security team, Wayne and Yannick. We were all staying at this luxurious resort and I felt like I was back in a family I had grown attached to.

When I arrived in my room, there was a gray packet that had been slipped under my door. It contained the tour rooming list (which listed everyone's names and room numbers), a schedule for the next couple of days, as well as a backstage pass and VIP tickets for both shows. I was mad at myself that I hadn't visited one of the earlier shows as well. Tour life was fun.

I perused the rooming list to find the person I thought might be closest to Michael. I wanted to let him know I had arrived and to make sure I would be able to see him somehow within the next two days. I called Charles Bobbit, who was now acting as Michael's road manager, and asked him to let Michael know I was there. The actual show at this point was secondary. I only cared about seeing Michael. At worst, I knew that Michael probably still had his meet and greets prior to every show. Surely he would be able to see me there. I relaxed in my room and decided not to worry about it.

As I settled in and opened my patio door, the tropical breeze whisked through the curtains. In the distance, I could vaguely hear the sounds of a ukulele strumming a lovely Hawaiian melody. I imagined that tourists were downstairs enjoying the nightly luau, feasting on a whole pig and drinking mai tais out of tall ceramic tiki mugs. All I could focus on, however, was the phone . . . willing it to ring. *Where are you, Michael?*

As the warm breeze transformed into a cool, brisk wind, I walked over to the patio to gaze at the glorious view. Stepping out onto the large tiled balcony, the wind started to get even stronger, blowing my long hair as if the oscillating fan from *Ghosts* was still in front of me. I looked up at the once deep-blue sky and dark clouds were approaching—silently creeping, threatening to destroy this idyllic paradise. A cold and mighty storm was brewing . . .

I awoke the next morning to the sounds of the hotel parrot that sat perched in the outside courtyard on the ground floor. He was a beautiful bird with vibrant colors of red, blue, and green, but he was annoying. No alarm clock was needed at this resort. The parrot was so loud—talking and squawking every morning—you had no choice but to wake up *early*.

I instinctively rolled over to look at the room phone, praying the red message light was on. Michael was known to call at all hours of the early morning, so I was hoping I had perhaps missed his call while I was asleep. No such luck. Tonight would be the first show, however, so I figured I would just see him there.

I walked over to the balcony to open the heavy curtains, expecting a ray of bright sunshine to infiltrate the dim room. But there was no light—only darkness. The ominous black clouds were still hovering . . . waiting . . .

I picked up the tour packet and searched for the day's schedule. Skimming the neatly typed itinerary, I noticed our call time was 4 PM. We were all to meet at the limo tour buses in front of the hotel lobby to be transported to the show.

I was part of the illustrious "B Tour Party," which meant I was to ride with the band, dancers, background singers, and any of the tour staff who interacted closely with Michael. The "A Tour Party" was always just Michael and his small immediate entourage. The "C Tour Party" consisted of the stage crew, including lighting technicians, stagehands, and any other tour members who didn't fit into any of the other categories. These categories existed for every show in every city. It had been the same on the Dangerous tour as well. Yeah, it wasn't hard to tell where you ranked on the totem pole with this setup.

Once we arrived at the stadium, there would always be a delicious catered dinner waiting for us in an empty room filled with round tables covered in white tablecloths. Preshow prayer, which I was not expected to attend, was usually at 6 PM, and then we would go to our respective dressing rooms to get ready for that night's show. Since I was a part of management and also a guest of Michael's, I was free to roam wherever I wanted during this time. I always felt out of place backstage because I didn't have an actual job to do. I had to patiently wait until the show started, hoping to find some other bored soul needing a friend to hang with.

On this show night, we boarded our bus and headed into Hawaii's version of traffic. Just as we were pulling away from the hotel, the forbidding dark clouds suddenly burst like raging, angry fireworks on the Fourth of July. Buckets of rain pounded like heavy rocks onto our bus. The torrential rain impeded our progress as we slowly made it to the freeway. What normally would have been a twenty-minute ride felt like it was taking forever. Wind mixed with rain whipped past our windows, creating a dangerous path. I stared out of the tinted bus window and prayed—*Please God . . . please let us all make it to the stadium safely . . . and wherever Michael is, please let him make it there safely too.*

I knew that January was rainy season in Hawaii, but why on earth did it have to rain on the only days of our show? I had been looking forward to seeing the beauty of Hawaii. So far the only thing I had seen were the four walls of my hotel room. Another problem—Aloha Stadium was an outdoor arena. Michael's fans would have to stand outside to watch this two-and-a-half-hour show . . . and Michael would have to perform in it. What a nightmare.

When we finally arrived at the stadium, our bus took the familiar backstage route of entering through the loading-dock ramp. As we descended into the imposing round arena, a huge sign perched above the ramp entrance greeted us. It read "Welcome Michael Jackson—Hawaii."

Immediately as I stepped off of the bus, a member of the Aloha Stadium staff placed a yellow rain poncho in my hand. I was very impressed with the hospitality of the Hawaiian people. No stone had been left unturned in giving Michael and his party a warm welcome.

As showtime grew closer, the heavy rain dissipated into a light drizzle. Magically, the rain would remain as a light mist for the entire show.

A small storm had started brewing inside of me, however. I hadn't received word of a meet and greet with Michael, nor any other communication from him. Not only had the weather turned cold outside, but the feeling in the arena was like ice. I felt like a little lamb lost.

The excited murmurs of the growing crowd seeped into our backstage oasis and my mood was lifted slightly. There was still one more night and one more show, so there was still hope. I decided to live in the moment and focus on enjoying the show. I couldn't worry about where Michael was and when he would see me. The rain may have dampened my spirits, but I wasn't going to let that ruin the entire night.

As the house lights dimmed, the dancers, background singers, and musicians scurried to take their places on the massive stage. They were all dressed in elaborate costumes, wicked makeup, and wild wigs. It was like a three-ring circus with Michael as the ringmaster.

I headed to my seat as a van with tinted windows slowly passed by me in the backstage corridor. The van traveled all the way to the entrance of the stage and parked. The side doors of the van opened and there was Michael. My heart dropped when I saw a little boy following him. The darkness in the arena made it difficult to see who the boy was. Perhaps it was one of his nephews or cousins.

Dumbfounded, I pushed my way through the frenzied crowd and searched for the VIP section, where my seat was located. As I ambled through the screaming girls and grown men dressed in high-water pants and fedora hats like their idol, my mind was in a state of confusion. Michael would rather spend his preshow time with a child and not even care to see me? And why was he now being driven to the stage? He could no longer walk the short distance from his dressing room? Was this all done to avoid people he didn't want to see . . . or face? Why did it have to be this way? Why couldn't things just be normal?

I made my way into the small, square VIP section located in front of the soundboard, raised above the middle of the floor seats. My anger was temporarily soothed when I saw where my seats were located—directly behind Michael's mother. Perhaps he thought that would be all I'd need to be happy. Sadly, however, the innocent thrill of seeing Michael just onstage no longer excited me. My emotions wouldn't even allow me to focus on the show at all.

I introduced myself to his beautiful and kind mother, reminding her that we had met on the *Ghosts* set. She instantly knew who I was and said she remembered meeting me. I admit, this interaction put me in a slightly better mood. And there was still the rest of the night ahead of us—anything was possible. I mean, Michael wouldn't fly me all the way to Hawaii, seat me behind his mother, and refuse to see me . . . would he?

The blinding white lights of Michael's show flashed before me, creating the perfect backdrop for my dazed mind. I was confused and didn't know how to feel. I sat there in a haze, watching the man I loved perform for thirty thousand worshipping fans—*Most of them would probably kill to be in my shoes*, I thought. I tried to put myself in *their* shoes and see things from their perspective, because I *was* once able to feel how they felt. Surely I could bring that feeling back, couldn't I? It wasn't that long ago that I was an enthralled teen screaming at Michael's every move on stage. I would have died just to breathe the same air as him. And here he was now, on that stage again . . . and I couldn't even force myself to be happy or excited. The magic was gone.

After the show, the downpour started again. We had all been invited to the official HIStory tour afterparty at a club called Maharaja in downtown Honolulu, not far from our hotel. It was being hosted by a local television show that was broadcasting live from the party. Like the troopers we were, Michael's entire tour entourage changed at the hotel and traveled through the rain-soaked streets of Waikiki to the club using our new yellow rain ponchos as umbrellas.

Although Michael didn't show, of course, I managed to have a great time. The host of the television program that was broadcasting recruited me for a sit-down interview. I was introduced as a friend of Michael's and part of his management team. The pretty Hawaiian hostess asked me questions in excited awe. "What is it like to be a part of his team? What is Michael like as a person? What has been your favorite part of being in Hawaii . . ."

At that moment, I realized how grateful I should be. All of my dreams had come true, and here I was upset at the very man who created it all. I was a part of Michael's inner circle and I hadn't even realized that I was taking it all for granted. This man had made it possible for me to visit Hawaii for the first time in my life—all expenses paid. He had given me the opportunity to act in two multimillion-dollar short films. He had allowed me to watch him work—enabling me to study a legend and master at the peak of his craft. Most important, he had given me a piece of himself that few would ever be able to experience. He had taught me how to love. How could I possibly be upset?

My trip to Hawaii ended without ever seeing or speaking to Michael. He had sent a message to me, however, through one of his assistants after the second night's show, apologizing for not being able to see me. He said he was feeling a bit under the weather. This was halfway believable only because the shows had been underwhelming. Michael lip-synched both shows almost entirely and it seemed like his mind was elsewhere. He just wasn't into it. Also, the cavernous atmosphere of the large stadium didn't lend itself well to a Michael Jackson concert. The audience didn't seem as excited or attentive as I had been used to seeing at his past shows, and that was largely due to the impersonal nature of the large, cold stadium, as well as his nonlive vocals. He barely interacted with the audience or his band. He was just phoning it in, it seemed.

The morning after the last show, a driver met me in the hotel's lobby to take me back to the airport. He loaded my luggage in the trunk and we headed back onto the streets of Honolulu. The weather was now stunningly beautiful.

I boarded my flight and sunk into the plush first-class seat. As the plane ascended over the sparkling deep-blue Pacific Ocean, I gazed down on the city below me. After two days of dark clouds, I could now see it all so perfectly clear.

19

An era can be said to end when its basic illusions are exhausted.

—Arthur Miller

Michael's first child, "Prince" Michael Jackson Jr., was born six weeks after the shows in Hawaii, on February 13, 1997. With such a momentous arrival on its way, it was no wonder he had been preoccupied. I felt selfish for ever being upset with him at all. Michael had always wanted to be a father. I was hoping that this life-changing event would set him on a healthier path, both mentally and physically. He would have four months off to enjoy his new son before embarking on the second leg of the HIStory tour.

I went back to Gallin Morey and tried to focus on anything other than Michael. Now that he was a married father, I realized it wasn't healthy for me to continue hoping that things would go back to how they once were. We had shared our moments and I should be happy with that. Or at least that's what I kept telling myself. I had always been a positive, happy person and I couldn't let these inexplicable events change who I was. I was still young, only twenty-seven, and I had my whole life ahead of me. It was clear that Michael was now focused on being a father, and I would have to accept that.

I admit it wasn't easy. I felt like an old shoe so easily tossed aside. I started regretting my every decision and replaying every moment over and over in my head. I dissected and overanalyzed every conversation, crying myself to sleep, yearning just to hear

Michael's voice. I couldn't imagine ever being with anyone else. During the day at work, my smile masked the pain and heartbreak that had invaded my entire soul. Some days I wondered if I would be able to go on at all. How could I live a life without Michael?

After the HIStory tour ended, Michael officially severed ties with Gallin Morey Associates. His relationship with them had become severely strained over the years, but it had been a good run. We helped him create two of the bestselling albums and tours in the history of music, countless number one singles, groundbreaking short films, and numerous iconic moments in time. He had spent almost the entire decade of the 1990s with the company.

And so had I. It's never easy to make a change, but it was time.

Mariah Carey signed to Gallin Morey shortly after Michael left. She was at the peak of her career at the time and her presence helped the company rebound from the loss of Michael. She came into the office often for meetings and was always nice and down to earth. Without Michael, though, it suddenly felt like a gaping hole was missing at work. Everything seemed off without him. I started looking for a way out.

One day, as I was reading one of the countless magazines scattered on my desk, NBA superstar Earvin "Magic" Johnson walked in. He was there for a meeting with Sandy. I had always been a Los Angeles Lakers fan, so it was very exciting to actually meet this legend. I had watched him win all of his championships over the years and I remembered sitting at my desk at our old location on Sunset when he announced he was HIV positive. Magic was a Los Angeles icon and also a friend of Michael's. A few years before, he had appeared with Michael in his Egyptian-themed video, "Remember the Time," directed by John Singleton.

He strolled up to my desk and leaned his six-foot-nine-inch frame over it to shake my hand and introduced himself. Charismatic and charming, he had a presence only superstars possess. After some brief small talk, he said with confidence, "You're coming to work for me."

It was just the opportunity I had been waiting for—a chance to change the scenery, meet new people, and try to forget about

Michael. After exactly seven years at Gallin Morey and seven months after Michael left, I turned in my resignation. It's never easy leaving a place you love and saying goodbye to people who have become family. But there was something about the fact that it had been seven years that made me feel secure in whatever decision I made.

Michael had always been obsessed with the number seven, plastering it on many of his personal wardrobe items, like shirts and jackets. He was extremely spiritual, and, according to the bible, seven is the number of completeness and perfection (both physical and spiritual). Michael had also written a song that was never released called "Seven Digits." I heard a demo of it and Michael explained that he came up with the title because "when you die, all you are is seven digits—on your toe tag the number they identify you by is seven digits long. After living an entire life, in the end all you end up as is a number."

I'm not sure how or why he knew that random fact, but Michael could be deep—not to mention morbid. In any case, after seven years, it felt like the perfect time to move on and see what life was like outside of that desk and the crazy world that surrounded it.

My new office was located at the historic Paramount Studios lot at 5555 Melrose Avenue. Magic Johnson had hired me to be the audience coordinator for his short-lived talk show on Fox, *The Magic Hour*. I was responsible for bringing in an audience daily and making sure there were some attractive ladies in the front row. Checking in with the guard and driving through those iconic gates every morning gave me goose bumps. My parking space was located in front of a huge fake blue-sky backdrop. Here I was entering another world that could only be possible in Hollywood. My life had become a succession of unbelievable events surrounded by larger-than-life figures.

Thankfully, my new job and Magic's powerful presence were just what I needed to take my mind off of Michael. The talk show and the job didn't last long, but I was grateful for the lessons I learned from Magic, like setting goals and striving for excellence at all times. He was a generous and wonderful boss who created a fun, family atmosphere at his office. To this day, I'm still proud to count Magic as a friend.

It was around this time that I attended an event held at the Sports Club L.A. on Sepulveda Boulevard. It was usually a gym, but for this event they had turned the basketball court into a dance floor. Ironically, the court was named after Magic Johnson. His name was painted in big letters on the wall. As I was standing alone in the room full of loud partygoers, I heard someone asking me if I would like to dance. I turned around and laid my eyes on one of the most beautiful men I had ever seen. His name was Shemar Moore. At the time, he was starring as Malcolm Winters on my favorite soap opera *The Young and the Restless.* He was so gorgeous it took my breath away. He was wearing a suit but his six-pack abs were visible under his tight shirt. His entire body was covered in muscles. He literally looked like a Greek god. I couldn't believe this hunk wanted to dance with me.

We danced the night away and he called me the next day to ask for a date. I was apprehensive about dating him at first, since I was still slightly terrified of men. Michael was all I knew and I had grown comfortable with the uncertainty I had always experienced with him. I didn't know if I was ready for a normal dating relationship but Shemar was persistent, and I agreed to go out with him. He took me to dinner at a restaurant in Century City called Houstons. We ended up sitting there talking for hours, shutting the place down. I found him to be different from other guys. He was a nice guy with class, not yet affected by the Hollywood life. He had goals and dreams of becoming a better actor, and his determination inspired me. He also liked to have fun, which is just what I needed. He won me over and we dated off and on for the next few years. Discovering that there was a world outside of Michael was liberating.

Shemar's focus was his career and he eventually landed a dream role in prime-time television, starring in the CBS drama *Criminal Minds.* I was also focused on my own career and our relationship evolved into a close friendship. Shemar is like family to me now and someone I can count on for advice and genuine support, which is hard to find in Hollywood.

Shortly after my job at Magic Johnson Enterprises ended, I ran into an old friend, Qadree El-Amin, at an event at the Beverly Wilshire Hotel. I had met him in 1990 when I first arrived in Hollywood as a young, wide-eyed aspiring actress/singer. He had given me his card at the time, but I never called him. When you're a pretty young girl, new to Hollywood, you receive lots of cards from men, and it's difficult to discern who is the real deal.

Qadree was an unassuming, somewhat shy man with a quiet dignity. He was always well dressed in a crisp tailored suit and his trademark baseball cap. After our first meeting in 1990, I didn't see him again for several years. One day, he came to Gallin Morey to meet with Sandy and he instantly remembered meeting me on that one occasion years before. By that time, Qadree had become one of the hottest music managers in the business. He managed Janet Jackson, Vanessa Williams, Deborah Cox, and the act he was best known for—Boyz II Men. All of those acts were at the pinnacles of their success at that time and Qadree's management company, Southpaw Entertainment, was a coveted spot for artists to land.

After chatting with him at the event at the Beverly Wilshire, Qadree offered me a job at Southpaw Entertainment on the spot, as a day-to-day talent manager for two of his newly signed artists, who were both former child stars—Tracie Spencer, an incredibly talented and beautiful young singer signed to Capitol Records, and actress Kim Fields, whom I had idolized as a child when she portrayed Tootie on the long-running sitcom *The Facts of Life*. In the '80s, I had posters of Kim plastered all over my bedroom wall, right next to my *Thriller*-era Michael Jackson posters. Now she wanted to expand her career into spoken-word performances. I jumped at the opportunity and immediately accepted the job offer.

As fate would have it, Michael Jackson was a huge fan of Boyz II Men and Qadree was a close friend. They were so close that Michael had been kind enough to open his home and allow Qadree to have his wedding at Neverland.

The offices of Southpaw Entertainment were like something out of a fairy tale. They were in a two-story cottage on Santa

Monica Boulevard in West L.A. It was situated amongst a group of four other cottages. These brick English Tudor buildings had been declared historical landmarks and looked like something right out of Hansel and Gretel. Ironically, they also resembled Michael's childhood home on Hayvenhurst in Encino.

Within my first few weeks, I learned that Michael was preparing for a charity concert in Korea called Michael Jackson and Friends, which would benefit the Nelson Mandela Foundation, among others. He desperately wanted Boyz II Men to be a part of this historic event. Michael's manager at the time, John McClain, called constantly to negotiate Boyz II Men's participation. Things weren't going very smoothly because of scheduling conflicts and prior commitments. But, as I said, Michael wanted them desperately.

One morning at about 11 AM, just as I was settling in and preparing my schedule for the day, the phone rang. "Southpaw Entertainment," I answered. It was a very small office with only four other staff members, so we took turns answering the phone.

"Michael Jackson for Qadree."

There was that old familiar voice, caressing my ear again like a melody sent by angels.

I honestly couldn't believe it. I had left Gallin Morey thinking I was starting anew, hoping to extricate myself from my intense feelings for Michael, and here he was again. It had been nearly two years since I last heard from him, and he was now a father of two children, Prince and Paris. Things had certainly changed, but he still sounded like the old Michael. I melted.

"Michael?" I said, excitement rising in my voice. "This is Shana."

"Shana? From Sandy Gallin's office? Oh my God! Hi!" He sounded even more excited than I was, if that was possible. "Do you work there now?"

I told him I did and that I couldn't believe he was calling. "This is just like old times," I said.

"I know," he enthused. Then, typical of Michael, he started excitedly talking a mile a minute, gossiping, telling me that our friend House had quit his job working for him out of the blue. "I couldn't believe it," he continued. "One day he just up and quit. I don't know why."

But I knew why. House had called me the day he quit. He was on the road with Michael in the middle of the HIStory tour in Europe. He was upset and worried. "I walked into Michael's room last night and he could barely stand up. I tried to hand him some papers and he fell over onto the floor. There were empty pill and minibar bottles everywhere . . . I handed in my resignation today. This is too stressful. I can't risk him having an overdose and dying while I'm here. I just know one day I'll walk in and find his dead body. Everybody would hold me responsible."

I didn't mention any of that to Michael, of course. I was hoping that those reckless days were over for him. Touring just wasn't good for him, I figured.

We continued our conversation. He asked about my job and I explained that I was a day-to-day manager for some of our artists—responsible for setting up recording sessions, creating budgets for tours, booking promotional appearances, and traveling with the artists to events. He sounded genuinely happy for me. "Wow. All of those years at Sandy's office paid off."

He told me that he really wanted Boyz II Men to do this concert with him and that's why he decided to call himself.

I distinctly remember hearing the classic song "I'm Not in Love" by 10cc playing loudly in the background as he spoke. At the time, it sounded like one of those haunting songs you hear vaguely at the edge of a dream. Michael was speaking loudly, almost competing with the song for my attention. I'm not sure why he didn't just walk into another room where it was quieter.

I recently searched for the song on the Internet, just to remind myself of the feelings I had during this conversation. The song, with its intricate harmonies and calming melody, feels like a cool breeze on a hot summer day. It washes over you, invading all of your senses and transports you to another place . . . another time. The lyrics were eerily similar to what I imagined Michael didn't have the courage to say to me during our last conversation. The song is about someone running away from his feelings, refusing to accept them. There's a line in the song that says, "Don't tell your friends about the two of us." And then, "You'll wait a long time for me . . ." The song revolves around the singer repeating, "I'm not in love." By the end of the song, however, he realizes he's deceiving himself. I believe that sometimes there are clues given to us by the universe that we may not discover until years later. To me, this song perfectly encapsulates the fight that Michael must have felt within his heart—sadistically denying himself the pleasure of experiencing real love for more than a brief moment, as if he felt he didn't deserve it. He had a pattern of getting close and then running away from people he cared about or who cared about him.

"When am I going to see you again, Michael? It's been way too long."

"I know. I'm out here at Neverland, but the next time I come to L.A., I'll stop by. Or maybe you can come to Neverland sometime."

I told him I would love that and to keep me posted about his schedule. He left his number and asked me to have Qadree call him.

It had taken me nearly two years to get over Michael. Him being married with two children helped that process along a bit. I had felt so defeated and used at the time. And I felt like I was chasing a married man, regardless of how real the marriage was. I couldn't bear the feeling of rejection and I had made a pointed effort to get him out of my system. Hearing his voice again, although exciting, didn't quite give me the same massive butterflies it used to, which was a relief. I felt like I was finally sober and free from a powerful drug I had been addicted to. But I have to admit, like all addictions, having this taste of his voice again made me start craving for more. A flicker of hope started stirring in my soul.

A few days later, I set up a conference call with Michael, Boyz II Men, and Qadree. On the call, Michael basically begged the guys to participate in the concert. He explained how important the charities were to him, specifically Nelson Mandela's and various other charities for children, and enthused that the concert would make history. He said that his plan was to have four more concerts like this one in other countries for the new millennium, which was coming up in less than a year. "They're going to be the biggest concerts ever," he said. "It'll touch millions of people all over the world."

Michael's enthusiasm was infectious, and Boyz II Men decided to rearrange their entire schedule in order to be a part of the show.

It was impossible to say no to Michael, and I have a feeling he knew that.

On June 25, 1999, the Michael Jackson and Friends concert took the stage in Seoul, South Korea. The show was considered a huge success, playing to eighty thousand screaming fans live in person and countless more on a widely viewed television broadcast. Boyz II Men were excited and honored to be a part of it. Qadree had traveled with the group and called me from backstage. He was almost always reserved, with an exceptionally calm demeanor. At this moment, however, he sounded more excited than I had ever heard him.

"The first thing Michael said when he saw me," Qadree exclaimed, "was 'Where's Shana? I thought she would come. Why didn't you bring her?'"

He went on to say that Michael couldn't stop talking about me.

"She is so pretty," Michael gushed. "I was so in love with her when she worked for my manager. And she is so sweet. I used to go in that office just so I could see her face. I made sure I had all of my meetings there."

He and Qadree had discussed me before, back in 1993 when I was working at Gallin Morey. Qadree had traveled with Boyz II Men to Monaco for the World Music Awards and Michael attended that year as well, with Jordan Chandler. Prior to that, Qadree had met with Sandy Gallin a few times at the office to discuss possible collaborations for Michael and the group. In Monaco, Qadree mentioned to Michael that he had met with Sandy.

"Did you happen to see that pretty girl at the front?" Michael had asked.

Qadree told him that he had met me when I first moved to Hollywood, a few years before.

"Oooh, well you better stay away from her. That's my girl," Michael bragged.

Qadree had never told me about that earlier conversation until this call from backstage in South Korea, and I couldn't believe he had kept it from me all of that time.

If I had only had a crystal ball to foresee the future—if I had only known then what would happen exactly ten years later.

If I had known, I would've driven straight to LAX after that phone call and jumped on a plane to South Korea. I wouldn't have wasted any more time. I can't remember why I didn't travel to that show. I could have gone. Why had things ended so abruptly between us in the first place? Why didn't I just try a little harder to remain in his life? Yes, he had gotten married and had children, but that shouldn't have stopped our friendship, at least. The love I felt for him was a once-in-a-lifetime kind of love. I should have fought to hold on to that. Instead, I'm now left with all of these unanswered questions and thoughts that still haunt me to this day.

20

> We do not really feel grateful toward those who make our dreams come true; they ruin our dreams.
>
> —Eric Hoffer

Michael invited me to Neverland a few months after that—and I ended up spending the entire day there alone.

Neverland was a somewhat long drive from L.A.—about two and a half hours. I remember taking that route from L.A. to the Santa Ynez Valley, where Neverland was located, so many times. I would hop on the 101 freeway, which took me through picturesque Santa Barbara, with the Pacific Ocean as a backdrop—once past Santa Barbara there was an exit that led through the long, curvy road that ended at the gates of Neverland. Before reaching Neverland, however, dusty farms and roaming cattle painted the scenery. There were endless miles of hills and valleys and not much else. It was one of those middle-of-nowhere places that you dream of retiring to when you no longer wanted to be bothered by the world.

When I arrived on this particular visit, after being cleared at the gate, I knocked on the door of the main house. Michael's chef, dressed in a white chef's jacket and tall chef's hat, warmly greeted me. He walked me into the kitchen and handed me a menu. He told me that Michael hadn't arrived yet but wanted me to make myself at home. I sat at the bar that surrounded the kitchen and chatted with the chef as he cooked the meal I had requested. He told me that the official Neverland meal was pizza and french fries, but I decided on a turkey sandwich and chicken noodle soup.

As private as Michael was, he made his home surprisingly open to his guests—almost too open. The only part of the house that was off limits was the upstairs bedrooms, where his children resided. Other than that, I and any other special guests had the full run of the house.

He was so kind and welcoming; I could see him easily taken advantage of. He was also extremely giving and never ever said no to anyone (except his record company). If you mentioned that you liked a new jacket he was wearing, he would take it off and give it to you. I don't think the word *no* was even in his vocabulary. Even if he wanted to say no, he would still say yes—never wanting to disappoint anyone. This caused problems because sometimes he would agree to something and then back out at the last minute . . . simply because he couldn't say no to begin with. He was polite to a fault and people expected him to always be that way. He made his friends feel special, like each one was the closest person to him. If ever that relationship were cut off, which it usually was without warning, his friends would become upset and start trouble. Michael was like a drug. He would give you a fix and then cut you off coldly. Many people couldn't handle this because they had truly become addicted to him—it would drive people (and parents of kids) crazy to no longer have access to him. This was the root of many of his problems.

The house itself was cozy but extremely cluttered. It was difficult to even walk through the living room. Scattered everywhere were ornate antiques, including a huge chessboard and castle replica, gold statues, and creepy mannequins that looked just like real people. Large framed pictures of his children covered the walls. They were dressed in fancy, regal clothing, looking like the perfect children. It brought tears to my eyes thinking that Michael had finally realized his dream of having a family.

Every comfort for guests that could be thought of was offered. Little things like having blankets waiting at the door that led outside, in case you were cold. It could get very chilly there at night and a warm blanket was exactly what you craved.

When dinner rolled around, I decided to have Chinese food, which the friendly chef cooked fresh in a wok. It was chicken fried rice, which was delicious. As I ate my food at the kitchen bar, he opened a cabinet. I noticed a full array of alcoholic beverages, including vodka and Bailey's Irish Cream. There were also countless boxes filled with bottles of wine, both white and red.

I chatted with the chef for over an hour, hoping that Michael would walk through the door. He had prepared separate plates of Chinese food for Michael and the children, covering them with plastic wrap, so I knew they had to be nearby. Night had now fallen and I started to feel that Michael was purposely avoiding me. The chef seemed nervous, as if he was covering for him. My instincts told me that Michael was already home. Although two years had passed, his refusal to see me in Hawaii still lingered in my mind. That incident had left a scar, making me feel insecure and unwanted. Now I was feeling the same way again. I knew Michael well enough to know when he was playing the avoidance game.

I felt sad rather than upset. Michael running away every time we got close had become a pattern. My self-esteem had sunken so low because of it that I just figured he never wanted to see me again. There were so many issues that had been left hanging in the air between us and there had been no closure. But Michael hated confrontation, and so did I. It was easier for me not to know the answers to all of the questions. I feared that knowing the truth would be too painful. I didn't really want to know why he didn't want to see me. The chef looked at me with compassionate eyes and offered me a glass of wine. I knew that a glass wouldn't be enough to make me feel better, so I grabbed the entire bottle and walked to my room, which was located in a guesthouse just outside of the main house.

Being alone at Neverland was creepy. Knowing there were cameras everywhere, I felt like I was being watched the entire time. There was no cell phone reception there, so the only connection to the outside world was via the house phone. I just knew that every time I picked up the phone to make a call, someone was listening. Once in my room, I meticulously searched through the flowers and behind the framed artwork on the wall, looking for hidden cameras and recording devices. I inspected the mirror in my bathroom looking for any signs that it contained a camera. I knew that Michael liked to spy on his guests, so I was leaving no stone unturned.

It was impossible to relax, so I decided to drive around the property. I hopped in a Bart Simpson golf cart, which was parked outside of my door, and placed my bottle of red wine on the passenger's seat. It was chilly and dark as I drove—the steering wheel in one hand and a glass of wine in the other.

I passed by the main house and noticed lights were on in the upstairs rooms. To me, this was all the proof I needed that Michael was indeed there. A wave of conflicting emotions surged inside of me.

Classical music blared out of speakers hidden in fake rocks as I maneuvered my golf cart over wooden bridges and narrow dirt paths filled with fragrant flowers. The music and my sadness and the darkness created a surreal feeling that I'll never forget. As tears welled in my eyes, I could feel my heart slowly letting go of the spell Michael had me under. I never wanted to feel this way again—so empty, lonely, confused. . . and rejected.

Michael never did show up on that visit, apologizing that he had gotten stuck "out of town." I found that hard to believe. Although painful, this rude awakening was exactly what I needed. I could honestly say that I was now truly over Michael. What a relief.

On September 13, 2003, for perhaps the first time in his life, Michael had a huge birthday party at Neverland. Growing up, he was never allowed to celebrate birthdays because of the Jehovah's Witness religion he was raised in. Even though Michael had disassociated himself from the religion while in his twenties, he still kept many of the traditions and values that had been so deeply engrained in him. One of those was the no-birthday-celebration policy. Deciding to have such a huge birthday party for his forty-fifth year signified a major change in attitude for Michael. I was proud of him for finally allowing himself to be open and breaking free of some of the chains that had psychologically held him back for so long.

I recall going to at least two other star-studded parties at Neverland that summer. I remember sipping sweet Mondavi wine with Paris Hilton and standing in line for popcorn behind Gwen Stefani at one party and being introduced to two stunningly beautiful teen girls named Kim and Kourtney Kardashian at another. They were both dating Michael's nephews TJ and Taryll at the time. Michael had wanted to open the place up a bit and gradually allow the public in to experience it. He started with these parties and they were a blast. These were mostly adult parties where alcohol flowed freely right alongside the cotton candy and popcorn.

He had also started attending other parties in L.A. with a group of new friends that included movie director Brett Ratner. I remember one late night receiving a call from my friend Courtney Barnes, who was at a Sean "Puffy" Combs party at the Beverly Hills mansion of billionaire Ron Burkle. I answered the phone and all I could hear was the loud thump of music.

"I have someone here who wants to talk to you," Courtney said. I heard the phone being passed to someone and the next thing I knew, *there was that voice.*

"Hello? Shana?"

It was Michael! At a Puff Daddy party no less. Courtney, who was a well-known entertainment publicist, had seen Michael and somehow I came up in conversation. He immediately dialed my number and put Michael on the phone. Michael sounded like he was having the time of his life. In fact, he told me he was having fun. He asked how I was doing. We tried to chat longer, but the music was so loud it was difficult for us to hear each other. He yelled over the music for me to call him later. He handed the phone back to Courtney before I could even think to ask for his latest number. Talking to Michael Jackson at 1 AM from a wild Puff Daddy party was such a strange occurrence I couldn't even wrap my head around it for days to come. This was a new Michael, and I liked it.

It was so nice to see Michael finally able to be himself and enjoy life like the rest of us. It had taken forty-five years for him to get to this place. Perhaps he was having a bit of a midlife crisis, but he now seemed ready to take on the world in a whole new and exciting way. The shy, meek public persona was gone and he was ready to mingle. I was hoping he would stay on this path. I think the public would have loved to see this new side of him. But Michael's life moved in predictable patterns. It never remained a smooth ride for very long. Sadly, trouble was always lurking just around the corner.

The ghosts of trouble were looming all over Neverland on the day of Michael's birthday party. It was being sponsored by local

L.A. radio station 102.7 KIIS FM and attending were a mixture of Michael's personal guests, celebrities, and some lucky fans who had won tickets off the radio. Neverland was in full swing with lines for rides and food like a real amusement park. The only difference was that everything was free.

I received a personal invitation, which had been delivered to me via messenger. The envelope featured the Neverland logo, a little boy on a moon, and the invite itself was beautiful. I took my friend Tita and her five-year-old son, Andre, as my guests. Like Disneyland, Neverland was always more enjoyable with children.

We entered through the gate off Figueroa Mountain Road and I parked in a dirt parking lot just in front of the second gate, which had the famous Neverland sign emblazoned upon it. Entering Neverland was like trying to access Fort Knox. There were two gates that you had to be cleared through. You also had to sign an agreement promising not to take photographs or to reveal anything that happened behind those gates. Hidden cameras were everywhere on the property to ensure these rules were not broken. Everyone who entered was recorded in a log by the security guard. Then, the black main gate of Neverland opened and you were transported into a world where childhood would never die. The lush green grass was perfectly manicured, the flowers bloomed in vibrant colors, and the scents of orchids and roses filled the air.

For special events like this one, animals would usually greet you when you reached the main house area. At this celebration, llamas, monkeys, and snakes waited for the arriving guests. It was like entering Willy Wonka's chocolate factory, minus the chocolate. This place was a peaceful paradise that gave you a sense of freedom and happiness.

Michael was not visible during the early part of the birthday celebration, but I could feel he was nearby. One of Michael's assistants picked Tita, her son, and me up in a Neverland golf cart that had been decorated as a Batmobile and was taken to the main house. Although it was September, the house was covered in Christmas lights, a touch Michael added to inspire the joy of Christmas every day of the year. As a child, he had not been able to celebrate Christmas because of his religion, and, like his birthday now, he was making up for lost time. It's difficult to imagine Michael not being able to celebrate Christmas. With all of its magic and wonder, it seems like a holiday made especially for him.

We were led through the cluttered house to the entrance of the foyer of Michael's bedroom, where I was asked to wait until I was called in. There were freshly baked chocolate chip cookies on a platter being held by a smiling and rotund French chef.

The chef was a mannequin.

These lifeless people inhabited every room of the house and were everywhere on the property, as if they were substitutes for friends that didn't exist.

I hadn't physically seen Michael in a few years and the anticipation was killing me. My heart was racing as I waited by the chocolate chip cookies, their sweet, buttery aroma tempting me to taste them. Just as I was about to give in to their charms, I was called in to the foyer.

And there he was . . .

In all of his iconic glory he stood, like an image from a magazine. He was in his full Michael Jackson regalia in front of his bedroom door. It was dimly lit and there were shadows of other statues, mannequins, books, and antiques surrounding him, making the entire scene surreal. He looked perfect and ready for the stage in a black shirt, sparkly tight black pants, and a silver sequined belt around his tiny waist. He was the epitome of a rock star. I instantly melted as all of my feelings came rushing back.

A knowing smile washed over both of our faces, like two friends who had shared forbidden secrets in a time almost forgotten. He staggered over to me and wrapped his long arms around me in a hug. It felt so good holding him close again. As I was lost in his arms, I smelled not only his ever-present perfume but also the distinctly strong scent of alcohol. His perfume could not mask that. It was now obvious why he was staggering. He was drunk. I was surprised. Then again, it was his birthday and he had every right to live a little. Perhaps he just wanted to enjoy his party. But I knew that Michael's personality wouldn't allow him to have just one drink. He did everything to the extreme. His intoxicated state became even more evident when he spoke.

"Sandy Gallin's office, remember that? And *Ghosts* . . ." Although he was excited to see me, he was slurring his words.

And then suddenly, he switched into a version of himself that could've only existed under the influence of something. Out of the blue, he said, "You were House's stuff weren't you?"

Appalled and hoping I was hearing him wrong, I said incredulously, "What did you say?"

"Yeah, you were House's stuff, admit it." He was speaking in an arrogant tone that I had never heard from him before, as he vulgarly readjusted his crotch area.

I was stunned. Just the fact that he had used the word *stuff* was disrespectful enough, but to accuse me of something so outlandish made me furious.

"Excuse me? What are you talking about? What do you mean 'House's *stuff*'? You know that's not true, Michael." My voice was seething in anger as I stared at him through indignant eyes. I had never spoken to him in this tone before. I'd always been pleasant and sweet, going along with all of the crazy drama he had created in the past. But we were both older now and better able to speak our minds. I was now thirty-three years old and not about to let him get away with this behavior.

He stepped back and blinked as if he had been struck with a right hook from a prize fighter. In an instant, I saw him literally snap back to reality. Hearing the unfamiliar anger in my voice must have made him realize he was being disrespectful and ridiculous. He started stuttering and became sweet, flirtatious Michael again.

"Oh, I'm just kidding," he nervously giggled. "I mean, *everybody* had a crush on you on that *Ghosts* set. I know I did."

"But Michael, you know that you were the only one I wanted."

I was trying to calm my voice back into its own sweetness. But I was still mad. My friend Tita and her son were witnessing this entire conversation, and it was awkward. There were so many unspoken words lingering in the air—so much that needed to be said—but this was not the time or place.

Was this his own way of making himself feel less guilty about the way things had ended? Perhaps his paranoia had gotten even worse. Or was he genuinely so insecure that he had deluded himself into believing I had cheated on him with his own assistant? Whatever the case, he shouldn't have waited seven years to bring this up. The alcohol, or whatever it was, had turned him into a different person with a whole new personality. I started to get a bad feeling about things. It was obvious he was on a reckless path.

After this exchange, he charmingly tried to smooth things over by inviting us to meet him in the arcade. He told me he was going to go there after he finished meeting with some other guests.

We walked out of the main house and headed back outside for the guesthouse that had been turned into a two-level arcade. As we waited for Michael, I took a look around. I had been to Neverland many times before but hadn't been in this particular room in years. The arcade had every pinball machine and video game you could imagine. All of the classic ones like Pac-Man, Centipede, and Donkey Kong were there, as well as new ones. Best of all—none of them required coins. They were all free, just like everything else on the property. The high-beamed dark wooden ceilings reminded me of a ski chalet, which was in the same architectural style as the main house.

Not long after I arrived, teen pop stars Nick and Aaron Carter showed up along with my longtime friend music producer Rodney Jerkins. Rodney had produced several songs on Michael's last album, *Invincible*, and he and I had become close friends over the years. I had visited Record One Studios in Sherman Oaks a few times during his sessions with Michael for the album and was a comforting ear for him when he was being pushed to impossible perfection by Michael. Michael was going through a particularly dark time during that era, with his addictions back in full swing. Many sessions had to be canceled because Michael would show up at the studio in no condition to sing, or wouldn't show up at all. Rodney was a God-fearing nice guy who had never even tasted alcohol or tried drugs, a rarity in the treacherous music industry. Michael loved those qualities about him.

This was obviously going to be a private, invite-only arcade visit—everyone else was made to wait outside. Michael strutted in shortly after we arrived. It was impossible not to stare at his face. Every time I saw him it seemed like something was different about it. This time, it looked like a pristine porcelain doll. It was so perfect it appeared unreal. His big brown eyes were surrounded by thin black eyeliner and enhanced by long, fluttery lashes.

We all gathered around and Nick Carter challenged Michael to a game. I think it was football. As Michael was playing, he kept saying that he wasn't very good at this particular game and that he knew Nick would beat him. He was right.

Michael was the perfect host, making sure everyone had a great time. We were all very happy to be able to share this private moment with him for his birthday. He seemed content to be among familiar faces and trusted friends—laughing and joking like old times.

Sadly, this would be the last time he would be able to celebrate his birthday—or anything else—at Neverland. Soon everything would change again, as it always did.

As day fell into night, a large white tent had been erected near the amusement park rides. The entire crowd of guests was told to gather in the tent to present Michael with a birthday cake. They stirred with excited anticipation awaiting Michael's entrance. He hadn't made an appearance yet at the actual party, so this would be the first time the partygoers would see him.

I stood next to him at the entrance of the tent as he waited to be introduced to the crowd. The screams made him bounce up and down with unbounded glee. He could barely contain his energy and joy. He was fired up. The love from the crowd seemed to infuse him with undeniable happiness. He was truly and genuinely ecstatic to hear how feverishly everyone was anticipating his arrival. It was a beautiful thing to witness. He thrived off of this adulation from the public. It's what kept him going when times were tough. His fans were truly the loves of his life.

He was in a good mood with boundless energy, but still there was a glazed emptiness in his eyes and it worried me. That magnetic sparkle that they used to have was no longer there.

I left around midnight to make the long, dark drive back to L.A. Although it had been a wonderful event and it was great to see Michael, a sense of sadness was all I could feel. I just couldn't help but think that fame had finally changed him. He had fought fame's cruel price valiantly his entire life, but now it seemed it had finally won. Although he seemed happy, I could tell there was something not right. This just wasn't the same Michael I had once loved. He was still kind and friendly to everyone, but he now had an edge bubbling just below the surface. Most people probably wouldn't have noticed it, but I had been dealing with him for so long I could always tell when things weren't quite right. He owned a piece of my heart and I could always feel if something was wrong. A pervasive sense of doom and sadness stayed with me for the entire two-and-a-half-hour drive home, and for weeks after. Something was about to give—I could feel it.

21

Success, fame, fortune—they're all illusions. All there is that is real, is the friendship two can share.

—Michael Jackson in *The Wiz*

Two months later, in November 2003, seventy deputies from the Santa Barbara police department descended upon Neverland Valley Ranch, search warrants in hand, investigating every inch of it. They completely destroyed the once peaceful paradise, rifling through every nook and cranny, looking for evidence of child molestation. Another family had accused Michael of unspeakable acts. I couldn't believe it. *Not again . . .*

Michael was arrested for lewd and lascivious acts upon a minor and supplying alcohol to a child. After the hell he had gone through with the allegations in 1993, I couldn't believe he would put himself in a position to be accused again. I was sad and mad at him at the same time. Seeing him being escorted to jail in handcuffs absolutely broke my heart. I felt so helpless. The stark realization that Michael could actually go to jail hit me like an avalanche. Tears streamed down my face as the endless breaking news reports dramatically covered every angle.

I couldn't believe they had actually handcuffed him. I felt like they were just trying to humiliate him. With all of Michael's unpredictable and erratic behavior, having sex with children was just not something that I would ever believe was in his nature. No one close to Michael believed it. I asked everyone who was around during the time the accusing family was at Neverland and everyone agreed that these allegations were a joke.

I've been around Michael when he was with children and he was truly like a peer to them. Sleeping in the same bed with them was highly inappropriate, of course, but it was all innocent fun to him. He wasn't a sexual predator waiting for the right moment to strike. He was haunted by a lot of inner demons and issues, but I don't believe that being a child molester was one of them. He clearly had an unnatural obsession with childhood, but he was genuinely attracted to women, not children. I think I would be a pretty good judge of that. He just wasn't your typical rock-star womanizer running around with a bunch of random girls. He was different and that shouldn't be vilified. It should be applauded.

Michael freely admitted he loved boyhood and being around children. So there was never a sense he was hiding anything. In fact, he was way more secretive dealing with me than he ever was with these kids. His whole mission in life was to stand up for the children of the world and to be a champion for them. He focused a lot of his attention on these boys and their families and when that attention started to dissipate, the parents would become upset. In the past, I had parents beg me to introduce their sons to Michael and some would try to push for him to spend more time with their child. It was like a competition with some of these parents. They knew that kids were his weakness and that he couldn't say no. The parents used that to their advantage. Some of the little boys who were close to Michael remain my friends today and they all still love and support him as adults. That, to me, says it all.

After hearing all of the lurid allegations and seeing none of his so-called friends stand up to support him, I decided I couldn't keep quiet any longer. It had been a decade since the first set of allegations surfaced and I wasn't able to speak out then. I always regretted not making a statement. I was one of the few people in contact with him during that time and I knew what was in his heart. I wasn't going to let this moment pass without setting the record straight about the Michael I knew. His image was in shambles and I couldn't sit back and remain quiet any longer. The world needed to know that there was a human being lost in all of the speculation and crazy media stories.

I contacted my friend in public relations and I was booked to tape an interview on *Entertainment Tonight.* Other than my interview in

Hawaii during the HIStory tour, this would be my first time sitting in front of cameras discussing Michael.

I was nervous and didn't know how he would react once he found out. Host Bob Goen interviewed me for about forty-five minutes, and they edited the most explosive sound bites into a three-minute segment. I was dubbed Michael's "secret girlfriend" in the interview, and I told the world that he was a normal, red-blooded man. I didn't go into any details because I knew Michael would not be happy if I did. Some speculated that he or his camp had put me up to giving this interview to repair his tarnished image, but that couldn't be further from the truth. I did it on my own. In fact, after the interview aired the next day, I received a message from Michael asking me not to do any more interviews. He said he was embarrassed and didn't want me pulled into the media circus that was swirling out of control. Although I was more than willing to put my own reputation and privacy on the line to help him, he still wanted to keep me a secret.

I didn't agree with a lot of his decisions. I never understood why he would prefer to constantly promote his love of childhood, be seen with little boys by his side, climb trees, or admit to sleeping in bed with kids instead of having me reveal that he was actually normal. It was as if he would rather the public think of him as an eccentric Peter Pan than to appear to be the man he was. If he had only presented his true self to the world, I think a lot of his problems would have never existed.

Although Michael was embarrassed, he said he was grateful that I was willing to stand up for him and be there in full support once again. I couldn't imagine not being there for him. No matter what had happened in the past, my love for him would never die. Although I had managed to contain it, that flame was still burning deeply.

A couple weeks after the interview, my old friend Nicole, who was still working with Michael closely, called to ask if I would help her organize an event at Neverland for Michael. He hadn't returned to his home since it had been so recklessly raided and this event would be a welcome back home of sorts. Apparently he was deeply depressed and this would help lift his spirits. She told me we had two weeks to plan this special event because it needed to be scheduled before Christmas. It was already the end of November, but I was more than happy to accept the challenge. We enlisted Jackson family publicist Angel Howansky and Michael's nephew Taj to help. They were both wonderful, offering to help in any way they could. We all cared deeply for Michael and wanted this event to be a success. We had daily conference calls figuring out how to pull this off in a matter of weeks.

I was given the task of calling all of Michael's celebrity friends to invite them. I was pretty familiar with the people who had claimed to be his friends in the past, or whom Michael had considered friends, so I made a list and called them all. I called some directly with phone numbers that Nicole had given me from Michael's contact list and contacted the publicists of the other celebrities whom I didn't have private numbers for. They all had excuses as to why they wouldn't be able to attend. None of them came.

I asked my old friend comedian Tommy Davidson, who was best known for his role on the sketch-comedy show *In Living Color*, to host the event. Having been a lifelong Michael Jackson fan, he jumped at the chance and did a great job.

In the end, the event was a success, with a great turnout of both fans and celebrities . . . but almost none who had previously been visible and known to the public as Michael's friend. Most of them had turned their backs on him during this, his darkest hour. It had never been clearer that Hollywood was filled with fake friends and phony people. Everybody wants to bask in your light when it's shining, but when the darkness arrives they're nowhere to be found.

When I arrived at Neverland for the event, the first person to greet me was Michael's oldest sister, Rebbie. She walked over to where I was standing and introduced herself to me, embracing me in a warm hug. I suppose she had seen my *Entertainment Tonight* interview. "Thank you so much for being there for my brother. I've heard so much about you! You are even prettier in person," she gushed. "I'm so happy you're here today. I've been wanting to meet you to tell you how much we appreciate you."

I was taken aback by her kindness. She had the same warm, gentle, and sweet personality that Michael possessed. Tears came to my eyes as she stood in front of me telling me how thankful she was. The Jackson family had been world famous for decades and yet they were still some of the nicest people you could ever meet. A couple of his brothers also introduced themselves to me and thanked me. I was stunned that they knew about me at all.

Michael was there too . . . barely. He arrived in a private bus and was welcomed with open arms by his staff and guests. The air was crisp and California cold on this dark winter's night in Neverland Valley. Michael was so heavily sedated he could barely walk. His steps were slow and measured like that of an old man. He wore dark sunglasses the entire time, even though the sun had already set. It was obvious he was going through hell—and this was well before his trial even started. He looked frail. He was always skinny but he appeared to be at least ten pounds lighter than usual. It just made me so sad to see him like this. He looked utterly defeated—all of the vibrant life he once had had been sucked out of him. The old bubbly Michael was completely gone. It was like witnessing a dead man walking. I'm not sure if he even knew where he was.

His entire family sat in the front row of seats that had been arranged for the show we had put together. Michael sat stoically in the middle, clearly in another world, sometimes forcing a smile at Tommy Davidson's funny jokes and impressions. All of the Neverland staff took the stage in their various work uniforms and gave speeches telling Michael how much they loved working for him. It was touching.

As the night ended, I was taken to a van where Michael was waiting to leave the premises. He had gone straight to this van after the show was over, not wanting to stay any longer at his former dream home than he had to. The raid had made him feel violated. Neverland now represented bad memories for him. He could no longer call it home.

When I reached the van, Michael was sitting there all alone. It was the saddest sight I had ever seen. Here was this once great superstar who had reigned on top of the universe for decades, sitting there looking like he hadn't a friend in the world. He had hit rock bottom.

I ignored the lump in my throat, trying to put on a happy face. But when I saw him sitting there, all alone in the dark, I was unable to fake it. This was simply awful. My mind raced trying to think of what I could possibly say to comfort him. Seeing me, he opened the door of the van and reached out his hand. I grabbed it and held it tight. Even his hand felt lifeless, rough and cold. His usual bright smile was missing and he couldn't even pretend to be happy. I tried to muster a smile, but as I spoke my voice cracked.

"I love you, Michael." It was the one thing I knew he needed to hear and all that I knew was real at that moment.

"Thank you. Thank you so much for everything. I love you too." His voice was soft and barely audible, as if he would cry if he spoke too much.

"I miss you. And I'm here for you always." Unable to hold back my emotions, tears formed in my eyes.

"I miss you too." Sadness engulfed his every word and his entire body.

We had said these words before, a decade ago. I was younger then and more naive. But we *both* were. The weight of the last ten years had taken its toll on Michael, and the pain was etched all over his face. He had never fully recovered. I suppose I hadn't either. So much had happened—I think it was easier to pretend like none of it had ever occurred. But seeing Michael like this reminded me of it all. And through all of it, somehow I was still there, holding his hand.

22

you take
a lover who looks at you
like maybe you are magic.

—Marty McConnell, "Frida Kahlo
to Marty McConnell"

Michael endured a long criminal trial and was found not guilty of all charges. The damage, however, was done. It was irreversible. Although he prided himself on being strong, that trial was his kryptonite. I don't think any human being could have emerged unscathed. He left the United States and remained out of the country for over a year.

I went on with my life, continuing to work in entertainment. But once again, fate would bring Michael and I back together.

"I would like to offer you the position of my personal touring assistant. Would you be able to relocate to Las Vegas by next week?"

The offer came from legendary magician David Copperfield. I had been flown out to the MGM Grand in Las Vegas to interview for the position after sending him my résumé. I'd met David many years before when he was working with Michael on some illusions for the Dangerous tour and we had become friends then. It had been years since I had seen him.

The first part of the interview was to sit front and center to watch his magic show. I was in heaven. I had been a fan of David's ever since he had his yearly TV specials back in the early '80s. My parents and I would sit with bated breath in anticipation of each magnificent illusion and every year they became more and more elaborate. We watched him make the Statue of Liberty disappear and vanish a 747 airplane. No other magician at that time was doing these kinds of large-scale productions. David was a pioneer in his field.

In my teens and early twenties, I was still a fan. I started recording all of David's specials. Obsessed with figuring out how each illusion was created, I'd watch each one over and over again in slow motion. I even started hanging out at the Magic Castle in Hollywood just to be around the world of magic. I would say I loved magic just as much as I loved music. So the prospect of working closely with another of my childhood idols was intriguing.

After watching the show, I met with David in his dressing room. He had seen my résumé beforehand and remembered my time at Sandy Gallin's office. I was hired on the spot. Another crazy adventure was about to begin.

On New Year's Eve 2006, I received a call from Nicole asking if Michael could come to that night's show with his children. She said that she knew it would make him happy to see me. I couldn't believe that he was back in the country, let alone in Vegas. It seems we had both moved there at the same time. The thought of seeing Michael again, on the first New Year's Eve I've ever had to work, instantly made the entire day better. We were going to have three shows that day, back to back, and I wasn't looking forward to it. One show was grueling enough, but three was exhausting. I had to be on my feet for the entire show, helping David transition into each illusion, as well as monitoring the audience for participants for the tricks. The days and weeks were long—sixteen hours a day, seven days a week. I felt like I was never really off the clock, because I also lived at the MGM Grand, where David's show had a residency. A smoky, cold casino filled with flashing lights and noisy, drunk tourists was basically my living room. It was a surreal and seemingly glamorous existence for sure. But it got old quickly. Michael's presence would surely make it better. David reserved the best table in the house for Michael, front and center.

Las Vegas on New Year's Eve is like no other place in the world. Crowds converge from all walks of life to be a part of this hedonistic celebration. Lights are impossibly bright, alcohol is flowing, people are everywhere, and everybody seems drunk off the energy. Everything is done to the extreme in Vegas. There's a reason why they say "what happens in Vegas, stays in Vegas." There was something about it that tempted you to be wilder and more carefree than you normally would.

Nicole gave me the number of Michael's main bodyguard, a gentleman named Bashir, and we coordinated Michael's arrival. I didn't think that happy times like this would ever exist again for Michael, but he had somehow managed to put the trauma of his criminal trial behind him and was seemingly back on track to being king of the world once again.

He arrived in a blue Lincoln Navigator being driven by one of his bodyguards. I waited by the backstage entrance, anticipating the moment I would see the man who had once been my entire world. I hadn't seen him since that last sad time at Neverland, before the trial, so this felt like a long overdue reunion.

I was the only member of David's staff allowed to interact with Michael. In fact, it became my only duty for the night, which was a welcomed relief. Usually on show nights my job was to solely be with David and it could be exhausting. On this last night of 2006, however, Michael was my only focus.

He walked in accompanied by his three children—Prince, Paris, and Blanket—along with his friend Omer Bhatti, who was from Norway. Omer had met Michael during the HIStory tour as a young fan and had become like family to him over the years. He was now in his twenties and was a talented dancer in his own right. Michael was wearing all black and was back to looking healthy and sexy. The moment I saw him, I could feel those old butterflies wildly flapping their wings in my stomach.

It took such a long time to get over him . . . I can't let the overwhelming presence of this man suck me back in . . .

And then our eyes met. His big, bright smile was back. His eyes swept over my entire body, looking it up and down, and he wrapped me in his arms.

"You're still looking good," he said. "Damn. You haven't aged a day." Like a phoenix risen from ashes, old Michael had returned.

I smiled and blushed. "Thank you, Michael. You still look good too."

He always knew exactly what a girl wanted to hear. Only he could make me feel this way. I was almost thirty-seven years old and happy to hear I hadn't aged. He still had that way of looking at me that sent shivers down my spine—making me feel special and intensely wanted. I regressed back to feeling like a schoolgirl whenever I was around him—shy and nervous.

I don't know why the public ever assumed he was asexual. His entire aura reeked of sex. Everything about him was sexual. He had a certain power that not very many men have. I've lived in Hollywood for most of my life and met all of the sexy hunks idolized by women. None could even come close to the magnetic allure that Michael possessed. I had witnessed grown men considered to be hardened thugs reduced to tears when meeting Michael. He was that powerful.

The chemistry between us was so thick, you could cut it with a knife. He was staring and smiling, just like he used to. I could swear nothing had changed. I was transported back to Gallin Morey, fifteen years before, when life was simple and love was still a glorious dream. He was on top of the world—an untouchable superstar. I was just a young girl falling in love. For a moment, I was lost in that memory of a time so far away and long ago.

He introduced me to his children and Omer. I couldn't believe that Michael was now a father of three children. It was weird to think of him being somebody's father. Although he was nearly fifty, he was still like a kid himself.

His children were amazing. Prince was the oldest and almost ten years old. Mature, wise, and beyond intelligent for his age, he was the serious one. He discussed in detail with me how he thought some of the tricks were done. He had an analytic, scientific mind and had all the makings of a genius. Michael and I looked at each other and smiled as Prince continued with his deep analysis.

Paris, on the other hand, was like a princess—eight years old and a pure girly girl—sweet, polite, friendly, and talkative.

Whenever I spoke, she'd look up at me with the deepest-blue eyes I had ever seen. They possessed the innocence and curiosity that could only belong to a child. She was the most outgoing of the three and a true sweetheart.

And then there was Blanket. He was four years old—impossibly cute and incredibly shy, with silky, long, straight black hair and curled eyelashes that extended for miles. Adorable and well trained, he did not speak to strangers.

I gave them each a program from the show and a stuffed duck, which was featured in one of the illusions. They were all very polite, remembering to say thank you. David asked them each for their names so that he could personally autograph the programs. When David got to Blanket, he asked for his name. Blanket would not say a word. He looked up at Michael with his big eyes, silently asking for approval.

"It's OK. You can tell him your name," Michael assured him. Blanket would not say a word until he got that approval from his dad. Michael couldn't help but smile proudly.

"My name is Blanket." His voice matched his looks—angelic, cute, and innocent. I glanced up at Michael and placed my hand on my heart. David smiled.

Even though Michael had been through hell in the past few years, he had managed to raise the most intelligent, polite, and friendly kids possible. He was a great father, it was clear. And Michael was the center of their world. They all looked up to him with respect and admiration. The love between him and his children was palpable.

After the introductions were out of the way, Michael immediately asked the question that was always most important to him. "Where's the bathroom?"

He had made the bathroom his first stop at every meeting or event I had ever attended. Some things never change.

I grabbed his hand and started walking him to the bathroom that was located behind the stage, in David's dressing room. As I guided him through the cluttered backstage area, stepping over illusions that were waiting in the dark, Michael's overbearing bodyguard, Bashir, stopped us.

"Nobody moves anywhere until I say it's all clear!"

Michael and I looked at each other with feigned scared expressions and started laughing as we shook our heads. Bashir seemed to be trying too hard to prove that he was good at his job. I mean, what threat could possibly be lurking backstage at a magic show? Michael told him it was OK and not to worry about it.

As I continued walking him to the bathroom, he excitedly started reminiscing about the filming of *Ghosts*. It had been over a decade since we filmed it, but every moment was clearly still vividly etched in his mind. Aside from his children being born, it was probably one of his few happy memories in the past ten years. It made me happy that he looked back on those times with such joy. Every time I had seen him or spoken to him within those last ten years, *Ghosts* was always the first topic of conversation.

"We had so much fun on that set, didn't we?" Michael said with the enthusiasm of a child reminiscing about his favorite Christmas toy.

"We sure did. I wish we could've stayed there forever."

"Me too . . . " Michael's voice trailed off as if he were thinking back on all of the tough times he had endured since then.

If only we could rewind the hands of time . . .

Whenever he mentioned *Ghosts*, I knew he was also remembering all of the other moments we had spent together during those days. We both were too embarrassed to ever actually mention that part of the experience in front of others, but it was impossible to not think of one without the other. We shared a silent understanding and I had proven my loyalty to him by never telling anyone, as he had requested. Perhaps I was also one of the few people who had not stabbed him in the back and he appreciated that. Whatever the case, talking about *Ghosts* made him happy. It made me happy too.

By the time we reached the bathroom, Michael had managed to recount every funny moment we had shared on that set. I had forgotten some of it myself. It warmed my heart to see him back to normal like this. He was clear and present and his memory was sharp. That bubbly personality was back, along with everything else that was the essence of Michael. He had survived the toughest time of his life and was still there standing like a king. That amazing man I had loved so deeply was still there.

I decided to wait until the lights dimmed to take Michael and the kids to their table. I didn't want the raucous New Year's Eve audience to see him and bother him for autographs or pictures. Once the lights dimmed and the show started, the audience would be distracted enough to not notice him walking to his seat at all. One thing I had learned from David was that it was easy to distract an audience's attention. You have to make them focus on one thing while the real action is going on in a place they would least expect. Michael knew a thing or two about that.

Before taking him to his seat, I told Michael to make sure to wait until I came to get him when the show ended. David was going to do a special trick just for him, and he didn't want Michael to miss it. It was a trick that David only did on occasion as an encore—making a group of randomly chosen members of the audience disappear. It was a spellbinding illusion, but I always hated when we did it. Because there were so many variables, anything could easily go wrong. But then again, I was a worrywart. David had been performing magic for decades, so there was really no way anything could ever go wrong. He was a pro. Yet still, I was nervous every time we did it.

Michael asked me which trick it was that David was going to do. He told me he had seen the show several times before and wondered if it was a trick he had already seen. He mentioned a few other illusions he thought it might be, but I told him I wanted it to be a surprise. He was genuinely excited and curious to see what this special trick might be. He loved magic just as much as I did and had obviously studied it extensively.

The illusion went off without a hitch and I gathered Michael and his kids, walking them backstage. I walked to a dark corner, waiting for the entire party to make it safely back into the private area behind the stage. Michael followed me. He wrapped me in another hug, kissing me softly on the lips, and held me for what seemed like an eternity. I closed my eyes as we stood there, lost in our own world. It was one of those hugs you give someone when you know it'll be the last time.

The first fireworks of 2007 burst into an array of colors and sounds above the Las Vegas strip, and they were exploding inside of me as well. The intoxicating scent of Michael lingered well into the early hours of the New Year. I was due to leave with David for a tour across Canada and the West Coast of the United States in a couple days, but all I could think about was Michael. He had once again ignited that ray of hope within my soul. No matter how hard I tried, he still had me.

23

Uneasy lies the head that wears a crown.

—William Shakespeare

The big wheels of the bus turned as I lay in my small, curtained-off bunk bed—the wheels of my mind turning just as fast. I was traveling with David Copperfield on a luxurious tour bus across Canada and the West Coast, en route to our first city. We were scheduled to perform a sold-out show in a different city almost every night for the next two months.

It was January in Canada, the middle of winter. I had never felt air so cold. I'd lived in California for so long I had forgotten what winter actually felt like. A blanket of white snow paved every inch of the path as our bus trudged along the road. We would sometimes stay up late watching the snowstorm develop in front of us while watching movies like *The Prestige* to kill the time. David and his three other assistants rode on this bus. The rest of the crew was on two other buses. Part of my job was making sure the two live scorpions that were traveling with us stayed warm and didn't die. They were being kept in a container and were part of one of the card tricks in the show. I must say, that was one of the worst parts of the job.

We hadn't really had a chance to discuss Michael's visit yet. Things moved so fast—these long bus rides were really the only time we had to talk.

David finally broached the subject, politely asking if Michael and I had dated in the past. The other assistants had been wondering too.

I had been so lost in those moments with Michael that I hadn't realized how others must have perceived us. You know how you can often tell if two people have been intimate just by observing their body language and reactions to each other? Or by how they look at each other? It's almost always a dead giveaway. Well, apparently everyone had seen these clues with us. The intense magnetic pull that Michael and I had was difficult to ignore, even after all of those years.

I just smiled and said, "No comment," which pretty much answered the question. I couldn't even bring myself to lie at this point. It was all too obvious. I think the years we had been apart had made that attraction and pull even more heightened, if that was possible.

After I returned from the David Copperfield tour, I moved back to L.A. and started working for Simon Fuller's 19 Entertainment, the producers of *American Idol.* I was responsible for the day-to-day management of *Idol* winners Fantasia Barrino and Ruben Studdard. I had always been a fan of the show, so it was yet another one of those dream jobs.

Amazingly, Michael moved back to L.A. at about the same time as I did. Once you have lived in L.A., it's difficult to stay away. Los Angeles was like a toxic ex-lover. You knew it was bad for you, but you just had to keep coming back to try it again, hoping this time would be different. The City of Angels appeared like a perfect paradise on the surface, but underneath lay a land filled with con artists and sharks. Everybody had their own hustle, only looking out for themselves. It was the boulevard of broken dreams, no doubt. But when you're in the entertainment industry, L.A. is the place to be.

When I heard Michael had moved back and taken up residence at an opulent mansion on Carolwood Drive in Beverly Hills, I was excited but worried. I just didn't think he was mentally ready to face this town of charlatans.

In 2008 Michael's presence could be felt all over L.A. This was his town—he had grown up here and, despite my worries, it was nice to have him back.

He had started making plans for a big comeback, one that involved movies. His dream was to create and star in films. Music and everything else had taken a backseat to this passion. *Ghosts* had been the last time he had produced and acted in a film and he was itching to get back on the big screen. The last time we spoke in Vegas, he had mentioned that his dream was to do a project on King Tut's life. King Tut and the Egyptian pyramids had always fascinated him.

Michael's friends told me that he was now suffering from depression. I figured that being able to embark on that King Tut project might brighten his spirits. Hoping to save the day, I started calling all of my industry friends to gauge interest in funding such a project with Michael involved. No one was interested. When I excitedly pitched the project to some of my high-powered Hollywood friends, they all said that Michael was too unpredictable and unreliable. He was considered a risky investment. Now I understood why he was depressed. Getting his career back on track, as well as his finances, was not going to be easy.

As I walked into the defunct Robinsons-May department store on Wilshire Boulevard, which sat directly next door to the iconic Beverly Hilton hotel, an eerie feeling of dread swept through me. I turned to my old friend, music producer Rodney Jerkins, who I had run into upon entering, "Is it me, or does it feel like Michael died?"

"No, its not you. That's exactly how it feels," Rodney agreed.

But Michael was still very much alive.

It was April 2009, and the department store was huge—and every inch of it was covered in Michael's personal items, taken directly from Neverland. The arcade games Rodney and I had once played with Michael at his birthday party were sitting there in front of us. The pimped-out black van I had once kissed Michael in was there too, staring at me like an apparition from a distant past. All of the special-effect masks from *Ghosts* were there. It was like my entire life with Michael was sitting before me to remind me of the good times we had once shared.

An overwhelming sense of doom followed me as I walked around inspecting all of the items. Tears enveloped my eyes. This felt like a funeral for Neverland—its entirety sitting in this cold, abandoned department store. I couldn't believe it had come to this.

Michael's new financial adviser, Dr. Tohme Tohme, had arranged for the entire contents of Neverland to be auctioned off. This display was for potential buyers to see the items available for sale. His reasoning was that Michael needed money, and this was the only way to get it. The property itself was also on the market.

Neverland was a place created from every fiber in Michael's soul. It was a place where time was suspended and the often-difficult real world didn't exist—a place that could have survived only with Michael's heartbeat. The entire pulse of the land lived off Michael's magic. It would now exist only in the minds of those of us fortunate enough to have experienced it. Sometimes it feels like it never existed at all, like it was a figment of my imagination. How could something so wonderful be no more? I truly believe that when Neverland was abandoned, Michael abandoned the childlike innocence that he viewed the world through as well. He had tried to cling so long to his myopic view of the world as a beautiful work of art, believing that he could turn back the hands of time and have the perfect childhood he never had. Back then, he truly believed in the magic and mysteries of life. He believed in the beauty of trees, flowers, birds, flowing streams, and animals. Neverland transported him to another place and made him forget there was a real world out there somewhere. And now it was gone. It's not hard to guess why he was feeling depressed.

To me, there had to be a better way than selling Neverland and all of its contents to get quick cash. This shouldn't have even been a possibility. Michael, I was told, was not aware of the auction until the last minute—clear evidence that his life had become a runaway train, every day bringing new unbelievable drama.

Rodney and I were in the middle of surveying the items when we both received a text at the same time informing us that Michael had managed to stop the auction. The items wouldn't be sold after all. A wave of relief engulfed my entire body. I was so happy.

Sadly, however, the madness didn't stop. The next two months would bring an avalanche of daily craziness. A pervasive feeling of doom filled the air all around Beverly Hills and that house on Carolwood Drive. Something bad was bound to happen—and I tried to figure out a way to stop it.

The warning bells had already starting ringing the month before, when Michael appeared in London at the O2 Arena to announce an upcoming tour called This Is It. He had appeared to be under the influence of something, slurring his words and not acting like himself. His behavior was so unusual that some had speculated it wasn't Michael at all. Many fans had never seen him like that before—talking in a deeper voice and carrying a cockiness he usually didn't display. I, however, had no doubt that it was him. This was exactly how he had acted when I was with him at Neverland at his birthday party. I suspected alcohol was the culprit at the press conference, just as it had been at Neverland. It made him act differently from how he'd acted on prescription pain medication. I'd grown to recognize the different personalities in Michael that each substance created. After almost twenty years, I was an expert.

That same month, *American Idol* had a Michael Jackson week. The idols performed only Michael's songs and many of his former background singers and band mates were there in attendance. I was still working for 19 Entertainment, the producers of the show, attending the show every week, and I was excited to be a part of this special show. I invited my old friend Nicole, who had still been working for Michael up until recent weeks. We had both started in Michael's world the same year—way back in the early '90s. Dr. Chopra had introduced us back then, thinking we would be a good support system for each other. Life in that world could drive anyone crazy and it was nice to have someone of a like mind to bounce the day's craziness off. After almost twenty years, we were still close friends.

After the show was over, Nicole and I had the bright idea to call Michael. He had been feeling down and we thought that maybe hearing from a few familiar voices might brighten his spirits. I ran onto the *Idol* set, pushing past hopeful contestants, and rounded up every former background singer and band member of Michael's I could find. I gathered singers Dorian Holley, Siedah Garret, and Darryl Phinnessee, as well as Michael's longtime musical director Greg Phillinganes. When I returned with them, Nicole had Michael on the phone. She handed Siedah the phone first. The look on her face when she heard Michael's voice on the other end of the phone was priceless. She was filled with joy. Dorian was next and then Darryl and Greg. They all excitedly told Michael that they hoped to be a part of the new tour, which had just been announced. When it was my turn to talk to Michael, Nicole quickly disconnected the call before we could speak. She said, "Aww, I'm sorry. I forgot to let you talk." I was seething. Michael had always warned me not to trust her and now I was wondering if he was right. I had always given her the benefit of the doubt because we had been friends so long, but this incident made me wonder.

Although the band members were all of the same faces from way back in my days on the Dangerous tour, the hopeful feeling of those days was gone. I felt in my heart that this tour would never make it to that London stage at the O2 Arena. It was scheduled to start in just four months and there was no way Michael could be mentally ready in that amount of time.

I had experienced the preparation for both of Michael's previous world tours over the last two decades. Even during those times when life hadn't taken as much of a toll on him, it was difficult for him to make it to the stage on many nights. The criminal trial had just happened a few years before and it was clear to me that he still hadn't recovered from it. But Michael had signed the contract. There was no way out.

Tohme Tohme had fired everyone who had once surrounded Michael, including Nicole. Michael claimed he didn't know anything about any of the firings, blaming it all on Dr. Tohme. "It's not my fault," he said. He had a habit of placing the blame on others so that no one could ever be mad at him. Michael's old manager from the '80s Frank DiLeo was also back. He seemed to be keeping Frank at a distance though.

A month after the *Idol* show, rehearsals for the This Is It tour started in Burbank at CenterStaging. Because I had worked previously with Michael and most of the tour staff, I had a standing invite to attend.

It was a hot May day in Burbank when I decided to attend my first rehearsal. It was heartwarming to meet all of the new young dancers, some of whom had just been born when we embarked on the previous tours. Everyone was buzzing around, talking excitedly about the apartments that were being rented for them in London, and not believing their luck to have been chosen for a Michael Jackson tour.

I hung with my friends Dorian Holley and Darryl Phinnessee in the singer's room. Two new singers had been added as well, including Judith Hill, who had taken Siedah Garrett's place. On a portable boom box, Dorian played the backing tracks to all of the songs from the previous tours to teach the others the harmonies. I sat there helping them with lyrics that the newer members weren't familiar with. Production manager Kenny Ortega came into the room to greet me. He instantly remembered me from the Sandy Gallin days and told me how happy he was to see me. Kenny had been working with Michael since the Dangerous tour. It was like one big happy reunion. All of the familiar faces were back and everyone was happy and excited.

Michael was there too, in the room next to us. I could hear the music to all of his hit songs loudly thumping through our wall. He had two bodyguards, including Alberto Alvarez, sitting in front of the door waiting for him to finish. I had seen daily reports on TMZ of Michael leaving Dr. Arnold Klein's office, and he appeared frail and out of it. I had also been getting daily calls from Nicole and other friends who were on the inside, and they were panicking. I had even spoken to one of Michael's longtime doctors and he told me that he was deeply worried. Everybody knew something was wrong, but nobody seemed to know what to do about Michael because Michael had shut everybody out.

I remember receiving a call from Nicole that same week. She was crying hysterically. "Shana, why is he so mean?" I was shocked at the anger in her voice. She could barely get her words out as she tried to speak through her tears. Michael had hired her back to work for him and it only lasted one day. She was sitting in her car in front of the Carolwood house when she called. "First,

Michael called and yelled at me for telling the chef what time to start work this morning. He told me that I had no authority and had no right to tell anybody what to do. He was also mad that I had given her my number. He didn't want us gossiping about him. And then, out of the blue, he asked me why I had so many Facebook friends! He told me that none of them were really my friends and that they were only my friends because of him."

"That's actually kind of funny, Nicole. He probably wasn't serious. Maybe he was kidding."

"No, that's not it," she sobbed. "After I hung up with Michael, I went to the kids. I hugged them and told them I loved them. They asked if I was quitting. I told them that I didn't want to but that their daddy was upset and that I'd help him find somebody to take my place. Prince told me he had to go to the bathroom, and when he came back he had his cell phone in his hand, 'My dad wants to speak to you . . . ' He had called Michael and told him everything I had said."

Reluctantly, she took the phone from Prince and, sure enough, it was Michael on the other end. He was on his way home from rehearsal. He screamed at her at the top of his lungs, "Why are you involving my kids in this?"

She told him that she had never had the chance to say goodbye to them before and she wanted to make sure she did this time. He screamed, "Are you quitting? You're lucky you work for me. I'm nice. If you worked for Barbra Streisand or Diana Ross, they would've kicked your ass!"

By this time, Nicole was crying.

"Why are you getting emotional?" he asked.

"Because I'm sick of this shit! And you know you're the one who fired me, not Tohme! Admit it! I can't take anymore of your shit!"

"Can you believe she's cursing at me?" he asked his driver.

She said that he called her back ten minutes later to apologize for yelling at her, asking if she was OK. He ended the conversation with a sweet and calm "God bless you."

I tried to make her feel better by telling her that Michael was probably just stressed out over the upcoming shows in London. He was clearly on edge and easily agitated because of the immense pressure he was under. She had been calling me every day prior to this expressing her hopes of getting her job back, so this turn of events was devastating for her. In the past, she had been so worried about his drug use that she had attempted to stage several interventions involving his family. These interventions never succeeded though, because he would always find out about them beforehand and become upset. I wondered though, if she felt he was so bad, why did she want so desperately to work for him again?

She had suggested that I get in touch with him and offer my services to be his assistant or homeschool teacher for his kids. She said she would rather me be there, someone she trusted, than someone new. She gave me his number and also an e-mail where he received messages.

A few weeks before, I had taken her by the Carolwood house, prior to her being hired back, to show her where it was. At first she didn't want to see it, fearing she would be tempted to ring the gate bell and ask to be let in. But I explained to her that we had already driven by it numerous times without her knowing. It was located just off Sunset Boulevard, a route we traveled often to get to our favorite meditation spot in Pacific Palisades, Yogananda Gardens/ Self Realization Center. That morning I turned onto Carolwood Drive. "This is the house, Nicole. Right there behind those black iron gates."

A group of fans were gathered across the street, including an entire tour bus filled with tourists. Carolwood had become a popular spot for celebrity gawkers hoping to catch a glimpse of the most famous man on earth.

As I circled around the property, Nicole started saying a prayer out loud. "God, please protect my babies. Please watch over them and keep them safe." It was heartbreaking to witness. Because of Michael's weakening state of mind and the presence of Dr. Tohme, who was keeping everyone away, Nicole had become very worried for the children.

I called my former boss and friend Qadree El-Amin and begged him to call Michael.

"Qadree, you have to get back in Michael's life. Get on that tour somehow and ask to be the road manager. He no longer has Bill

Bray or Wayne Nagin. He needs someone there to protect him. Here's the number. Please call him." I pleaded as if my life depended on it. Qadree called Michael and left a message and so did I.

Michael's assistant ended up calling us both back separately. The assistant relayed a message that Michael would call me soon and that he was sending his love. I could hear Michael in the background relaying the message to the assistant. "Tell her I'll call her back soon. And tell her I love her!"

For Qadree, the assistant gave him Frank DiLeo's number and asked him to set up a meeting.

Qadree and Frank met at the Beverly Hilton about a week later. Qadree asked him how Michael was doing. Frank said that he was doing just fine.

"He's lying," I told Qadree as he recounted the conversation to me. "There's no way he's doing fine. He's just trying to make it seem like you're not needed there to protect him. If he doesn't have someone with him he can trust, he's not going to be able to do this tour. If he were his normal self, he would've called us both back personally. You know that." I don't know how I knew these things, but my instincts were always correct when it came to Michael. I had been dealing with this drama far too long not to know the outcome. Michael's life moved in patterns. This was the "summer before the big tour drama" that happened every single time.

Michael's father was also trying to get to Michael to free himself of the alleged negative forces of Dr. Tohme, who had become a villain in everyone's eyes at this point.

The week of June 15, 2009, Nicole called me again. She was frantic. "Shana, you have to go back to rehearsal. Please go this week if you can. Just write Michael a letter and offer to help him with the kids. You're the only person I trust with them and I know he trusts you."

"What if he doesn't want to see me?"

"He'll be happy to see you, Shana," Nicole pleaded. "Stop making excuses. Just go. The children need you . . . *Michael needs you . . .*"

That's all I needed to hear. I don't know how I kept getting pulled back into it all, but I was willing to do anything I could to help. "If we could only figure out a way to stop this tour," I responded. "All of the problems would be solved. He's not strong enough to do this. Why can't anyone else see this?"

The tour was scheduled to start in London in two weeks, which meant the days I would be able to attend rehearsal were dwindling. How on earth could I write a letter to this man within the next few days and ask to take care of his children? What would be the proper words to use? To me, this would be further embarrassment for him. I didn't want him to think that I felt he needed help. He had always been a very proud man. He wouldn't want me to think for a second that he was weak. On the other hand, I had known Nicole for twenty years and was certain she wouldn't ask me to do something this drastic unless it was a dire emergency.

I admit, I was trying to talk myself out of going and kept thinking of everything that could go wrong. I had an open invitation to attend rehearsals every day but I had only gone that one time in May. I don't know what held me back. I think it was because I knew Michael wouldn't want me to see him in the state he was in. I didn't want to see him that way either. I had seen him walking to his car at the one rehearsal I attended and I had never seen him look so frail. It was obvious something was wrong and it gave me a very bad feeling. I also felt that if he really wanted to see me, he would've called me himself. I didn't want to force myself on him. I was torn.

Nicole's words haunted me, however. I didn't even ask why she was so adamant that it was imperative I go to rehearsal as soon as possible. The tone of her voice was all I needed to hear. We had been through this type of drama before with him . . . but something about this felt different. Michael was different.

"Nicole, I wouldn't even know how to be a homeschool teacher for the kids. I don't have any training."

"I didn't have any training either. It's easy and I'll help you. There's a store on Wilshire where you can buy all of the school materials."

She also didn't know about the secret rendezvous Michael and I had shared in the past. Being around Michael in this different capacity might be a little awkward. He had never been my boss. The dynamics would be very different. I noticed he treated his employees much different from how he treated his friends. Clearly, he could be difficult to work for. In almost twenty years, he had never shown me that side of his personality. Sandy and Jim had a difficult time managing him at times, but he was always sweeter than pie with me—even with all the crazy drama we had gone through. He was an absolute dream to work with every day on *Ghosts,* which was probably the longest film production he had worked on in years. I also saw how he treated others on that set and everyone loved him. Maybe I was just blinded by love. It was definitely hard for me to wrap my mind around this latest, easily agitated version of Michael. How could he have changed so drastically? The stress of the tour had to be the culprit, I figured. Or perhaps it was just Nicole who pushed those buttons in him. Regardless of all of these thoughts running through my mind, I knew that I had to see him. I could no longer put it off. Nothing could be more important than helping Michael get his life back on track. I decided I would go to rehearsals, which were now at the Staples Center, and present a letter to him offering my help for the tour.

Every day of that week, I pulled out my notebook and tried to think of the words to tell Michael I wanted to help. I stared at those blank pages day after day.

I called Dorian Holley and asked him to leave my name with security at the Staples Center for Friday, June 26. I figured I'd give myself the full week to think of what to say in the letter. Wednesday, June 24 came and I spoke to Dorian, who was on a break from rehearsal.

"You're still coming on Friday right? Michael's here today and things are looking better." He had expressed concern to me in the days prior that Michael had good days and bad days . . . on the days he actually showed up.

"Yes, I'm coming for sure! I'll call you when I'm on my way on Friday." They were scheduled to leave for London the following week, but I still had the feeling that Michael would never set foot on that stage, that he would figure out a way to cancel the entire tour at the last minute. I had seen it happen before and his behavior had all the makings of a cancelation coming up. I started hoping that he would check himself into rehab again, or get some kind of help along those lines. It had worked before and it could work again. But he no longer had Sandy and Jim or any reputable person guiding him. Frank DiLeo was around, but he had been pretty much shut out. All of the people who might have saved Michael from himself in the past were gone. He was in a vulnerable place with seemingly no way out. Something drastic needed to be done.

24

I never dreamed you'd leave in summer.

—Stevie Wonder

June 25, 2009, started off like any other day.

I woke up to the California sun beaming brightly through the window in my apartment on Whitley Avenue in Hollywood. I had finally moved out of the valley to the "other side of the hill" and the heart of Hollywood, just off of Hollywood Boulevard.

I took my morning walk to Starbucks, stepping on the stars that lined the iconic street. I always loved taking this walk. It reminded me of how far I had come—from that young girl in Largo, Maryland, dreaming of moving to the land of the stars to now actually living here. Most of my dreams had actually come true. Sometimes I couldn't believe it myself.

Birds were chirping as the smell of frying bacon mixed with freshly brewed coffee wafted through the open doors of cafés cooking cheap breakfasts. Stores filled with Marilyn Monroe T-shirts, five-dollar sunglasses, and key chains with pictures of the Hollywood sign sat waiting for eager tourists willing to spend money on anything that bore the symbol of this boulevard of broken dreams.

I ordered a stronger drink than usual—a red eye (drip coffee with a shot of espresso). I figured I needed the extra boost to help motivate me to write that letter to Michael. I would be seeing him the next day, so I could no longer procrastinate.

I walked back home and pulled out my blank sheet of notebook paper. I had been staring at this page all week hoping words would magically come. *How do I convince Michael that I can help him?*

I turned on the morning news and saw breaking news interrupting the usually routine broadcast. I figured it would be another high-speed police chase—there seemed to be one every day. I turned up the volume on my television and waited with anticipation to see what this news might be.

The anchor had a sad tone in his voice, "Actress Farrah Fawcett has passed away at the age of sixty-two."

This was a shocker. Even though Farrah had been battling cancer for quite some time, I believed she would eventually beat it. She was a fighter.

I called my mother to tell her the news and we discussed the sadness of Farrah dying so young. My aunt Vera, who had taken me to New York to the Michael Jackson concert back in 1988, had also recently passed away from cancer at the young age of fifty-six. We both agreed that life was short and you never knew what tomorrow might bring.

I looked through my closet to find an outfit to wear the next day. Michael hadn't seen me since New Year's Eve in Las Vegas. I had to look my best. Of course, I couldn't find a thing in my closet so I decided to travel to my favorite mall, the Glendale Galleria. It wasn't often that I traveled to Glendale. There were closer malls. Today, however, I decided to venture farther out, hoping to find that perfect outfit. I had combed through all of the clothing stores near Hollywood that week and hadn't found a thing. The Glendale Galleria was huge; surely there would be something there.

I searched every store in Glendale, but was still not able to find anything I liked. As I was rummaging through the racks at Macy's, I received a text message from my friend Lonnell Williams.

"TMZ is reporting that Michael had a heart attack and he is being rushed to UCLA Medical Center."

I responded, "lol. Really? OK. I'll check out the website."

I had become so used to Michael dreaming up elaborate excuses to get out of things I just figured this was another one of those stunts.

I called Dorian Holley, who had been at rehearsal with him the night before. Maybe he would have more details.

"Hey, Dorian. Did you hear that Michael had a heart attack and he's being rushed to the hospital?"

"No, that can't be true. Where did you hear that?"

"It's on TMZ," I laughed.

"Why are you laughing?"

"Oh, Dorian, you know he's faking. I knew he would come up with something to get out of these concerts. I'm glad actually. I was so worried that he wouldn't be able to figure out a way to get out of this. This is perfect!"

Dorian wasn't so happy. He was looking forward to these shows. "Yeah, it can't be true. I was just with him last night. He was fine. I'm just going to head to rehearsal. Hopefully Michael will be there when I get there. I'll call Kenny Ortega and see if he's heard anything."

I then called Nicole, who was in Europe.

"Did you hear that Michael had a heart attack?"

"No. Where did you hear that?"

"It's on TMZ. This has to be his way of getting out of these concerts. I just spoke to Dorian and he said that Michael was fine at rehearsal last night. He's going there now to see if he can find out more information."

"Where are you?" she asked.

"I'm at Macy's in Glendale."

"Please go to the house on Carolwood and find out what's really going on. Can you go there now?"

"OK. I'll head over there."

I left the clothes that I was holding on the first available rack and bolted out the door. I hopped in my car and my mind was thinking a million thoughts as I merged onto the 134 freeway at Brand Boulevard. I called Dorian back to see if he had any updates.

"Kenny spoke to Frank DiLeo and things aren't looking good," Dorian said.

"What do you mean 'things aren't looking good'?"

"Frank is at the hospital. It's not looking good at all . . ."

I hung up the phone and suddenly things weren't so funny anymore. This seemed real. The tone of Dorian's voice was one of sadness and concern.

As I was passing by Forest Lawn Memorial Cemetery, my phone rang. It was my mother.

"Pull over to the side of the road." Her voice had a worried tone that I had never heard before.

I looked to my right and there was Forest Lawn. I couldn't pull over on the side of the freeway, so I took the exit that led to the cemetery. After I found a safe spot to park, I asked her what was wrong.

"We lost him, Shana."

"What do you mean?"

"TMZ is reporting that Michael has passed away. He's gone."

I responded with a nervous chuckle. "Are you sure? Maybe this is all a hoax. You know how the Internet has fake stories all of the time."

"I don't know, but it's on TMZ right now. Check for yourself."

Before I could check, Lonnell texted me again, "He died?"

No, this can't be true. I typed in the TMZ website on my cell phone, worried for the headline that might appear. It took forever to load.

MICHAEL JACKSON DEAD AT THE AGE OF 50.

No.

No. This just can't be true. Maybe he's faking his death to get out of these concerts. That's it! That has to be what it is. This was the only way and he figured out a way to do it.

I called Nicole back.

"Hello?" she answered, her voice riddled with the fear of what I might say.

"Did you hear?" I thought I had it all under control, but my voice broke and tears gushed out of my eyes. I couldn't even get the words out. It was too surreal to even say. "Did you hear the news?" I was full-on hysterical by this time. Nicole dropped the phone. She didn't need to hear me say those words. My tone of voice said it all.

Michael was gone.

The words we had been worried we would hear for months had become a reality.

I didn't know where to go or what to do.

So I just went home.

No need to go to Carolwood anymore.

"I never dreamed you'd leave in summer . . ."

Stevie Wonder was singing on the stage of the Staples Center, where Michael had danced his final step and sung his last song. His golden casket sat in front of me. And I cried.

I had been holding it together up until this point. But when Stevie sang those words, it hit me hard. I cried so hard a stranger next to me offered me a tissue. The lyrics expressed perfectly how I was feeling.

I never dreamed he would leave that summer.

There I sat, surrounded by Michael's family and friends. I looked in front of me and there was Janet, La Toya, Rebbie, Randy, Jermaine, Tito, Marlon, and Jackie—we were all there together, just like at Neverland six years before. Except there was Michael—*in a casket.* How did we get here?

My mind flashed back to being seventeen years old at the Helmsley Palace in New York. The Jackson family seemed like untouchable icons back then. And here I sat, together with them, mourning their brother's death. Michael was the king of the world then—young and handsome, full of dreams, hopes, and laughter. Everything was possible then. And now it was all over. No longer would there be any hope. This was truly *it.* The roller coaster of everything we had gone through finally halting to an abrupt and final end.

"No more lying friends wanting tragic ends . . ."

Stevie continued to sing, expressing every emotion and word as if Michael were singing it himself. I looked around at all of those friends who hadn't been there for him in his darkest hour when I invited them to Neverland in 2003. They were all there now—a little too late. Stevie's lyrics couldn't have been more prophetic.

I had never experienced a more surreal and emotional moment in my life. It was like I was sitting through a sad scene in a movie, except it was real. Magic Johnson spotted me crying and walked over to give me a hug. No words needed to be said. We were all feeling the same way. Kobe Bryant stood next to me in stunned silence as Michael's young daughter, Paris, broke down in tears as she was giving a heartfelt speech.

Frank DiLeo was walking around in a daze. He looked shell-hocked. In fact, everyone had that look on their faces. Confused shock is what I would call it. No one had any answers, only questions . . . and guilt.

All of these people could have saved him, I thought. *If only we had all tried a little harder . . .*

Why had I procrastinated so long to go to rehearsal? I should have gone every day that I was able. I knew something was wrong. Why didn't I do something sooner?

Those questions will haunt me forever.

Yes, I am sure guilt was the pervading emotion in many of our minds.

Guilt, sadness, regret . . .

And a lifetime of memories.

People have asked me over the years if Michael was a "normal guy." Well, no, he wasn't. There was something truly magical about him. No other human being possessed this rare quality that he had, and I am certain there will never be anyone quite like him again. He had a unique energy that radiated through him and he didn't have to do a thing for you to feel it. He didn't have to sing or dance—all he had to do was stand before you and you could feel his power. Yet, for all of his magnetic intensity, he was still just a human being, and I think people forget that sometimes.

He wanted so badly to be remembered as the greatest entertainer who ever lived, to be the best who ever did it. I hope that history is kind to him, and that people will remember him for who he *actually* was—a man who dared to create the most spellbinding show the world has ever seen, who lived to entertain and make people happy, who sang and danced his heart out until the very end. A man who worked hard his entire life and suffered greatly just to share his God-given talent with the world—who wanted nothing more than to love and be loved.

But most of all, I hope people will remember that he was simply—a man.

EPILOGUE

It's not often you get to witness your own death, but Michael did just that during the filming of *Ghosts.* It was a moment that will always stand out in my mind—a moment that would haunt me.

Michael was crumbled in a heap, lying on the floor. We were all crying, staring at his lifeless body.

"Look at Michael's dead body," said Stan Winston, the director. "Imagine he has just died . . ." And just like that, tears welled in my eyes. It wasn't hard for any of us to produce real tears—everyone in the cast had grown to love Michael. We all thought of him as a friend.

"Imagine that you'll never see him again . . ."

I didn't have to pretend. Just the thought of losing Michael was enough to send tears rolling down my face. Then someone reached over to wipe my tears and a soft voice whispered in my ear, "I'm right here."

It was Michael, in costume as the mayor. He was standing next to me as we filmed a scene of him lying dead on the floor. *He's alive. It's not real,* I told myself. *He's right beside you—where he's always been . . . where I hope he'll always be . . .*

As we stood together staring at his make-believe body lying motionless on the floor, I felt torn. It looked so real. Anguish and relief surged through me all at once. The thought of Michael dead was unfathomable. He was so energetic, so full of love and life. I glanced over at him just before the cameras started rolling. He was in a trance now, staring at himself lying there.

"Aww, you're dead," I joked, trying to lighten the mood. I didn't know what else to say or do. He looked so sad—I just wanted to make him smile. It was usually easy to make him laugh, but not this time. He just stood there looking at me with the saddest eyes and didn't say a word. I felt like an insensitive fool.

When the cameras started rolling, Stan walked us through the emotions again. "Imagine that this is your friend Michael lying in front of you. He's gone and you'll never see him again. You'll never laugh with him, smile with him, have fun with him. He's gone forever . . ."

There wasn't a dry eye in the room. Loren, the African American boy, had tears streaming down his face. Members of the cast were hunched over, as if in pain. I didn't want to play this game, to pretend anymore, but we filmed this scene several times, having to relive the pain of Michael's death again and again. Michael was right there next to me, feeling the emotions too.

Michael, dressed as the mayor, was directed to turn angrily and walk away. "Let's go!" he yelled to all of us. We were instructed to ignore him and continue to stare at dead Michael lying on the ground in front of us. With tears in my eyes, I stood there looking at the dead body. Then I felt someone tapping me on the shoulder. I turned to see Michael, dressed as the mayor, a few inches from my face, staring into my eyes.

"I said, 'Let's go!'" he yelled, directing the line at me. It was an unexpected change. Pure improvisation. He hadn't done that in rehearsal. I was so surprised I almost smiled and ruined the take. We filmed the scene six times. Every take was exactly the same. At some point, it was as if the cameras were no longer there. Michael and I were having our own moment. I looked deep into his eyes with a silent pleading, trying to express in a language without words that I didn't want to go—that it was the last thing I wanted to do. I wanted to stay there and protect him forever. But Michael was asking me to leave.

What was once a scene in a movie, a dress rehearsal of the saddest day in my life, has become an unbearable reality. Sometimes when I'm alone in my room, away from the distractions of the demanding world, in the chilling quiet of silence, Stan's words still haunt me. *You'll never laugh with him again. You'll never hear him call your name. You'll never glance across the room and see his smiling face. Michael is dead now. He's gone forever.*

I'm still waiting for him to yell, "Cut!"

ACKNOWLEDGMENTS

Thank you to the following individuals. Without their contributions and support, this book would not have been written:

Yuval Taylor, Michelle Williams, and Chicago Review Press: Thank you so much for believing in me! I couldn't have done any of this without you. You are the best!

Sandy Gallin and Jim Morey: Thank you both for all of the crazy times and memories! You two were the best bosses a girl could have—and the best managers a King of Pop could have! There will never be another place quite like Gallin Morey Associates.

Janice Mangatal: I'm blessed to have the most wonderful mother in the world. I love you!

Todd Mangatal: To my big brother—I love you.

Hana Ali: You are truly the greatest. Thank you for everything!

Scott "House" Shaffer: Your memories and support have been invaluable. Thank you for all of your jokes and for making Michael smile.

Jill Marr: I appreciate your kindness. Thank you!

The Michael Jackson fan community: Thank you to Michael's fans all over the world! You were truly the loves of his life.

Qadree El-Amin: Thank you for being a true friend. I am so grateful for your advice, guidance, and support.

Reginald Hudlin: Thank you for your motivation and encouragement!

Gregg Mitchell: Gallin Morey's finest! Thank you for your priceless recollections.

Anthony "Chicago" Hall: Thank you.

Tove Stodle: Thanks to you and Magne for your friendship and kindness. I cherish it. And to all of my friends in Norway—I miss you.

"Nicole": Thank you for the decades of memories—the good, the bad, and the crazy. Sending you love.

Prince, Paris, and Blanket: Your daddy was an amazing man. Thank you for being a blessing in his life.

Nicky-Al Peerdeman: My Facebook assistant in the Netherlands! You are such an inspiration. Thank you for everything! I love you!

My Facebook community of friends: You guys have been there when I needed you most. Thank you!

Thank you also to the following for your friendship, advice, and support: Bonnie Berry LaMon, Esq., Frank K. Wheaton, Esq., Earvin "Magic" Johnson, David Copperfield, Shemar Moore, Omer Bhatti, Dr. Deepak Chopra, Vincent Cirrincione, Dorian Holley, Tirina Simons, Erik Schnur, Evelyn Bates-Jackson, Tracy Laney, Angel Howansky, Terri Bingham, Lonnell Williams, Dr. Marcella Wilson, Bryan Alexander, Sherryll Atkins, Courtney Barnes, Olga Fogel, Darrell Walker, Bryan Loren, Tita Martin, Andre Allen Jr., Duane Nettlesbey, Laura Mitchell Wilde, Susan Mangatal, Lisa D'Angelo, Valerie Brossard, Nancy Lewis, Kenny Semer, Sheila Gillis, Linda Lyon, Michelene Insalaco, Geoff Cheddy, John Himelstein, Xen Lang, Evan Charnov, Cheryl Cobb-Debrosse, Nancy Wolfson, Zola Mashariki, Annice Parker, Gail Berman, Nelson Hayes, Wayne Nagin, Yannick Allain, Bill Whitfield, Dennis Ashley, Gary Hearne, Connell Black, Darryl Phillips, Monty Nkhereanye, Rodney Jerkins, my Gallin Morey Associates family, the Bell family, and the Jackson family.